IMAGINATIVE POSSIBILITIES

LATINX AND LATIN AMERICAN PROFILES

Frederick Luis Aldama, Editor

IMAGINATIVE POSSIBILITIES

CONVERSATIONS WITH TWENTY-FIRST-CENTURY LATINX AUTHORS

Javier O. Huerta and Maceo Montoya

UNIVERSITY OF PITTSBURGH PRESS

Published by the University of Pittsburgh Press, Pittsburgh, Pa., 15260

Manufactured in the United States of America
Printed on acid-free paper
10 9 8 7 6 5 4 3 2 1

Cataloging-in-Publication data is available from the Library of Congress

ISBN 13: 978-0-8229-4831-5
ISBN 10: 0-8229-4831-1

Cover art: Jose A. Arenas. *Infinita.* 2017. Oil on wood. 48 x 48 in.
Cover design: Melissa Dias-Mandoly

CONTENTS

IMAGINATIVE POSSIBILITIES

INTRODUCTION

IMAGINATIVE POSSIBILITIES

We are both writers and avid readers of twenty-first-century Latinx literature. We have engaged in conversations about this ever-growing body of work at several levels in the past two decades, as fellow writers, as instructors, and as friends. We have found a genuine sense of community in these literary circles—meaning that we have met and bonded and followed each other and other Latinx writers. It is always great to hear of a new author or a new book from an already familiar author. We talk at conferences; we talk after readings when we catch the authors when they come through town on their book tours; we talk when we bring authors to our campus; and we talk on social media. We knew many of the writers in this book before this project, and of the others, we knew their work and have wanted to meet them. There is a strong sense of support for each other, and it is from this sense of community and conversation that we approach this book of interviews.

WHY WE CHOSE INTERVIEWS

We decided on interviews because we think of author interviews as their own literary genre. When we first started to write, or were trying to write, we'd turn to them to learn about the writer's process. What most appealed to us were the glimpses into a writer's ritual: where they wrote, how many words a day, whether they wrote their first drafts by hand or typed them, the books they turned to for inspiration—the mechanics of actual writing more so than the discussion of its contents. How one *becomes* a writer can be a mystery, especially for the aspiring writer full of desire but lacking in guidance. What good author interviews do is show the artist for the human being they are, full of doubts and insecurities and with plenty of obstacles to overcome. In our opinion, the best author interviews are less a manual of how to become a writer and more a manual of how to persevere as one.

As Chicano writers ourselves, we found two collections of interviews especially influential: Juan Bruce-Novoa's *Chicano Authors: Inquiry by Interview* and Frederick Luis Aldama's *Spilling the Beans in Chicanolandia: Conversations with Writers and Artists*. Both books made us feel as if we were part of something larger, a literary heritage. These influential books gave us an essential glimpse into the mindsets of those who helped establish the tradition in which we were engaging and trying to contribute. Two decades into the twenty-first century, that tradition has only expanded and evolved, and a whole new generation of creators has come of age. While the collections mentioned have focused on just Chicanx writers, our collection broadens its reach to Latinx writers as a whole. The cultural and historical differences between Latinx communities, which are reflected in our respective literatures, are all the more reason why it's important to see these artists side by side. Latinx literature is not monolithic. It's not one voice but many. These conversations highlight the vast range of approaches to thinking about identity and community as well as about craft.

In Tomás Rivera's interview in Bruce-Novoa's *Chicano Authors*, Rivera describes his discovery of Américo Paredes's book *"With His Pistol in His Hand,"* a scholarly work that tells the story of Gregorio Cortez and explores the significance of corridos in the border region. Rivera explains how coming across that book in the library while a graduate student in the late 1950s revealed several things to him: first, it was possible for a Chicano (Paredes) to publish; two, it was possible for a Chicano (Cortez) to be the central subject of a story and to be represented as a complete figure as opposed to a racialized stereotype; and three, it opened a whole world of "imaginative possibilities," one in which Rivera realized that he could write about the stories that mattered to him. Just as Paredes had documented Cortez "para siempre" (forever), Rivera could document the stories of the migrant farmworkers of his youth.

Eventually, those stories would become his seminal novel . . . *y no se lo tragó la tierra*. This moment from Rivera's interview captures what is most powerful about the literary interview: how a single moment of discovery can awaken not only one's creative potential but also one's humanity.

Our book, *Imaginative Possibilities: Conversations with Twenty-First-Century Latinx Authors*, is a collection of interviews with contemporary Latinx creators that seeks to engage the writers' processes, aesthetics, and creative trajectories and how they see themselves within the larger body of Latinx literature. They speak to new trends and developments in Latinx literature and current preoccupations and struggles in their creative work as well as reveal anew the powerful process through which they find their voices and declare themselves artists. Within this book, twenty-one authors discuss how they found their own paths, and over and over, we see how the intervention of one person or the discovery of one book can open a door to a world of imaginative possibilities.

HOW WE SELECTED THE AUTHORS

Bruce-Novoa's book was the first interview collection, whether Chicanx or Latinx, to bring together authors as part of the same literary movement or tradition. He focuses on what can be described as the first wave of Chicano authors, such as Tomás Rivera, Rolando Hinojosa, and Rodolfo Anaya. Aldama's *Spilling the Beans in Chicanolandia*, along with other interview collections from the 2000s such as Hector A. Torres's *Conversations with Contemporary Chicana and Chicano Writers* and Karin Rosa Ikas's *Chicana Ways*, focuses on the second wave of Chicanx writers. Another important collection to note is Bridget Kevane and Juanita Heredia's *Latina Self-Portraits* because it expands to include Latinx writers more broadly—in this case Latinx women writers who were part of the second wave, such as Julia Alvarez, Judith Ortiz Cofer, and Denise Chávez.

We're now in a moment where a significant number of Latinx authors have emerged and it makes sense to demonstrate connectedness between the different Latinidades, even while we keep in mind the diverse and separate traditions among Latinx writers. Defining literature in group terms can be imperfect, even problematic, whether that's generational or ethnic. One of the positive achievements in the twenty-first century is that there are many more books by Latinx writers published every year, but a related challenge is trying to conceive or define a generation that is both expanding and in constant flux. For this reason, we adapted the question from Bruce-Novoa in which we ask the writers themselves to reflect on the milestones so far of Latinx literature in the first two decades of the century and which directions they see Latinx literature heading. In doing so, we let a representative group of writers define and conceive the generation by hearing what achievements they prioritize, what writers inspire them, and what trends most excite them.

Since our purpose in this book of interviews is to capture the voices of Latinx writers in the twenty-first century, we decided that the most logical way to organize the interviews is chronologically based on the date of the authors' first publication. This provides us more context for when the authors entered the literary scene, and in this way, the table of contents can be read as a timeline—of publications, of influences, of divergences, and of mentorship. We chart important inroads, whether that's publishing with large commercial presses or covering new thematic ground, and as we move toward the more recent publication dates, we see these inroads built upon and expanded with an increasing number of voices, venues, and challenges to the way we conceive of Latinx literature.

The key development in Latinx literature(s) of the twenty-first century has to be its expansion in terms of perspectives. Bruce-Novoa interviewed writers that were mostly men and Chicano. In *Spilling the Beans in Chicanolandia*, Aldama expands the selection of writers to include more women and queer writers. For our project, we recognize voices that now have a significant presence in Latinx literature: the centrality of queer writers and the emergence of Central American (American) diaspora writers, Afro-Latinx writers, and undocumented migrant writers, among other groups. These new voices aren't just expressing new perspectives but are offering critiques of the Latinx literature that came before, such as nationalistic hegemony, erasure of Indigenous groups, and anti-Blackness in Latinidad. We can only really understand this generation through a multiplicity of voices. How they conceive of their work within a larger community of writers ultimately will determine the outlines of that generation. We hope that this collection attempts to broaden those outlines rather than narrows them by acknowledging multiple or intersectional identities, embracing hybridity, and breaking down borders.

This book is composed of conversations—authors speaking about their own work within a broader context of their particular literary tradition and Latinx literature as a whole. Our hope is to demonstrate how varied the voices in Latinx literature are, but any book that attempts to be representative of a particular group or identity, especially one as large and varied as the umbrella term *Latinx*, will likely fall short. We already know there are voices and demographics and important perspectives that we haven't included. We interviewed twenty-one authors, but we easily could've interviewed twice that number and still felt that authors doing important, innovative work were left out. What is heartening to see, as many of the authors discuss, is the sheer number of Latinx writers that are publishing work today. As poet Willie Perdomo mentions regarding the anthology he coedited, *LatiNext*, his hope would be that those not included in the anthology would create their own anthologies. This is not to shirk responsibility for whatever gaps this collection might have, and as much as we challenge the burden placed on individual artists to be representative of a larger identity, we understand that a collection like this cannot escape it. We encourage the dialogue that results as a way to learn and grow. Many of the authors we interviewed spoke with excitement and anticipation about the next generation of Latinx writers because they were so unapologetic in challenging the status quo, including accepted ideas long considered sacrosanct, and pushing the dialogue in new directions that are ever more complex, nuanced, and individuated. We share their enthusiasm and hope that this collection can be one that those authors build upon and challenge.

HOW WE DEVISED THE QUESTIONS

Again, we acknowledge the validity and necessity of critiques against the heteronormative, nationalistic, and patriarchal nature of the movements and literatures of previous generations of Latinx writers. As we will see in the interviews, the authors we have included in this book have been some of the more prominent voices in those critiques, both in their literary works and in their thinking. But what we want to argue for is that amid this contention there is also a significant continuity between the Latinx writers of the twentieth century and the Latinx writers of the twenty-first century. For that reason, we decided to use several of the questions from Bruce-Novoa's inquiry to emphasize and explore that continuity. A central question, for example, in Bruce-Novoa's interviews is: "Do you perceive yourself and your work as political?" Just as Bruce-Novoa wanted to get a sense of how the writers and their work were connected to the Chicano Movement, we also wanted to inquire about the authors' connectedness to and awareness of twenty-first-century movements, including the struggles for justice and rights for migrants, Black and Indigenous peoples, LGBTQ+ and trans communities, and women, all of which taken together illustrate the intersectionality of the Latinx population.

There is a genuine excitement and curiosity in Bruce-Novoa's inquiry into the new cultural phenomenon that was the emerging literature of the Chicano Movement. We feel a similar excitement and curiosity about the emerging twenty-first-century Latinx literature. Despite being a scholar of Chicano literature, Bruce-Novoa didn't frame his questions with a certain interpretative framework or theory. Instead, he invited the writers to define for themselves their work and influences, their sense of place and community, and their responsibility as artists as well as the milestones and directions of their literary movement. Since we conceived of this interview project as fellow writers, we also believed in approaching this project with an openness that would invite and allow the interviewees to offer their own interpretations of these complex and significant ideas.

In *Spilling the Beans in Chicanolandia*, Aldama also acknowledges the importance of Bruce-Novoa's book of interviews and the influence of it on his own interview project. While Bruce-Novoa interviewed the first generation of Chicano writers, Aldama interviewed what he calls the "second wave" of Chicano authors. Although Aldama sees Bruce-Novoa's book as a model, he makes the case for a more organic approach to the interviews. While Bruce-Novoa asked the same questions of each author via a survey, Aldama met with the authors individually and asked questions that paid attention to the particulars of the authors' literary works. As writers ourselves, we also favor asking specific questions sensitive to the nuances of each author's books in addition to questions addressing common themes and concerns. Thus, our methodology became a combination of both Bruce-Novoa's predetermined questions and Aldama's more organic, individualized approach. This resulted in fruitful conversations on diverse themes and creative concerns as well as a degree of unpredictability. There are certain resonances throughout the collection—for example, the impact of the pandemic, the formative moments in their journeys as writers, the political nature of their work, the future directions of Latinx literature—but just as often the conversations deviated from the script as we readily followed the authors' responses and preoccupations.

WHAT WE FOUND

We realized that our interview project would be influenced by the COVID19 pandemic. This was the main reason why we conducted the interviews over Zoom. But we also felt it was pertinent to ask the authors about their writing during this time, especially the shelter-in-place phase of the pandemic. Our authors describe experiencing a certain pause in their lives—not a pause of reflection but one of uncertainty. It was not uncommon for the authors we interviewed to experience a lack of productivity during this pause or, even more to the point, a lack of connection with their literary selves, at least during the initial weeks and months of the shutdown in 2020. Our authors communicated an eventual drive to be and feel human during this crisis and, along with that, a need to reconnect with reading, writing, and the literary life. This would lead to authors finding themselves again not only as persons but also as writers. For several of them, this reconnection involved a redefining, through either exploring different genres or a recommitment to their creative life.

We must also make note of the sense of loss during the pandemic and the accompanying grief. For some of our authors, this includes personal loss, losing someone in their family to COVID19 or knowing of someone who passed away from complications from the virus. But our authors also observe a sense of national grief, including reflections on the deaths of George Floyd and Breonna Taylor and the resulting protests for racial justice. In one interview, the poet Aracelis Girmay connects the pandemic and the protests and speaks about poetry being a place of quiet and contemplation that she hadn't been prepared to go to given the turmoil around her. There is a general sense that for most of our authors, COVID19 and their experiences with this crisis compelled them to question their purpose as artists. Despite having established careers, the authors express having been at a crossroads, asking themselves how they will make the rest of their work, literary or otherwise, more meaningful in the years to come.

The Importance of Place and Community

In the canonical Chicano poem "Un Trip through the Mind Jail," Raúl Salinas ends his poem with a roll call of neighborhoods, including Segundo Barrio in El Paso, East Los Angeles, and other neighborhoods known for being ethnic enclaves. The previous generations of Latinx writers were often writing as representatives of their communities, and based on these interviews, it's clear that twenty-first-century Latinx writers still speak from a certain place, neighborhood, and community that is central to their work. This involves neighborhoods and places with a long Latinx presence and rich literary history, such as Willie Perdomo's Harlem, Erika L. Sánchez's Chicago, Tim Z. Hernandez's San Joaquin Valley, and Oscar Cásares's Rio Grande Valley.

But some writers have started to shift the attention from those traditional neighborhoods and communities to new places. For instance, Los Angeles has long been central in the works of Latinx writers, especially Chicanos, but Yesika Salgado, a Salvadoran American writer, focuses on the neighborhood of Silver Lake, and Guatemalan American novelist Héctor Tobar tackles the entire landscape of Los Angeles, including wealthy suburbs, to explore class tensions. This slight move to another community can also be seen in Jennine Capó Crucet's decision to locate many of her stories in Hialeah. Little Havana may be central to our imagination of the Cuban American experience, but Jennine Capó Crucet shifts the camera to the side to show us a more settled, middle-class, and largely second-generation Cuban American community. We also see major shifts in sense of place. For instance, Lorraine López writes about Latinos in the South, a change in focus that aligns with the growing Latinx population in the Southern states, and Ivelisse Rodriguez, in her stories about Puerto Rican women and their failed search for love, relocates our attention from New York City to a lesser-known Puerto Rican enclave in Holyoke, Massachusetts.

In addition, the authors we interviewed remain interested in the conversation about place in relation to migration and exile. The countries of origin—Mexico, Puerto Rico, Cuba, El Salvador, Guatemala, Peru—show up in the works of these writers along with their distinct histories and relations to the United States. In the twenty-first century, and particularly with the writers we interviewed, we see that this relation to the home country is complicated. This might be especially present in the emergent literature of undocumented migrant writers, as can be seen in the novels and memoirs written by Reyna Grande. She writes about the distance between Iguala, Guerrero, and Los Angeles, and as with other undocumented persons, the distance is felt even more because of the inability to go back. The longing for the home country is also present in the works of Ana Menéndez, especially in the Little Havana depicted in her stories populated by Cuban émigrés waiting for the opportunity to return to Cuba. This leads to a conversation about displacement and diaspora. Aracelis Girmay speaks of both the rootedness and the routes of her mixed heritage Puerto Rican and Eritrean family, and Urayoán Noel talks about how his neighborhood in the Bronx greatly resembles the neighborhood where he grew up in San Juan, Puerto Rico, and the "ghosts" of the lives now gone that he finds in both places.

The Persistence of the Political

The poet Carmen Giménez talks about how art happens in movements, artists surrounded by other artists and art forms, nourishing, inspiring, and challenging each other, often reflecting charged political moments. It was the civil rights movement in the 1960s that gave rise to the cultural renaissance in the Latinx community. Cultural galleries and community art centers sprung up across the country, such as the influential Nuyorican Poets Cafe in New York City, as did Chicano/Latino publishing houses, such as Quinto Sol at UC Berkeley. Chicano/Latino studies departments were established that provided a receptive audience for these emergent literatures, with readers hungry for work that instilled cultural pride and spoke to their experiences in a country that maligned their language, cultural, history, and identity. In Bruce-Novoa's *Chicano Authors*, the range of answers to the question about the political nature of the authors' work is surprising given the political wellspring that their writing emerged from and the political stridency identified with that generation of cultural activists. Each author interprets *political* in their own way, some defensively as though they had grown wary of the expectation that their work should be so overt. Overall, they came down on the autonomy of the artist as their first priority.

A half century later, the authors we interviewed didn't seem to have any qualms about the term *political* or feel the need to quibble over definitions, nor did they appear to feel the same anxiety over whether claiming the political nature of one's work undermined their commitment to their craft. To be political was obvious, to deny it seemed naive. Their politics were embodied, in some cases literally, as both Eduardo C. Corral and Carmen Maria Machado state, in essence, that to inhabit brown bodies, queer bodies, fat bodies, or migrant bodies in this society was to be political. Others felt by virtue of claiming an identity, whether Chicanx or Latinx, was to understand oneself in relation to the mainstream. Instead of being viewed as a hindrance to one's work, just about every author articulates this ingrained aspect of their work as a unique entry point for their creative voice and a necessary responsibility. This responsibility often led to a discussion of literary citizenship and how they could best contribute to knocking down barriers to access. This is perhaps best exemplified by Rigoberto González, who says that when he writes he looks around for his communities and asks himself how his work is serving them. For many authors, this willingness to serve includes their role as teachers, participating on boards or judging prizes to ensure Latinx books are considered, or being very intentional about using their work to inspire dialogue and open minds.

Influences and Traditions

This book is interested in exploring traditions and continuity as much as departures. However spontaneous it may feel, an artistic movement springs from a tradition, whether building on the pillars erected by prior generations or knocking them down. It's one of the reasons why we asked every author what tradition they saw themselves inheriting or a part of. Overall, the authors acknowledge the importance of early Latinx writers, including the role of individual mentors such as Judith Ortiz Cofer, Juan Felipe Herrera, Helena María Viramontes, Martín Espada, and Francisco X. Alarcón and the impact of Pedro Pietri, Miguel Algarín, and the Nuyorican poets. These mentorships often in turn inspired the authors to be mentors to younger writers, knowing how important these interventions can be. Other authors talk about the experience of immersing themselves in early Latinx writing to find inspiration but more importantly departure points for their own work.

In general, however, we found that the authors are hardly siloed in their reading. The influences are vast and as varied as perusing a used bookstore. They speak to an unbounded love of literature and storytelling rather than feeling that being part of a literary tradition confines one to that tradition. Cuban American author Ana Menéndez cites the importance of Italo Calvino and Georges Perec on her most recent project. Chicano author Daniel Chacón discovered a decades-long affinity for Emanuel Swedenborg by way of Jorge Luis Borges, and Peruvian American author Daniel Alarcón speaks movingly about the early years of his writing journey when an obscure record or a dog-eared book could be a potential discovery and influence. If there is one constant theme, it is that the authors repeatedly speak about the importance of the Black tradition in their work, often because it was the first literature they were exposed to that aligned with their own experience of otherness. These influential authors include James Baldwin, Langston Hughes, Audre Lorde, Toni Morrison, Octavia Butler, and Percival Everett. Author Manuel Muñoz speaks about how young Latinx literature was in relation to other literatures, and how he could turn to Black literature for a greater range of voices speaking about issues of race and identity in complex ways. It is the relative newness of Latinx literature that makes this question of influences so essential, because it informs our understanding of how a literary tradition grows—not in isolation but in communion with other literatures.

Experiences in Publishing

The authors interviewed largely view the future of Latinx literature with excitement and optimism, while acknowledging the obstacles that remain, particularly regarding access to a wider audience. Latinx authors are publishing in all venues, from large commercial presses to independent and academic presses, as well as creating their own publishing houses. The interest of commercial publishers in Latinx authors continues to be viewed with caution, especially as there have been moments in the past decades where that promise has focused on a select number of authors rather than a comprehensive and lasting commitment to Latinx literature. Latinx authors continue to struggle to get the support they need from big publishers and have learned it's not just about getting published that matters but also about the marketing support that results in reviews, awards, and getting books into readers' hands. Several authors referred to the 2019 *American Dirt* controversy and how it demonstrated that a white author with a work of questionable literary merit about a Latinx immigrant can still receive the kind of lucrative advance and industry support that most Latinx authors can only dream of. As a result of the controversy and others like it, commercial publishers have made attempts to diversify their books as well as their employees. It remains to be seen whether this change will be lasting. What's clear, however, is that most of the authors we interviewed, even those published by commercial publishers, are clear-eyed about the industry's unreliability. Waiting for it to change has been a decades-long process. Finding ways to hold it accountable is one path, embracing alternative publishing venues is another; but the main focus for these authors remains on the writing, their love of the craft, their willingness to share their knowledge with the next generation of authors, and their desire to open doors so that the road to a literary career isn't so difficult for subsequent generations of Latinx authors.

Future Concerns and Directions

We asked the authors about the future directions of Latinx literature in the twenty-first century and invited them to think about this question in their roles as editors, publishers, teachers, literary critics, and readers. The authors we interviewed have a special insight into this question because most of them have engaged in editorial and publication projects that group other twenty-first-century Latinx writers. Of course, many if not all of our authors teach and, in that role, also have the opportunity to be invested in the direction of contemporary Latinx literature. The writers appreciated the opportunity to speak beyond their own writing when considering these future directions.

In terms of themes and genres, several writers speak about the ecological concern of climate change and the connected turn to the speculative. Carmen Giménez comments that in reality we couldn't write about anything else but the issue of the impending climate disaster, and Jennine Capó Crucet expresses immense concern that Miami will be under water during our lifetime, transforming her stories about place into elegies. In general, there seems to be an openness or desire for more speculative fiction or genre writing, including from authors like Gabby Rivera and Carmen Maria Machado who have turned toward comic book projects with Marvel and DC, respectively. This shift has been felt more markedly perhaps in Latinx literature, which for the most part has been perceived as fiction based on literary realism. What this turn to speculative and genre writing demonstrates is that there is an openness for Latinx writers and other writers of color to broach other topics, other styles, and other genres than what have traditionally been used or that they have been expected to use. This turn is not an escape from that sense of responsibility or commitment to one's community but instead a new way to tell those stories.

Most notably, the majority of the authors we interviewed express the importance of highlighting voices that haven't been heard before. Their goal in previous editorial and publication projects, as well as in their role as mentors, was to include a greater range of voices speaking to the specificity and intersectionality of their experience. Several authors speak about moving beyond a generalized identity and forcing themselves to dig deeper to create multilayered works addressing not just ethnic identity but other identities such as queerness and disability. While this work is already being done, a general sentiment among the authors in their role as mentors is to encourage further exploration of these complex identities and promote publishing opportunities for these new voices. Yesika Salgado mentions how exciting it is that when people ask her for Latinx book recommendations she can now offer diverse choices based on their background and interests. Other authors acknowledge the need for more multilayered works that engage transnational, multilingual, and hemispheric conversations. This all points to multiple openings and possibilities—possibilities that are only now being imagined—as we continue into the twenty-first century.

WHAT WE TAKE AWAY

The exciting part of a project of this nature, reading literature encapsulating a time period and conducting interviews over the course of two years, during a pandemic no less, is that we were conscious of offering a snapshot of time. We joked often—especially when we expressed regret that we hadn't interviewed a particular author—that we wouldn't stop at twenty-one authors, that we would keep interviewing authors ad infinitum, creating endless spinoff collections focused on specific subsets within the umbrella of Latinx literature. But these conversations are happening already, across the country and even transnationally, in all different kinds of forums. Our goal in this book is to bring attention to these ongoing conversations as well as document them for future writers, readers, and scholars.

We can't predict how subsequent generations will interpret the conversations within this collection, but we know the impact this project has had on us as readers, writers, and friends, how meaningful it was to immerse ourselves in the work of our contemporaries, to enter virtually into their homes, and to have deeply personal conversations about the craft of writing and the stories they hold dear. There were always questions and points of inquiry that we didn't get to. Most of our conversations could have continued far beyond the allotted time. We always would stop the recording, say our goodbyes, and end the Zoom session, returning to the solitude of our respective workspaces feeling inspired, much as we did when we were aspiring young writers devouring the literary interviews of a previous generation. We're grateful to the authors in this collection for their time, their insights, and their candidness and for sharing their artistic and personal journeys. We hope that, taken together, their journeys create a roadmap for understanding Latinx literature in the first two decades of the twenty-first century but also serve as inspiration for the future writers who will shape Latinx literature in the decades to come.

1

WILLIE PERDOMO

Willie Perdomo's poetry is inextricable from New York City; specifically, East Harlem, the neighborhood where he was raised. His earliest influences in person and on the page were those that opened him up to the possibilities of the language of his neighborhood and community, including Ed Randolph (known as the "Mad Poet of Harlem"), Langston Hughes, and Piri Thomas, whose memoir, *Down These Mean Streets*, gave Perdomo permission to explore his Black and Puerto Rican identity. Born in 1967, Perdomo made a name for himself in the spoken word scene in the 1990s at the Nuyorican Poets Café. His early work for a literary agent gave him an insider's knowledge of the publishing world, and unlike many poets, certainly Latinx poets, most of Perdomo's poetry collections have been published by major publishers, including his first book, *Where a Nickel Costs a Dime*, which was published by W. W. Norton. Perdomo attended Ithaca College before dropping out to write his first book, preferring to write from his life experience, which often entailed hanging out with friends on street corners. It wasn't until his forties, and already two successful poetry collections behind him, that Perdomo completed his bachelor's degree and then received his MFA at Long Island University Brooklyn. His MFA thesis, which makes use of the dramatic mode to channel the story of his musician uncle and the big band scene in Spanish Harlem in the 1970s, became his third poetry collection, *The Essential Hits of Shorty Bon Bon*, published by Penguin Books and a finalist for the 2014 National Book Critics Circle Award. His 2019 collection, *The Crazy Bunch*, brings alive Perdomo's own youth, telling the story of a group of friends during one weekend in Harlem amid the violence of that era. Perdomo has also authored two children's books, *Visiting Langston* and *Clemente!*, and coedited an anthology published by Haymarket Books, *The BreakBeat Poets Vol. 4: LatiNext*. Perdomo spoke to us from New Hampshire, where he teaches English at Phillips Exeter Academy. He divides his time between there and New York, where he was appointed state poet laureate in 2021.

Javier: How has the pandemic impacted your writing? And can you speak more generally about your writing process?

Willie: I was on spring break and we had to escape from New York City because it had become a Level 4 hot zone. The city was about to be locked down. I remember the drive back to New Hampshire and feeling that "normal" was no longer a thing, that what we knew to be a given in the before times was no longer the case. The way I dealt with it creatively was to stay busy in terms of my practice. I decided to write haikus, of all things. I wrote about a hundred haikus in a month and a half. Every day I would say, "I'm going to write one," and one led to two, and two led to three. I whittled the manuscript down to about seventy-five haikus and made a book out of it. They turned out to be like daily nano-meditations. I had breathing space in New Hampshire. The campus was shut down, but the grounds were open, so I had time to take walks as long as I kept a good distance from other human beings. But when I started hearing about caskets being left outside storefronts in New York City, I knew that somehow any attempt at writing realistically was going to fall short in the after times.

I was also trying to take as many notes as I could about what it meant to be present to the moment, but in December 2020 my mother died from COVID complications. Two weeks after she passed away, my mother showed up in a dream. I was in Puerto Rico at the time and had taken leave from work. In the dream, we were in a playground, and I was my current age and she was younger. We weren't at the playground together, though; it was as if we were just passing each other by. She asked very simply, "Where are you going?" That alone was enough for me to wake up and start writing. The writing was now a response to her question. Journeys, you know. All it takes is a good question from someone that you love to start the writing process.

MACEO: I'm so sorry to hear about your mother. I've been poring over your works and it's clear how much of an impact your mother had on you as a person as well as on your work. In thinking about her influence as well as others, can you speak about the formative moments in your journey as a writer?

WILLIE: My mother was a documentarian. She used to keep journals, notes, predictions from Walter Mercado, and dialogue from popular movies like *Mahogany* with Diana Ross. She had elegant handwriting. I came up in a time where they taught you cursive in school. My handwriting was not the best, but I would be amazed seeing my mother's cursive go from left to right margin on a notebook page. I was fascinated by loops and crosses and the sudden appearance of words on a blank page. I didn't understand that she was *writing*, but I knew that once she put pen to paper, whatever was on that paper was saying something. So, one day during my first-grade year at school, we're doing art and crafts, and I took a pencil and some stock paper and started writing in zigzagging lines from left to right. I was imitating my mother. No words, just zigzag, zigzag, zigzag, left-to-right zigzags until I accumulated a few pages. In my mind, I'm looking at the pages and I'm like, "Damn, I wrote a lot right here." It was an act, a physical act. The other part that my mother influenced was reading. I was one of those kids who by the second grade was reading at a fifth-grade level. Books were my best friends. They were portals to other worlds that were not reflective of living in East Harlem and what that meant to me as a child in the mid-seventies. Books were like subways for me. I would hop on a train and read a book, and then get off when it was time to get off and think about what it meant to be in someone else's world. It fed my imagination.

Can't forget music. Music was my mother's dream space. Nothing like a good Ray Barretto album to get my mother in a narrative space. When I wrote *The Essential Hits of Shorty Bon Bon*, I realized that the book was part of my dream life. When I was a kid, I would fall asleep at parties—baptisms, sweet sixteens, marriages, Noche Buena—while salsa and boogaloo played in the background, so music became part of my dream life. That comes out in the sonic charges of my book.

I went to a public school in East Harlem, but my sixth-grade teacher, Ms. Friedlander, suggested that I apply to a private school. And I did. I had a hard time navigating East Harlem and private school downtown. I was one of maybe five students of color at that time at Friends Seminary, and searching for an identity was difficult. Who are we and how do we belong to something? Where are our levels of acceptances when we're socialized? That led to some altercations, arguments, fights, and anger that was compounded by a chaotic home life and the violence that I was surrounded by. Processing that was a major challenge. I had a mentor named Ed Randolph, who I still know to this day, and he was a receptionist at Friends. I found out later that he was known as the "Mad Poet of Harlem." He was a contemporary of Sekou Sundiata. One day, Ed read some poems during assembly, and the poem rocked me because it took place uptown, and was written in what you might call an "uptown tongue." I didn't know you could do that with poetry. In the classroom, I was reading Chaucer's *Canterbury Tales*, Joyce's *Portrait of the Artist as a Young Man*. It took me a while to understand that Joyce was a writer that really heard language, and I unconsciously understood that one could use one's country, one's block as material for poetry.

The moment that really broke the writing dam wide open for me was reading Piri Thomas's *Down These Mean Streets*. That was the book that changed my career path. I was intent on being a professional: a lawyer, a doctor, a corporate banker, so that I could make bank and get an apartment on Park Avenue. But I read *Down These Mean Streets*, and man, Lexington Avenue just came to life. It felt like an electric pop-up book. I saw my block in three dimensions after reading Piri. The names, the love story between him and Trina, the search for manhood . . . all of it just transformed my perspectives. There's a point where Piri writes, "Can one actually become a man without going through hell?" It felt like every man around me was going through some sort of private hell. I understood that intuitively. But the biggest gift that Piri gave me was a sense of being Boricua and Black. Those were the true wings on the same bird. That was important for me because, again, I was going to a school that was white-dominant and a lot of kids thought I was Black. They didn't know I was Puerto Rican until I started speaking what little Spanish I knew. Piri Thomas gave me the impetus to start exploring my identity and rejoice in the power of self-definition.

Something else happened around that time. I was in shopping for schoolbooks in Barnes and Noble on Eighteenth Street and Fifth Avenue in New York City, and I came across *Selected Poems of Langston Hughes*. Langston was on the front cover, in front of a typewriter, and he's looking at the camera tentatively. I skimmed through the book and saw flashes of words like "Harlem," "Lenox Avenue," "numbers," and "jazz." Again, my block, my barrio, was living on the pages. Harlem was the canvas and the streets were rich with imagery.

I wasn't a very good college student. I was very distracted, but the library was my hangout spot. Whatever I wasn't getting in the classroom I would search for in the library at Ithaca College. I broadened my engagement with the arts. One day, I'd be interested in photography and I would start looking at street photography from Paris, from New York City, or photos by Puerto Rican and Black photographers. I found Roy DeCarava that way. The next day, I might want to be an impressionist painter, so I'd go pick up a book on Monet or Cézanne, or maybe an abstract expressionist painter, or painters and sculptors like Jacob Lawrence, Benny Andrews, Augusta Savage, and Romare Bearden. I wanted to know what made an artist. Mind you, I was terrible at drawing. My exploration fed my writing. You might call me a documentary poet, with my emphasis on capturing imagery. That comes from my love of photography. It was also at Ithaca that I found Miguel Algarín and Miguel Piñero's *Nuyorican Poetry*, and I was like, "Finally." I found the missing link. At that point, I had already read through the Harlem Renaissance, some romantic poetry, a little bit of Shakespeare, Beat poetry, New York School of poetry, and San Francisco Renaissance poetry, so finding a book of Nuyorican poetry was tectonic.

I dropped out of Ithaca and enrolled in the City College of New York, where I met Raymond R. Patterson. I knew his work because I had already read the seminal anthologies *Black Voices* and *New Black Voices*, so I signed up for his creative writing class. He introduced me to Jean Toomer's *Cane*, which was a pivotal book for me. Toomer was engaged in hybridity. Not only were there poems in the book but there was short prose and a play. If you look at my work from *Where a Nickel Costs a Dime* to *The Crazy Bunch*, you know that I'm invested in the mixture of genre, mixture of form, so that it's not just one aesthetic or genre at play.

I lasted a year at CCNY. I wanted to be a writer, so I dropped out to write. Around that time, the Nuyorican Poets Café had just reopened. For me, besides being a published poet, the Nuyorican was my mecca. I started reading my poems aloud all over New York City. Reading poems aloud made me think about audience and editing, but I wasn't yet aware of how seductive and destructive having a live audience might be. I didn't find my writing practice until I went back to school when I was forty—finished up my bachelor's degree and then I got an MFA right after that. That's when I started to discover my approach to notebooks, annotations, and curating my reading around a specific project. That's when I discovered my practice.

JAVIER: How did you publish your first collection with a major publisher, W. W. Norton, and can you speak about your early experiences with publishing?

WILLIE: Back then, you could still find Black newspapers on newsstands. *Amsterdam News* was the most prominent, another was *The City Sun*, and the newspapers would have literary supplements once or twice a year. I started submitting my poems to them, and on occasion one or two would get accepted, so I was starting to accumulate publication credits. For me, it was always about publishing, writing a book, before I stepped to a microphone. But it was really being at the Nuyorican Poets Café and being part of an underground scene that catalyzed my first book. I wrote my first book while I was touring in Europe, New York, Vermont, a little bit in DC, and finally wrapped on my mother's kitchen table. Every publisher I submitted to rejected the book except Henry Holt and Company and Jill Bialosky at W. W. Norton. I went with Norton. Jill's one editorial suggestion was to remove "Ni***r-Reecan Blues." By that point the poem had become a benchmark of mine and I refused. The original title for my first book was "Papo's Poems." One summer day, I went to the New York Public Library on 125th Street between Third and Second Avenues, and I came across Arnold Adoff's anthology of Black poetry in the twentieth century. I'm sitting there reading, and suddenly I see a poem called "Prime," by Langston Hughes, which I hadn't seen in his *Selected Poems*. There's one couplet that goes, "Uptown in the section of the ni***rs / where a nickel costs a dime," and the eureka flash was instant. I said, "That's it: *Where a Nickel Costs a Dime*."

After my first book, I got lost, man. I got lost on Lexington Avenue. I started chasing dragons. I was out of school, but I was still touring. Poetry was still a passport for me. I was going to Europe, the Caribbean, but the streets had more of an allure for me than the academy, than school, because I felt I was one of those writers who had to live it to write it. I was what William Carlos Williams would call "in that line between observer and participant," but I became more participant than anything else. All of that shows up ten years later in *Smoking Lovely*, which I also submitted to Norton. They had an option on my second book, and they rejected it. They wanted me to write a memoir, which I wasn't interested in. So my second book was done by a small press—Rattapallax. It was the homie, the profe from New York University, Urayoán Noel, who made me see what I was trying to do in *Smoking Lovely*. I try not intellectualize the artistic process or analyze my own writing. That's dangerous. But according to Noel, I was addressing the commodification of spoken word and the gentrification of New York City. The book is a testimony, a book of witness. Still, I wasn't satisfied with the book for a long time.

MACEO: Your first two books are, in a way, responses to the present, but your second two books, *The Essential Hits of Shorty Bon Bon* and *The Crazy Bunch*, hearken back to earlier eras. Both capture something that has been lost. How would you characterize this turn to the past?

WILLIE: By the time I got to LIU Brooklyn campus, I was not interested in poetry. I was done with poetry. I wanted to pursue playwriting. I was taking a class with Jessica Hagedorn. I had written a monologue, and she was so excited about the monologue that she sent me a note that said, "You need to start writing plays, poet." The writing prompts in workshops became my transport lines. The first line that arrived for *Shorty* was "What I remember between first & last track is how I replied to all those voice-sweet pretty boys." That was a visitation from my uncle, Pedro Perdomo. I ran with that voice, man. I started asking my uncle's ghost about the year he recorded with Charlie Palmieri's band, the Cesta All Stars. The conceit is constructed around an afterlife, and I'm Shorty's guide. How close is the content to my uncle's life? It's removed by maybe a block or two, for sure, but doing research for the book was the true reward. I read interviews with congueros and musicians like Joe Cuba. There's a poem in *Shorty* called "So Cool" where he says, "So cool that I made the king"—referring to Tito Puente—"bite his tongue," because Tito Puente used to play with his tongue wagging. I was echoing some of the braggadocio I found in interviews. *Shorty* became my graduate thesis and was eventually published by Penguin. By the time I got the Penguin deal, I was hired at Phillips Exeter Academy, so my life was moving away from the city.

The Crazy Bunch. Bro, that book came in heat. In 2014, I'd been away from New York for almost a year, working and living in New Hampshire. My wife and I were watching an HBO documentary, *Time is Illmatic*, about the making of Nas's album *Illmatic*, and there was one moment that hit me hard. Nas's brother is walking with his entourage down a path in Queensbridge Houses, and he points to an empty bench and says, "That's where Ill Will was murdered." Ill Will was Nas's best friend. By the end of the documentary, I was crying, and I told my wife, "Baby, I'm back." I ran to my study, opened up a notebook, and wrote, "You remember, that was the summer of Up Rock, quarter water, speed knots, pillow bags, two-for-five, Jesus pieces, and Bambú. The Willie Bobo was turned up to ten, and some would've said that a science was dropped on our summer." Boom, just like that. Once that door to a traumatic *and* joyful past opened, I was going to ride that subway train to the last stop. In that one opening I found a framework, a chronicle, and a controlling diction. Once again, the book started with a visitation in the form of a question. I had about twenty-five pages by the time I sent it to my editor at Penguin and he bought it outright. *The Crazy Bunch* was the most fun I ever had working on a book. Toward the final draft, I was in residence at the Montalvo Arts Center in Los Gatos, CA, as a Lucas Arts fellow. I was chilling out in my studio one night, having a couple of drinks, around midnight, one o'clock in the morning, and I know the writing is going well because I start to dance. That has been my measurement since. Dancing while I write. Ntozake said she used to sweat when she wrote. I dance. I was literally hanging out with my book, and before I realized it, the sun was coming out, the birds were singing, and I'm still revising. I broke night with my book. This was me living in the book. It wasn't me writing the book, I *was* the book at that moment. That's the way it felt, at least. I also realized that a writer needs to be in a space where you have enough tranquilidad in your life, enough emotional capacity to process traumatic images. I needed to be in a space where I could look back at the '90s, at my homies, and give it a frame. It's very much an inside book, and I was okay with that because, ultimately, I was writing *to* and *for* the crew.

MACEO: You cite Gil Scott-Heron as teaching you how to use poetry as a mode of definition and awareness as the ultimate weapon in citizenry. Can you elaborate on what that means to you?

WILLIE: The definition of what it means to be a human being in this world even if your body is always under assault, under suspicion, seen as a threat, inhuman. How does one find humanity when you see the bodies of friends brutalized, arrested, and cuffed? The definition of what it means to be a Boricua from New York City. The definition of what it means to live in East Harlem. Through that definition we're given access, a window into a particular experience, that if you look closely enough, with enough detail and specificity, the experience just might speak for a larger picture. How do we define our language? How do we take the definition of words that we've heard before, maybe seen in the dictionary, and flip them so they become part of our lexicon? The definition of what it means to be political as a poet, or in a literary context. You're addressing a specific moment that has political overtones. How are you defining that moment in terms of what you're hearing, the blood that is spilled, the violence that is documented? That's part of the definition process as I see it. You don't want to give the poet too much responsibility, though. Poets can bang shit up if they're not careful. You can't hold every poet too responsible to be an agent of change, even though by default, once you relay a poem to a reader, once you relay a poem to an audience, someone in that audience, someone in the private act of reading is going to be transformed. There are so many elements to what Gil was saying, but basically you have to be a witness and you have to be present. It's not about what you've done in the past, it's about being present to this moment, and how that moment is going to influence the way you define being a teacher, being a poet, being Boricua, being a Spanish-speaking person from the Caribbean, being Puerto Rican, being a husband, being a dad, not being from *there*, not being from *here*, but being all the things you are.

MACEO: You once described how at one of your early readings at the Nuyorican Poets Café, the vanguard of Nuyorican poetry, Pedro Pietri, Miguel Algarín, Bimbo Rivas, was there, and after they heard you read, Pedro Pietri said, "You're one of us." Can you describe the impact that tradition of poets who came of age in the 1960s and '70s had on you—particularly, how you understand the politics of your poetry?

WILLIE: As a Puerto Rican writer in the diaspora, I experience the world through more than one consciousness. I'm listening to the world in Spanish, through Blackness, through an archipelagic lens, through hip-hop, through bomba, through boom bap, through the MOMA. You start looking at the world consciously, looking for its promise. There's a moment where Langston Hughes was getting a stipend every week from white patrons, and he's walking near the Waldorf Astoria and he sees a homeless person. He has a hard time reconciling the privilege that he has with the reality that he sees on the street, and his writing undergoes a change. I'm bringing that up because by the time I got to Algarín, to Pedro, to Sandra María Esteves, by the time I get to Puerto Rican writers like Pedro Juan Soto, Jesús Colón, and Julia de Burgos, to writers like Amiri Baraka and Martín Espada, I was experiencing attempts to reconcile what it means to have been called a second-class citizen and showing the world that you are more than that. There's nothing second class about being Puerto Rican. In fact, being Puerto Rican requires elegance. We write poetry to survive. You're writing to make sense of being treated less than, to give a human form to what is called the "inner city," to living with more than one language and being discriminated against for that language.

Those early writers gave me permission to address the world from a survivalist lens and to also understand that to be able to read and write in this world is a privilege. For a long time, it was against the law for me to know how to read and write, let alone speak Spanish. The poet's act is a decolonized act when a poet takes control of a language that wasn't made for them. I'm engaged in a level of vernacular that is not standard usage, but I'm going to use it anyway because I'm taking control of that language. The political act is a defining act as well because sometimes we can be engaged in a level of linguistic nationalism that's unhealthy. If I don't speak proper Spanish, then I'm less than, I'm not authentically Puerto Rican. The Nuyorican poets were resisting that too. Fortunately, the dialogue in the vaivén dynamic of being Puerto Rican and translating Blackness is getting deeper and richer. I think poets have a lot to do with that.

JAVIER: In your role as a writer, a teacher, a mentor to younger poets, as well as one of the editors for *LatiNext*, what have been the milestones of Latinx literature so far in the twenty-first century? What directions do you see Latinx literature in the US headed as we continue in this century?

Willie: I think one of the things that I saw working on *LatiNext* was how conscious we were of letting the reader know that we are from a diaspora, from the Spanish-speaking Caribbean, that being Dominican, Puerto Rican, Colombian, Mexican, Peruvian, hyphenated, and Latiné was not a homogenic proposition. Being a Puerto Rican poet, I have to acknowledge the influence of many traditions and many cultures. You see a movement now that's tapping into our Indigeneity. That's really a journey back home. Now, the term *Latinx* itself might be a little problematic if you are from the Caribbean meta-archipelagos because you have to acknowledge the African in you. Part of the anthology's ethos was resisting a singular definition of what it means to be Latiné and how erasure is not an option.

I was also seeing the level of experimentalism in the writing, poems in different shapes, approaches to how one writes in Spanish and English. Raquel Salas Rivera insists on having his poems in Spanish and in English. That was unheard of twenty years ago. That's important to our literature right now because why should your reader's first exposure to a poem be a translation if your native tongue is Spanish? That's a political act in itself. Then there's a refreshing multigenerational aspect to the work. There are a lot of Latinx writers out there trying to get the work done. Half of them didn't end up in the anthology, and the hope is that they would create their own anthology. Today's Latiné poets address trans violence, femicide, the effects of colonization and imperialism, love, joy, our food, and our traditions. It's a very exciting time to be a writer who is Latiné or Caribbean or from the diaspora or bilingual or experimental. All these lineages and approaches to language have been there, but to what extent have we been exposed to it? We have to understand that there's a tradition, a solid history for what we are doing, but this moment is also about moving forward into something that we might not have seen or might be.

Maceo: How have you come to understand the different stages of a poet's life in their work?

Willie: What's important for a writing life is thirst and that thirst for writing that which you dream about, thirst for a few more stories that I want to tell before it's time to check out. As a young poet, I can tell you in all truth that I wrote a lot of those poems in *Where a Nickel Costs a Dime* from the corner of 123rd Street and Lexington. I wasn't standing there with a pen and notebook. No. You don't take out a notebook and start writing the shit you see. You don't do that in the street. You just hang out and live, and hang out and live, and hang out and live. If I told you how many of the countless hours I spent standing on the street corner, you'd be like, "What?" But it was for a reason, not the season. Now it's all dream, memory, and imagination. Writing *The Crazy Bunch* was a sort of purging process. Now I'm thinking about this question that my mother asked me in a dream: "Where are you going?" What is it about being in Puerto Rico that gives me a level of peace that I don't find in the States? What is it about the 24-hour novel and walking through the city that inspires me? What is it about the stage that is talking to me right now? What is it about the reunion I had with my boys in a place called Hell Gate Circle that makes the perfect title for a play? What is it that we're coming back to when we sit down to write? In the last couple of plays I've been trying to write, everyone is trying to reclaim something that has been lost. What has been lost, and how do my plays become reclamation projects? I still love poetry, and I'm always going to be a poet, but in a way, the first line of the poem might not excite me as much anymore. What does excite me is all these voices coming to visit. What is it that they want? Why is it that they're saying these things? As you keep writing, you arrive at a certain truth. That's the bonus. And that's the goal: How am I moving closer to the truth?

—November 21, 2021

2

HÉCTOR TOBAR

Born in 1964 in Los Angeles to Guatemalan immigrant parents, Héctor Tobar began his writing career as editor of *El Tecolote*, a community newspaper in San Francisco's Mission District that sought to represent the community and its struggles, including its resistance to marginalization and inequality. Eventually, Tobar would bring that journalistic mission to some of the country's most important newspapers, including a long career at the *Los Angeles Times*, where he would dedicate himself to writing about the Latinx community, bringing their historically silenced or overlooked stories into a larger civic conversation. Tobar has published both fiction and nonfiction, including *Deep Down Dark: The Untold Stories of 33 Men Buried in a Chilean Mine, and the Miracle That Set Them Free*, which was a finalist for the 2014 National Book Critics Circle Award and was turned into a feature film entitled *The 33* (2015). In his long and prolific writing career, Tobar returns often to the subject of class and inequality, particularly in his novels set in Los Angeles, *The Tattooed Soldier* and *The Barbarian Nurseries*, where the city looms as large as any character and is rendered in meticulous detail. For both the subjects of his books and his perspective as a writer, Tobar draws on his upbringing as the child of Guatemalan immigrants, where he saw firsthand the struggles of his parents to feel seen and valued. He spoke very movingly of the impact that his father's voracious appetite for learning had on him. "I was lucky that my father was a big history buff," he told us. He remembers when he was in elementary school, his father brought home a maroon-bound US history textbook that they pored over together: "For him to have a son become a writer is just the absolute lo máximo." Tobar spoke to us from his home in the Mount Washington district of Los Angeles, near downtown. After a three-decade career in journalism, he has recently taught at the University of Oregon and is now at the University of California, Irvine, where he received his MFA and where he now holds appointments in Chicano/Latino Studies, Literary Journalism, and English.

JAVIER: How has the pandemic impacted your writing? And can you speak more generally about your writing process?

HÉCTOR: I was very fortunate that I was able to spend the worst months of the quarantine with my family. We were doing things that we hadn't done in a long time because my kids are older. For the first time in many years we had dinner together every night and we had a movie night every Friday. That felt very nurturing. The other part was that I got a fellowship at the Radcliffe Institute at Harvard University for a year, so I didn't have to teach. I was working on a new book, which will come out next year, called *Our Migrant Souls: A Meditation on Race and the Meanings and Myths of Latino*. I worked on this book every day.

I'm a morning writer. I usually write about two or three hours a day in the morning, unless I'm in the process of revision, in which case I might add a midday or afternoon session to that. At different times of my life, I've gotten up very, very early, especially if I'm working a full-time job. I might be up at four or five in the morning, and definitely with my last novel, *The Last Great Road Bum*, I was writing that novel while commuting back and forth between Los Angeles and Oregon and teaching. Very often my writing time was at four thirty or five o'clock in the morning until seven or eight. Lately, I've been able to sleep in until about six or six thirty and work until about eight thirty or nine. Then, usually, the afternoons are for revision and sometimes for a rougher construction of writing, where you're just throwing ideas on the page that are not formed. Then the next morning when I start, I'll smooth them over, and that's basically been my rhythm of work for several decades now.

When I worked in Mexico City, I was the *LA Times* bureau chief in Mexico City. I would work at lunchtime. I remember very vividly when I was intensely into a particular passage or chapter, I would take the printout of my chapter on the bus in Mexico City. Since the traffic is so bad and the buses always move so slowly, it was pretty easy to work on a piece with paper and pencil. For me, being a writer is a lifestyle, it's always with you and it just shapes all these different moments in your day. I'm pretty much always working because even when I'm relaxing, an idea will come to me.

JAVIER: You write nonfiction and you write fiction and you're also a very successful journalist. How does your journalism impact or influence your literary work?

HÉCTOR: I started off as a journalist and my first job was with a community newspaper in San Francisco called *El Tecolote* in the 1980s. Before that, I'd never really had an idea that writing was a profession. Then I got my first job as editor of that newspaper, I got paid $9 an hour back in the mid-1980s, and then I got a job at the *LA Times.* I dedicated myself to becoming the best journalist, but while I was a journalist, I realized after a while that there were real limitations. First of all, when you're a journalist, what you can say in writing, in the printed word, is mediated by this corporation and by its corporate structure. I could have a great idea for a story about poverty in central Los Angeles, for example, but my ability to bring that to print is going to be dependent in part on my ability to navigate this corporate bureaucracy. After a while, that becomes very frustrating. Of course, the corporate bureaucracy has its blind spots, it has its biases, it's an upper-middle-class white-run institution, was then, and pretty much still is. I had this hunger to express my full voice, to talk about in my writing what I was actually seeing in the world as a reporter. I went and applied for several MFA programs, and I got into only one, the one at UC Irvine. Then ever since, I've been going back and forth between journalism and fiction and creative nonfiction. I've discovered a symbiosis between them. There's a way in which these two different crafts feed off each other. Journalism took me as a very bookish, shy person, an only child of a Guatemalan immigrant family, and it made me go out into the world. It made me go into the federal courthouse to interview attorneys and defendants. It sent me off into Watts in South Central LA and other places in LA I had never been. It just showed me the world, and it made me want to write. Then, when I decided to become a fiction writer, I was able to express a deeper emotional and political understanding of the reality that I had seen as a reporter. *Deep Down Dark*, my book on the Chilean miners, was an attempt to write a really big book of literary nonfiction. I couldn't have written that book if I hadn't been a novelist before. At that point, I had written two novels, *The Tattooed Soldier* and *The Barbarian Nurseries*, and being a novelist taught me how to enter into the emotional landscape of a piece, the textures, the natural landscape of a story.

MACEO: In both of your LA novels, *Tattooed Soldier* and *The Barbarian Nurseries*, the city is acutely observed. You're not only giving the reader the detail to establish the setting, but you're also often giving a geography or history lesson. How did you come to see the city as a character in itself? And from a craft perspective, how do you go about collecting that level of detail?

HÉCTOR: From a very early age I wandered back and forth across Los Angeles and back and forth across the class and ethnic lines of Los Angeles. My father worked in Beverly Hills. I grew up in East Hollywood in what's now called Little Armenia and he would work on the Westside. As an adolescent, I remember going with him and his bosses to a fancy dinner at a place like Trader Vic's in Beverly Hills. When I became a reporter, I got to go to all sorts of places I had never been before, and I think that when you are an only child, you are acutely aware of your surroundings. I was a real map geek when I was a kid. I remember owning the Thomas Guide maps, which if you're an LA resident of a certain age, you grew up with these things in the age before GPS. I had this thick map book and I would look through it as a kid and I knew all the freeway names—this is the golden age of freeway construction. I knew that the State Route 2, which is the Glendale Freeway was going to go all the way to the beach and become the Beverly Hills freeway. So I grew up knowing all of this stuff about the city's geography. It was just something from an early age I was into. When you become a reporter and you're in a city, or you're a writer, you realize that you're communing with history everywhere you go, even in a city as notorious as Los Angeles for erasing its history, even that kind of city has all these stories that are layered on top of one another. When I became a writer for the *LA Times*, I realized that I could add texture to my stories. I could add a sense of perspective and context just by telling the residents of LA the history of their own city, a history that had been erased.

In terms of craft and details, something that I learned as a young reporter was just to go out and observe. There's no substitute for going and being in the physical presence of the thing that you're writing about. When I was writing *The Tattooed Soldier*, for example, I knew that I had these scenes in central Los Angeles and I was living in Orange County at the time. I would take the train into Los Angeles and wander around LA and Pico-Union and take notes because I had been trained to do that as a reporter. I remember standing under the freeway underpasses and coming up with metaphors and similes to describe how the ivy was growing there. The central lesson that you learn in journalism is that real life will always surprise you. When you report and you research a work of fiction, you're recreating that sense of surprise. You're giving the reader the sense of discovering something, and so I've spent my whole life looking for the specific terms that I can use to describe something. When I was working on *The Barbarian Nurseries*, my kids were small and we were living in Mexico City and we came back to visit LA. We went to the Huntington Gardens, and I gave my kids pieces of paper and said to them, "Go out and write the names of all the plants that you see that are interesting." I was studying these gardens, which later helped me construct the succulent garden at the beginning of *The Barbarian Nurseries*. The journalistic craft aids the fiction craft by teaching you to be observant and to be on the hunt for terminology.

JAVIER: In *The Barbarian Nurseries* you give us stories of people from all over the world that are now in community in Los Angeles. The tension between the local and the international is there in all your work. In *The Last Great Road Bum*, Joe Sanderson is from the Midwest, but he's traveling all over the world and sending letters back home. In *Deep Down Dark*, it's an incident in Chile that was used for national purposes, but it was an international effort to rescue the miners. Why is this global interconnectedness important for you to represent in your books?

HÉCTOR: The heart of it goes back to the idea that I was a child of empire. Some of the earliest political stories my father told me were about the 1954 coup in Guatemala. He was giving me these lessons when I was 8, 9, 10 years old about Guatemalan history and politics. My parents were immigrants. They were, in a certain sense, exiles, although the reason they left Guatemala was because my mother was pregnant. I always had the sense that I was part of this international system of injustice, so when I got to college, I was originally going to be a premed major, but then I met all these radical professors who were basically telling me, "Yes, imperialism is a thing, dude, and we can teach you about it." I changed my major from biology to sociology and Latin American studies. I studied all these sociological theorists of empire, and the inequality of the core and the periphery, and how these systems of exploitation worked. When I was writing for the *LA Times*, very often I was doing little allegories about inequality and about capitalist injustice. My novel *The Tattooed Soldier* was about empire, and it was about Los Angeles as this imperial city that finally has to pay the accounts for all the crimes of empire. All of my books have in one way or another been concerned with this idea of power and empire and the individual, especially the Latinx individual as someone trying to make a life within this system. That's also what drew me to Joe Sanderson's story, because I could link this Latin American revolution, the Salvadoran uprising in the cities and the mountains of Morazán and Chalatenango, and I could link that to midwestern family life. I could take the intimacy of midwestern family life, which I spent a lot of time constructing and trying to capture in all its glory and its specificity, and I could link that to this imperial war with US bullets in the bodies of the massacre victims in Morazán, which is what we see in the climax of *The Last Great Road Bum*. One of the pedagogical functions of my work is to try to teach the reader and show the reader those connections.

MACEO: In *Translation Nation* you talk about the importance of Che Guevara in your household and how your parents held him up as this ideal that you associated with Latin America. I was thinking about that in relation to your interest in Joe Sanderson and how he left home to fight for others, and whether you were drawn to him because of this childhood reverence for the Che Guevaras of the world?

HÉCTOR: Oh, absolutely. When I found out about Joe Sanderson, I was working as a foreign correspondent in Mexico City, and the first thing I thought was "Blonde Che." I remembered hearing that he had this diary that he kept until he died and that the Salvadoran rebels had saved it, and I thought of Che's Bolivian diary, and I thought that I could recreate that kind of document but told through the eyes of a blonde 5'11" white guy. I was very much drawn to the romanticism and idealism of it. The political aspects as well. Joe was someone who started off as a Republican. He supported Nixon in the 1960 presidential election and ended up dying with a group of Marxist-Leninist guerrillas. One of the things you learn when you write novels is that you have to write about the whole person, which is the opposite of journalism—daily journalism, especially. You are writing about people as issues. If you're going to write about school funding, for example, you go out and you find a bunch of people to talk about how the public schools impact their lives. So really the story is about the issue. But when you write novels, you can't approach novelistic characters that way. They have to be fully embodied people.

And so what is the full person? Who is the full-person Joe Sanderson? He was a dreamer. He was someone who disappointed his mother over and over again. He was somebody who traveled the world, and when I thought about writing Joe Sanderson's book, I thought I could just go around the whole world like he did. I could recreate the entire world of the 1960s and '70s. He saw all of these different conflicts in East Africa, in West Africa, in Asia, in the Middle East. He witnessed the aftermath of the civil wars in Yemen. He was in Israel and Palestine just before the Six-Day War. Finally, he was in the war in El Salvador as a participant. That just really swept me away. The idea that I, the bookish, shy, upper-middle-class Los Angeles dad, could, in this book, become the road bum, the wanderer, the guerrilla fighter, the guy romancing the woman on the boat between Rio de Janeiro and London. I interviewed the woman that Joe romanced. I was lucky enough to meet her and interview her. So, yes, that aspect of it was just absolutely thrilling, because that's part of why we become writers: to feel powerful and to feel we're transported into other people's lives. I so much enjoyed trying to create a work of art from Joe's life. For the time that I spent with him, I got to be an American Che, and when Joe died, when I wrote the last sentence in which Joe died, I wept. I wept because it was over. I was no longer going to be able to be the guerrilla fighter.

JAVIER: What literary traditions have you inherited?

HÉCTOR: When I was an adolescent, my father made me read *The Jungle* by Upton Sinclair. I very vividly remember that book for its denunciation of inequality. It's an immigrant story. Maybe that's why my father liked it too. That was an early influence. Later, when I went to college, I spent a lot of time in the university town where I lived, Santa Cruz, in the used bookstores, and I gravitated toward African American literature. Richard Wright was a very important early influence, his book *Native Son*. The anger in that book and the rawness of it really blew me away. Toni Morrison and Alice Walker were also very important to me. In college, I learned how to read and write in Spanish, and I read Pablo Neruda. His book *Odas elementales* was very important to me. It was the first book of poetry that I ever read. Those were some very early influences. Then when I became a newspaper reporter and I started hanging around with other writers who had literary aspirations, we would pass around lists of books to each other. I remember reading *Invisible Cities* by Italo Calvino, the Italian writer, and I took a quote from one of the fanciful cities that he described and put it on my computer terminal at the *LA Times* because I wanted to write about Los Angeles the way Calvino wrote about this imagined city, which turns out to be Venice. At that time, I also read Don DeLillo, and his high-energy prose blew me away. Sandra Cisneros was also someone who made me think that I could become a writer. She was one of the first writers I ever saw speak in person. She did a reading from *Woman Hollering Creek* at the old now-defunct Santa Monica bookstore Midnight Special. It was because of Sandra Cisneros that I decided to pursue an MFA.

MACEO: Your prominence as a journalist has given you a powerful megaphone, but I imagine that must also be a heavy responsibility, especially when you're one of the few Latinos in the newsroom. Can you speak to that responsibility?

HÉCTOR: I was very much aware at the *LA Times* that it wasn't just a sense of responsibility but one of power and vision. I tell this to my students: if you grew up working-class, if you grew up feeling marginalized or grew up in a place like Huntington Park, or East Los Angeles, or El Monte, and you're used to having people belittle you or think of you as less, or if your mother and father are undocumented, or if you're in a mixed-status family and you feel like the forces of the world are arrayed against you—well, in fact, that state of being gives you a second sight; it gives you a deeper vision. And I felt that way at the *LA Times*. I felt like all these well-off white people in this newsroom have no idea what's really going on in the city, but *I* can see it. I really know what's there. I always felt so powerful. I felt that I had something unique to say, and that that was my own personal route to feeling *myself* empowered.

That overwhelming sense of being a representative of your people can be a really difficult thing to deal with as a writer. I think it's one of the things that infantilizes a lot of Chicano/Latino cultural creation, because we feel that we can't share things that reflect poorly on our people, and so it would be hard to be, for example, a Latino Harold Pinter if you didn't want to share the fucked up dysfunction in your family. I think I was fortunate enough to have had the bulk of my career unfold before things got so polarized, because now every piece of journalism, very often books and films, they're weaponized in struggles between ideologies. They play out in social media and other places, but primarily in social media, and it's a hard thing to navigate. Of course, I'm writing a book that's about race and identity, and so I'm about to enter the fray, so that's a difficult thing to deal with. I think that as I've become older and more experienced, I've come to realize just how impossible a situation that is, if you were to think about it all the time and you were to think about what's the right thing to do and what's the wrong thing to do. I think the only right thing to do all the time is to tell the truth, and to be loyal to the fullness of the truth, and to be open minded, and to try to see things that are not immediately obvious, and bring those truths to the readers.

JAVIER: One of the issues of Latinx representation in US media is seeing Latinas depicted over and over as domestic workers. One response to this problem is to say that we should depict Latinas as lawyers, doctors, business executives, etcetera. But a different type of response to this problem, which I believe you take with *The Barbarian Nurseries*, is to represent the dignity and complexity of the character Araceli, who is a domestic worker. Why did you decide on a domestic worker as a protagonist?

HÉCTOR: Araceli is my alter ego in that novel. She's me because she is an intellectual trapped in the body of a servant. In the Los Angeles of my time, "Guatemalan" is synonymous with "hired help." If you say, "There were five Guatemalan guys in my house yesterday," that usually means that they were there to work on something in your house. It doesn't mean that they were there to talk about *El Señor Presidente* and Miguel Angel Asturias. Araceli witnesses the injustice and the inequality in Southern California firsthand. I started that novel in the wake of Proposition 187 in California in the early '90s; that's how many years passed between the time I started that novel and when it finally made it into print in 2011. I was just so angry and so upset by the media campaign and the anti-immigrant sentiment that took over talk radio. I wanted to write a story about an immigrant person caught up in a crime, someone like the protagonist of Camus's *The Stranger*. I made Araceli a servant and I wanted to totally subvert the stereotype. She's not lovey-dovey, she's not a mothering type, and she's an intellectual with frustrated ambitions. I'm proud that I created this character before I was fully aware of just how common it is for Latin American and Latina young women to be asked to subsume their dreams in the name of a brother or in the name of the family. It's just so common. Araceli is expressing those frustrations. She also has these sardonic views of the world and an intimate knowledge of the American Dream. She gets to see it from the inside and see how empty it is and see how stressful it is and see how the pursuit of the American Dream is destroying the family she works for. I was always concerned about writing a novel from the point of view of a housekeeper, but once I committed to it—committed to writing from a woman's perspective, too—it was a tremendous learning experience for me. That's why the novel took me so long to complete: because I had to rewire my machista brain to see the world the way Araceli would see it.

MACEO: My first reaction to reading all your books is that they're so different from each other, but one of the common threads is the way that class keeps us siloed and unable to truly see one another.

HÉCTOR: I grew up with this idea of social class. When I went to college, I became a Marxist. I was a very annoying Marxist for the five, six years that I was in college. I remember coming back to Los Angeles after my first couple of years of Marxist instruction—of course, I'm being ironic—in Santa Cruz and just seeing LA in a different light. "Oh my God, this is a society shaped by class struggle. This is amazing." I'm interested not just in the political aspects of class but also in the emotional aspects. For example, with the Chilean miners, each one of those guys reminded me of my dad. They were ambitious, and this job in this horrible mine allowed them a taste of a middle-class lifestyle. My father worked in hotels and worked parking cars as a valet, and that gave him a vehicle into the American middle class. These men in Chile, that was their life, their dream, and they were also flawed in all these different ways. Sometimes their ambition led them to have more than one family at a time. Of course, at the end of the book, they realize after they've been through this horrific, traumatic event that the one truly valuable thing in their life is love. It's the love that surrounds them. The love of the family, the love that the country of Chile has expressed for them as symbols of working-class Chile. Yes, absolutely, I've always thought of my books as lessons about class and reflections on class divisions.

JAVIER: Can you say more about how you see your work as political or pedagogical? And is that different from saying didactic?

HÉCTOR: When you're a Latino writer, just to write itself is a kind of political act because it's an act against an ideology of silence, a social structure that imposes the notion that we cannot have artistic or intellectual aspirations, or that they don't matter. In that context, if you become a writer who carries his or her or their Latinx identity into your work, then you're doing something subversive because our culture operates on the idea that the Latino people in this country are subservient—they're the ones who pick the crops, they're the ones who clean the bathrooms. To me, becoming a writer was a political act. It's something that is extremely impractical. You're not going to necessarily make a lot of money out of it, but you're doing it because you have this love for the idea of being human. My father's mother was illiterate. For him to have a son become a writer is just the absolute lo máximo because his whole life was trying to overcome that stigma, that sense that he was from a people who were not fully human. To me, there's something just inherently political in the process of being a Latino writer dedicated to writing about his culture.

But there is a very serious problem with then taking that idea, that our work is a political act, and becoming didactic, and just aiming to illustrate a point or essentially prove the most obvious point, which is that Latinos are people who always get fucked over. The solution to that is to be absolutely committed to the exploration and perfection of your craft and to be committed to your own voice and to what you feel your voice needs to say. That's why I'm proud that every one of my books is different from the one before, because you can see me teaching myself something new. My first novel, I had never written a novel before. Then my second book, I'd never written a book of literary nonfiction, then my next novel was this big sweeping story of class and domesticity, *The Barbarian Nurseries*, and on and on, and on and on. Each book, I've been teaching myself to do something new, and I think that that's the process that really makes you a writer, and that's also how I deal with the pitfalls that can overcome a Latino writer.

MACEO: When it comes to craft, I think one issue for Latinx writers is audience and how that audience shifts. One of your predecessors at the *LA Times* was Ruben Salazar, who was one of the first Mexican Americans to write at a major daily. He felt that his role was to translate the Mexican American experience, or the Chicano Movement, for a white mainstream readership. Do you see your role as a translator of the Latinx experience to this outsider audience?

HÉCTOR: I think that the best way to translate "an experience" is to be fully inside of that experience and to write about it with all the gravity, the seriousness, and the discipline that you would write about any subject. When I was at the *LA Times*, very often it was clear to me that I was writing stories which were translating or explaining one part of the city to another. For example, I did some of the first pieces in the *LA Times* about the Latinization of South Central Los Angeles. In those stories, I was telling the rest of LA, "Look, this is happening—Latino and Black people are now living together." But in doing that, I wasn't treating my subjects as exotic; I was writing about them from their own perspective and writing about them from the inside. I think that you have to really commit to the point of view of your subjects; at the same time, you have to have distance from them. It's a real dialectic that you're involved in when you write about a community or a place. If you think of yourself as a translator, the big potential pitfall is that you're accepting the perspective of the outsider. You're writing about a Latino barrio, but you're writing about it to explain it to the sensibility of a white middle-class person, which means that you have to accept that white middle-class sensibility as dominant. I would never approach a story that way. My job as a novelist, or as a literary nonfiction writer, is to be completely immersed in the reality I'm writing about and to explain it in its fullness, illustrate it in its fullness, enter into its madness, its beauty. What ends up being the "translation" is our common humanity. The common humanity that we have with a Chilean miner or with a Mexican house servant. The white old senior citizen in Kansas can identify with Araceli as a woman who's ambitious and is misunderstood in many ways, and that shared humanity is what brings us together, bridges this gap—not trying to explain something to someone on their own terms.

Maceo: At the end of your first novel, *The Tattooed Soldier*, we see how the bloodshed in Guatemala is connected to the bloodshed and anger in Los Angeles following the Rodney King riots. You wrote this book in the 1990s; the wars in Central America had just ended. We of course know that the bloodshed there continues to this day, and the protests after George Floyd's murder revealed how little has changed since Rodney King. Did you have a sense when you were writing your first book how indelible these issues would be?

Héctor: When I was younger, I always thought that the United States would one day face a reckoning over class inequality, the inequality I'd grown up with as a kid. Then, during economic booms, before the anti-immigrant movement started, I believed that I was writing books that would soon become dated because I thought LA would find a way to incorporate all these new immigrant peoples and allow them to thrive, like my family had thrived. With *The Barbarian Nurseries*, I thought that the plight of the undocumented would be over, maybe even before the book came out, that immigration reform would be passed and that eleven million people would get their legal residency and eventually their citizenship, but those things didn't happen. I'm not shocked that they didn't happen, but I'm also saddened. I'm saddened because I can see the clouds of a coming civil war. That really scares me. I can begin to see the end of the project called the United States of America deep into the future.

I now see those events of the early 1990s, the growth of the anti-immigrant movement, the burning of Los Angeles, as deeply tied to everything that's happened since in the United States, not just in California. Because the conflicts of the early 1990s gave birth, in part, to the anti-immigrant movement, which eventually gave birth to Trumpism. The inequality and violence in American cities gave birth to this Black uprising against police brutality. It continued until the American people saw on their telephone screens and on their computer screens a Black man being tortured to death by a police officer and it caused this social explosion. I'm surprised by the specificity of it. It's like I could feel that all of this was going to happen, but the actual way that it happened, the video of George Floyd in a Minneapolis neighborhood, the actual campaign of Donald Trump with his pompadour and his red hats, delivering these speeches in his New York Queens accent, "Build the wall," and the fact that "build the wall" became a chant in high schools in Oregon when I was teaching there. The specificity of it is nauseating and surprising. The fact that it has all happened, yes, I think it was foretold. It was foretold in American history.

I'm proud of *The Tattooed Soldier* being so far ahead of its time. I originally sold that book for $5,000 to a very small boutique publishing house called Delphinium Books. That book has now gone through two more publishers and at least two dozen printings. It was a very political book. It was raw and angry, and that's not where Latino literature was in the late 1990s. We weren't really supposed to be writing books like that. And to see it embraced—the readership for that book was still in kindergarten when I wrote that book, and now I have people come up to me and say, "Mr. Tobar, your book changed my life. I read it when I was in community college," or, "I read it at university." Every book, I imagine a different reader. For my most recent book, I'm imagining this young Latino couple who are in college or just graduated from college and are really upset by the state of their country but also love reading and love literature. I want to give them a book that they can read to each other. That makes them feel that something that they always understood has been explained. That's who I'm imagining my reader to be now.

—February 18, 2022

3

DANIEL CHACÓN

A passionate Chicano student activist at California State University, Fresno, in the 1980s and '90s, Daniel Chacón has no qualms about identifying as a Chicano writer. In his 2019 story collection, *Kafka in a Skirt*, he offers us a path to contextualize his work: "This is a work of Chicano literature. Most readers will know that before they buy the book or before they open it, and Chicano literature is one of the fibers of the Latinx literary fabric." At the same time, Chacón has refused any boundaries on what Chicanx fiction should look like. Yes, he's interested in identity, and since his 2000 debut collection, *Chicano Chicanery*, his stories have explored what it means to straddle cultures, nations, languages—all very Chicanx themes—but he pushes these concepts beyond the limiting dichotomy of Mexico and the US, Spanish and English, brown and white, and seeks an honest reckoning with authenticity. In Chacón's 2008 short story collection, *Unending Rooms*, he ends with an essay, "Borges and the Xican@ (in b flat)," that addresses the insecurities of the Chicano writer. He reflects on his own isolation and comes to understand that while he may not fully belong in any of the worlds he moves, from the barrio to academia, he *does* fully and wholly belong in the world of literature, the "place where language is made." Born in 1962, Chacón's fiction reflects his biography as a Fresno native with working-class roots who now calls the borderlands home as well as a globetrotting international writer who delights in metaphysics and literary play, ushering readers from one dimension to another. In addition to four short story collections, Chacón is the author of the novel *and the shadows took him* as well as the YA novel *The Cholo Tree*. He was also a coeditor of *The Last Supper of Chicano Heroes: Selected Works of José Antonio Burciaga* and the editor of his late friend, the poet Andrés Montoya's posthumous collection *A Jury of Trees*. Chacón is the host of a literary radio program, *Words on a Wire*, and a professor in the MFA program at the University of Texas at El Paso. He spoke to us from his home office in El Paso.*

JAVIER: How has the pandemic impacted your writing? And can you speak more generally about your writing process?

DANIEL: I had to write when I could, and the only time I could was early in the morning when everyone else in the house was sleeping. Now my daughter is three years old, but during the lockdown she was a baby and required full-time attention. I would get up very early in the morning, usually around four o'clock, and I would stay in my office until the sun came up and the baby woke. That was the only time I really had to write or to think deeply. I think going into a text—that is, reading—is just as important as creating a text—writing—and those mornings became my best reading and writing time. It was beautiful, so peaceful.

I read a lot of physics, mysticism, neuroscience, and to be frank, I don't have the mind of a scientist, so it's hard work for me to understand basic physics and brain science. I have to really push myself to understand. For some people it comes easy; they read it once and a light goes on. But it's a challenge for me, so if I read neuroscience books in the afternoon, I don't retain much, or understand much. But in the morning, I can focus. I reach flow. I'll be walking around the inside of a human brain, and before you know it, the sun is shining in my eyes. The pandemic made me aware how much I can focus in the early morning. I love it. Even now, I get up at 4:00 a.m., even though I don't have to anymore.

Writers love to reach flow—that state of focus so intense that time disappears. But to get there, it helps to have uninterrupted time. During the lockdown, I couldn't write in the daytime because my wife was teaching full-time online. She's a pre-K teacher. Can you imagine the challenge of teaching four year olds online? I had a more flexible schedule than she did, which meant that I was spending a lot of time taking care of our daughter. That's not to say that she didn't do anything. Because it was tough on her as well, and together we learned how to make sure the needs of our kids were met.

I would get small blocks of time to work during the day, but that was generally department work, as I was chair of the Creative Writing Department, and as challenging and time-consuming as it could be, you don't really need to reach a flow state to sign papers and attend meetings. If I wanted to write, I had to do it in the dark mornings, when everyone else was sleeping. I would light candles and write, not wanting the sun to come up, because when it did, that meant—like it or not—my writing day was over. I got used to those quiet hours. I got addicted to them. And even if I got little sleep, I would still wake up at 4:00 a.m. I'm blessed to have a home office with a balcony that overlooks the mountains. When the sun comes out, it lights up my windows and I blow out the candles. I go downstairs to start my day as Daddy, department chair, radio host—everything but being a writer.

One of the results of writing like this is that my fiction got incredibly short. I welcomed it because I love short short stories. During the quarantine I wrote a collection of stories, and no story was over two double-spaced pages. Most of them were just a paragraph or two. The other effect the lockdown and pandemic had on me was emotional. During the lockdown I quit Facebook, because every time I got on, the world seemed to be falling apart, and even people I loved dearly were posting some crazy, delusional shit. It was toxic. So I go off social media and even gave up reading the news for a few months, which was hard. FOMO. But it gave me time to think about my priorities. It gave me time with my daughter, and I loved it. I love being a father, and the pandemic allowed me to realize what I hope I would have realized even without it: being a dad is more important to me than writing books.

MACEO: Your story collection *Unending Rooms* includes an epilogue that very movingly describes your insecurities as a writer; specifically, as a Chicano writer from working-class Fresno contending with the feeling that a literary life wasn't for someone like you. It felt like the description of a creative breakthrough. Can you speak to that breakthrough and what it has meant for your work since then?

DANIEL: You're referring to the essay "Borges and the Xican@ (in b flat)." It takes place when I was a new Chicano professor at a midwestern university. I was the only Hispanic faculty member in the English department and one of the only ones at the university, and my department chair asked me to teach a Latin American literature class. "That would be such a great opportunity for our students," she says. "You can teach Borges and stuff." I didn't know anything about Latin American literature, or Borges. I knew Chicano/a literature, but I was very young, and I hadn't studied Latin American literature other than, of course, some Neruda and Roque Dalton, poems that helped fuel the Chicano literary soul. But I hadn't studied Cortázar or Borges or these other names that sounded so familiar. It was my first tenure-track teaching job as a fiction writer, and I didn't want anyone to know I was a phony. Or felt like one. Like I didn't deserve such a job. Like I faked my way into academia. I didn't want to tell the chair that I knew little about Latin American literature, because at that university I was their Latino diversity hire. I represented all of Latin America and Spain, so I agreed to teach it.

The town I lived in didn't have a bookstore, so one weekend I drove a few hours to the Barnes and Noble in Sioux Falls, South Dakota, and I found this thin book by Borges called *Everything and Nothing*. I read it, but I didn't understand shit, nothing. I felt so stupid. Borges can be incredibly erudite. Talk about somebody who has spent a lot of time going so deeply into a text that he not only uncovers levels of his own imagination but runs into other imaginations and thinkers, others who have gone into those same texts, and he has conversations with them. I felt left out of those conversations. Who was Coleridge? Swinburne? Swedenborg? What was Kabbalah? He seemed to be having all these conversations that I wasn't part of. I felt pretty insecure, like, "Maybe I don't deserve this job." I'm supposed to be teaching at a university and I can't even understand this literature?

Of course, there's the other side of me that wouldn't let that happen. The assertive Chicano activist side. I knew teaching this class could be an opportunity for me, and I needed to do my best with it. I just kept reading Borges. I went to the library at the university and got everything I could by him, and the more I tried to understand Borges, the more I noticed how he loved writing about mystical ideas, some that I'd encountered in the past. The research that led me to science started with mysticism, and Borges loved writing about it, thinking about it, and imagining he could enter into mystical worlds. But the most important connection I made with Borges wasn't about what he wrote but about who he was. I realized how insecure he was. He was never really able to get women in his life until María Kodama when he was already world-famous. He was very awkward and insecure around women, and the ones he fell in love with didn't return his affection. This insecurity is evident in his famous false humility, often referring to himself like Paul the Apostle as the least of writers, undeserving. A man of no importance. I found out that behind every story he wrote, there was that little insecure boy whom his grandmother called "Georgie," a boy in love with ideas and playfulness, and I began to see him. He had this line that just blew me away when he was writing about Shakespeare. He writes that Shakespeare "hid himself in the subtextual corners of his work." I realized Borges was doing the exact same thing. Even though he was writing about Shakespeare, he was really writing about Georgie.

I was suddenly able to enter into his work. He was taking these incredible concepts, mostly based on mysticism, Kabbalah, and Swedenborg, and the Bible, and was just having fun with them. That was his playground. After that I think it changed my work, because it also allowed me to integrate what I've always been interested in, and I've always been interested in mysticism. He was like a kid playing with metaphysical blocks. Years later I would read in an interview that he read the Bible voraciously, but not as a spiritual text but as "fantasy literature." That's what he said—for him, the Bible was fantasy literature, and not just the Bible but other kinds of philosophical and mystical texts. His story "Three Versions of Judas" is amazing. When I started out as a writer, I read the Bible every day. I would go every day into the text and I would just try to go deeper and deeper into it. As we know, to go deeply into a text is to go deeply into yourself, into your own subconscious. This concept in Kabbalah is called *Lech Lecha*, "go into yourself." God tells Abraham, "Go! Leave your father's land and go into the land that I will show you," but literally what he's saying is "*Lech Lecha*, go into your *self*." When you go into a text, when you go into the landscape and you uncover meanings, you are uncovering levels of your own subconscious. To do exegesis of any text, any sacred text, is to find something that's already within you. You're going deeply into yourself. You're shaping the world in your own image. I was reading the Bible for years, every day, and that led me to reading mysticism. Eventually, I arrived at the Jewish mystics, the Kabbalists, thanks to Borges, and I had an amazing year in

Buenos Aires, the city Borges loved most. Maybe none of this would've happened hadn't I challenged myself to understand Borges.

JAVIER: What have been the formative moments in your journey as a writer?

DANIEL: I sold a novel to a trade press, and I got enough money that I was able to take a year off from the university. I went to Buenos Aires. It was a city I had been to twice before. Each time I went to that city, or at least initially, it was because of Borges. I visited his house and I visited the library where he was director when he was blind. This year off, I rented an apartment in Buenos Aires, serendipitously the exact same building in Recoleta where Bioy Cásares used to live and where Borges and Bioy used to write their detective stories, The Seventh Circle series. As I was there, I started to look more into Kabbalah. I would go into these esoteric bookstores and find basic books about it. Then one day, I was at this outdoor café where Borges used to sit all the time, called La Biela. In fact, they even had this kitschy statue of him inside the restaurant. I was at that café one morning, and I was reading the Sunday newspaper, and there was this big article about Emmanuel Swedenborg and the influence he had on the most famous person in Argentina: Borges. I had never heard of Swedenborg, except that Borges might have brought up his name. But I'm reading this article in La Biela and it talks about how weird Swedenborg was for a Christian mystic, and that one of the ideas that Borges admired is that nobody was sent to hell. People choose hell. I can't go into it right now, but it was really a fascinating idea, and I was hooked.

I went into Swedenborg. I read everything I could by him, and I just started to make connections. It was incredibly transformative for my writing. There is a basic concept in esotericism, "As above, so below," attributed to Hermes Trismegistus, but Swedenborg explained it so amazingly well in his book *Heaven and Hell*, calling it "correspondences." And he had a tremendous influence on poets. And something happened while I was reading Swedenborg that rarely happened before. As I was reading, I felt like I was walking through a city having a conversation with him. It was weird, but it allowed me to really understand the ideas. I was blown away.

When I left Buenos Aires, I was talking to a friend about some Kabbalistic concept that fascinated me, and she said, "That's physics!"

I go, "What?" So I started to go into lay books for physics and did that for ten years or so. I found the ideas to be mind-blowing and it took me to levels of the imagination I didn't even know I had access to. I even taught a class, a graduate seminar on physics and the creative writer, where we take the metaphors and play with them. Now I'm going deeper into Kabbalah. I'm going into shamanism. I'm going into esoteric systems, uncovering all these great ideas. It's all transformative because I'm still excited about it. I guess the way it affects my writing is that I understand on a more visceral level how to reach creative realms I once thought lucky to get a glimpse of. I have come to realize that the most important thing for me as a writer is the imagination, the ability to enter into imaginary realms, talk to imaginary creatures, even entities and thought beings. To use a worn-out quote from Einstein, "Imagination is more important than knowledge." I'm having more fun now writing fiction than I ever have.

JAVIER: You've talked about Borges and the tradition of mysticism. What are some other literary traditions that you feel you've inherited?

DANIEL: I'm a Chicanx writer. When I became a writer, it was parallel to my political consciousness and awareness—that is, my Chicanismo. I wanted to write stories that uncovered oppression and that wanted to do something about it. I was an activist, and I wanted to wake people up. That was my initial identity. But then the poet Andrés Montoya told me, "Don't think of yourself as a Chicano writer, think of yourself as a Latin American writer." When I started studying Borges, I remembered that, and I started looking into Cortázar. Now I'm into some Argentinian writers that are really blowing me away. The fact is, it was good advice, because the Chicano literary community then isn't like what it is today. Today, the Chicanx literary community is really more of a Latinx literary community, and it's huge. Back then, it was very small. If there was a Chicanx writer, you knew each other or they knew of you; everybody did. I was entering that community when it was still small. It's not that way anymore. Especially where I work at University of Texas, El Paso, in an MFA program that is bilingual and most of our students are from Latin America. I think the communities are coming together for me in ways that I could only imagine earlier in my life. I *am* a Latin American writer. I identify with Latin American writers. Although now I think maybe Andrés was wrong. Maybe it's not "be a Latin American writer." Maybe it's "be a multiverse writer." Be a fucking multiverse writer. I'll always be that Chicano boy trying to understand ideas and feeling insecure because he's not so smart; or like Lorna Dee Cervantes says in her great "Poem for the Young White Man," I'll always have that "nagging feeling that I'm not good enough." But perhaps that leads to humility, and that's something everybody could use a little bit of.

JAVIER: Your first book is called *Chicano Chicanery.* You said once that you gave it that title because you just wanted to see how people would say, "Chacón's Chicano Chicanery." What was behind your choice to center chicanery in your first collection?

DANIEL: Going deeply into a text is to go deeply into the subconscious, and I don't think you need to go very deeply to find me in those stories. There's the one about the guy who lives in Portland, the newscaster who wants to punch every white person that he sees. That's what Andrés and I felt like at the University of Oregon when I wrote that story. We were at a point where we were angry because it was so white and so liberal. That liberalness sometimes irritated the shit out of us. We wanted to punch a liberal. I know it sounds horrible, but that's what it was like. When you're in such a liberal, all-white community you begin to see how cultural biases and racism seep through their language and into their behavior, in spite of what they think of themselves, in spite of the fact that they will literally say, "I don't have a racist bone in my body." I wrote most of the stories from *Chicano Chicanery* when I was in Oregon and they reflect different parts of my experience as a Chicano from Fresno. I was so young and often confused, telling myself that I didn't deserve to be a writer, that I wasn't qualified to be a writer. When I got a rejection notice, even if it was from the *New Yorker*, it hurt. It was evidence that I wasn't good enough. To use the cliché, I was my own worst enemy. I don't deserve this. I'm not good enough. Sometimes we use the chicanery on ourselves, to subvert our own successes.

MACEO: In your novel *and the shadows took him*, Joey Molina performs being a cholo, or a gang member. There's also a degree of performance in *The Cholo Tree*, where, similarly, he's expected to perform roles that people expect of him. How do you view this element of performance in your work?

Daniel: Before I wanted to be a writer, I wanted to be an actor. Ever since I was a kid, that's all I wanted to be. At family gatherings when I was seven, eight, I would get my cousins together and write little scripts, and we'd go perform them for the adults. I just loved to hear them laugh and the applause afterwards. That just fed me. Clearly, what's at the center of this is my intense egotistic need to get attention. There's no question about that. I think all of us have that need on some level, but it's what we do with it that matters. I know that on some level, that's what I wanted. I was a kid wanting attention. But you transform that energy into something positive. When I started to write, I wrote pieces that were performance oriented. I used to write plays all the time. I used to direct and stage them at different places. Eventually, it became fiction, and I'm still dealing with characters who are performers. I think that when we interact with others, whatever goals we might have, we're performing in a sense.

Maceo: Your characters are also performing identity. They are never comfortable in their own skin, always feeling like they have to pretend in order to be accepted. To what degree is this a reflection of your own experience, your own life?

Daniel: I'll go back to that first time I read Borges. The story was called "Everything and Nothing," and it's about Shakespeare. One of the lines I connected to was that when Shakespeare wasn't on stage performing or when he wasn't creating his dramas, he didn't know who he was. He felt like he needed that performance in order to find himself. The line that struck me, and I'm paraphrasing, was "He was surprised when he told other people how he felt about this and they didn't feel the same way." Other people had an identity. He didn't. He needed to keep trying on these different masks. I think there's an element of that to me as a writer. I don't know who I am, so I try on these different masks. One of the biggest struggles of my life is identity, which is probably also why I'm such a Chicano writer, because that was one of the initial themes of Chicanx literature: Who am I, where do I fit in?

Javier: What is the connection between metafiction and metaphysics in your work?

Daniel: One of the things that I began to realize about consciousness is that we create a story about who we are as individuals. I have a Daniel Chacón story. Daniel Chacón was born, he did this, and this, blah, blah, blah. I have more or less control over the themes of my story, but we also have a story about reality. Most of us have two stories, a story about self and a story about reality. That story about reality might be based on the metaphors of physics. For instance, the world started with the big bang, there was this great expansion, and the world works this way, but I don't know the math. I'm just telling a very thin metaphorical story, and it's the same with myself. When I tell a story about myself, my memory, or the details, have absolutely nothing to do with facts. We know this. We encode memory based on meaning and emotional impact, not details. Every memory that we have is false, on the material level. The story we tell about ourselves is false. And we constantly change the meaning and content of our stories.

Not only that, but when you ask someone about their life, their story is going to be different from what they might have told a year earlier, or even ten minutes earlier. The cognitive scientist Daniel Kahneman did these great studies on the different ways that human beings think about their lives. One of the things that he says is that the meaning or the value of your life in any given point in space-time depends on your mood. So if you ask somebody who's having a shitty day, "How would you rate your life?" they're going to rate it differently than if they had a good day. Which means that their reality changes from day to day. When you go from year to year, and when you go from seven years to seven years—where physics tells us that you're an entirely new set of atoms—you're not the same person. There's not a single atom that exists in you that existed seven years earlier. All you carry is coding, memory, pattern recognition. The story always changes. The story in other words is false.

Once I was able to understand that, it was incredibly, incredibly empowering. Liberating. If the story of myself is false, then every story ever told is false. The energy behind it is not false, and, in fact, energy is the only real thing about me. The story of Daniel Chacón is false, but Daniel Chacón is a living organism with energy that is encoded to survive and procreate. But I don't need to survive or procreate, thank God. I've already procreated and I'm doing pretty well surviving, but even though those aren't my imperatives anymore, the energy is there. The drive. I have this incredible energy, like everybody. If I am a created story, I can change the details.

You can start playing with matter. That's where metafiction comes in, because you are very conscious that the story that you are telling or the story that the reader has played in their mind is false. It's a wink, wink. This doesn't really exist. Look backstage. What are you going to see? You're going to see that the landscape you thought was real is just painted, suggestive of a reality. It's all fake. Everything. But in a good way. Because if it's fake, that means all that really matters is our energy. Call it a soul, call it a meaning, call it the Spirit of God, call it the energy that lives within all of us. That seems to be what matters most. Not the details of the story. Details of the story are to be played with by the writer, and the individual if you are so inclined, to create the story you want.

Maceo: How has that influenced the way you've framed your collections? For instance, each story is a room to be entered in *Unending Rooms*. In *Hotel Juárez*, you have not only rooms but also loops. And then in *Kafka in a Skirt*, you've imagined all the stories existing in a sort of cloud system called "The Wall." This framing seems central to your work.

Daniel: In *Kafka in a Skirt*, all the data is stored. That is, "The Wall" in the subtitle is a data storage company, like iCloud or Dropbox. Everything you've ever written in your Notes, every document you've ever written and deleted, every photograph, your tweets, your Insta posts, your feelings, your grocery lists—it's all somewhere in the cloud. For example, when you use your Notes app to write down what you want at the grocery store, and then later you delete it, it's not gone. It's in your "Recently Deleted Files," and after that it's stored somewhere. If you had the processing power to take that information, you could represent consciousness. I think by the time I die, there will be so much of my consciousness stored in the cloud that my daughter could get a Dead Daddy app, and she could ask it questions, and it would respond very closely to what her real daddy would've said. It knows me. And this was the creative landscape within which I organized the stories in the collection. I write the stories, sometimes for years, and then I put them together and I see what is emerging, and that's how I organize a collection of stories.

And that's where "The Wall" came in. I knew I wanted to say something about the wall, about Trump's wall to separate families and to separate Mexicans from Mexicans, but it seems like I also wanted to say something about big data and how it is affecting our ability to make optimal choices. Everything is stored in the cloud, and in the future, when we are able to process that on more effective levels, it could mean that your consciousness is not going to die even when your body does. But what it means mostly for us now is that the algorithms created based on your information are incredibly accurate, and they can manipulate you. This is all very obvious and very well known. So in the collection, The Wall is, on one level, the wall that separates Mexico from the United States, but it's also a border that represents powers or entities that are able to control you because of the information that they have. You cannot penetrate it. You cannot climb over it. But it is used to control you.

MACEO: Given all that you've talked about, the fact that our lives are just data, the false narratives that we try to place on top of the infinite possibilities that surround us, do you perceive yourself and your work as political?

DANIEL: I suppose everybody's a political animal, and as a Chicano with a political consciousness coming from an oppressed community, I don't think I could ever write a book that doesn't have the struggle somehow embedded within it. And going back to *Kafka in a Skirt*, it's a collection of stories, some of them weird, some of them based on imaginary realms. But ultimately, I felt the need to say something about what was going on with "the border crisis." That's what they called it, although the border has always been in a crisis state, especially for Mexicans. But during the time that I was writing *Kafka*, immigrants from all over Latin America were coming to the US-Mexico border, thousands of people in these caravans crossing the landscape to get to the border, one of those border crossings right here where I live in El Paso–Ciudad Juárez. I remember going to Juárez one day, and usually on the way back it might take you an hour at most, but there were so many people there it took all day before we were able to get back. Boo-hoo, right? Poor little us. What was stunning is how many people were living on the streets waiting for some opportunity that would never come for them to be able to just cross to the other side. Thousands of people were camped out, families camped out, children not yet separated from their families playing ball in an alley. And when the US under Trump began to separate the children from the parents, it got surreal. That's Nazi stuff. But we let it happen. Well not we, because we—the Chicanx community, and some people of conscience—fought it. But our government, that which represented the people, had no problem with locking up children. How could I not say something about that? As feeble as my message might have been, I go on record fighting such blatant racism and crimes against humanity.

JAVIER: What are the milestones of Latinx literature so far in the twenty-first century, and which directions do you see Latinx literature taking as we continue in this century?

DANIEL: I think that we really need to look out for writers like Mariana Enriquez and Samanta Schweblin. They're both from Argentina, and they're both writing these incredible stories that are being translated all over the world. I think they're the emerging Latin American writers of our time, and they are going to set the tone in many ways. They're both women, and they're both in your face, presenting us with narratives that don't hold anything back, and both of them are rooted in or dabble with the occult.

JAVIER: Do you think there's a possibility for US Latinx literature to also be in that conversation?

DANIEL: I think it's happening right now. Latin America and Latinx-USA are coming together like never before. I believe that in ten years it's not going to be AWP with just a Latinx component; I think the community is going to be Latin American with an English-language component. Latin American writers and US Latinx writers are coming together. It's happening at UTEP, that's for sure. I actually get more invitations for readings and talks in Latin America than I do in the US, more internationally than I do in the US, where Latin American writers along with other international writers are constantly getting together; not in an insulated way that North American writers do, but with an international and global perspective on poetry. I think we're going to all be Latin American writers.

MACEO: Your first book was delayed for a couple years, but the result was that it was published in 2000, so all of your published work has happened in the twenty-first century. You've been a part of and witnessed different trends. Can you speak to this era of US Latinx literature and how you've seen it evolve?

Daniel: Originally, in Chicano literature, we just could not get published, period. Early Chicano literature, Chicanos were just trying to get published, but nobody wanted to publish them. Occasionally, there was some writer who broke through and got published by New York, but it was very difficult. So we published ourselves. At Fresno State, Chicano writers were always getting rejected by the official English Department literary journal, at the time called *Common Wages*. I later became the editor and changed the name to *The Joaquin Review* and diversified it, but before, they just wouldn't take our work. So we started our own journal, *Pachuco Children Hurl Stones*, which still exists today. That's the traditional Chicanx way, yes? Don't wait for the white people. Don't wait for the oppressor. Don't wait for anybody else to publish you. Publish yourself.

The greatest example of this tradition today is FlowerSong Press. They are transforming Latinx literature, and they're going to have a deep influence on the future of Latinx writing because they're publishing about fifty books a year. Unprecedented. Every book that they publish has the ability to reach a worldwide audience because of the digital information age, because of social media, because of all these things that we have access to. If you are good at promoting your book, your book is going to take its place in the canon. To be picked up by a "legitimate" press used to be the writer's goal, but the idea of a legitimate press doesn't exist anymore. We are asserting ourselves in the publishing world. We are taking control. There are so many voices out there now. There are so many Latinx books that are being published, there's no way I can keep track of them. I think it's a beautiful thing. Finally, we're taking control. Some people, young people especially, know how to get people to buy their books. They're really good at it. In fact, the young generation is going to be so good at it, that a lot of the writers we're going to read in the next ten, twenty years are there because of their ability to assert their work. They believe in their work, and they should believe in their work.

—June 17, 2021

* A portion of this introduction was adapted from Maceo Montoya's review of *Kafka in a Skirt: Stories from the Wall* in the *New York Journal of Books* (www.nyjournalofbooks.com).

4

ANA MENÉNDEZ

The titular story in Ana Menéndez's *In Cuba I Was a German Shepherd* is grounded in humor, nostalgia, and the way that exile can warp our understanding of our past and ourselves. The jokes related by the widower Máximo to his domino-playing friends slyly speak to larger truths about the Cuban exile community and place sadness and yearning on the same level as the need to laugh. It is that mix of heaviness and lightness that typifies so much of Menéndez's work, including her 2011 experimental novel, *Adios, Happy Homeland!*, which is presented as a personal anthology of Cuban writers put together by Herberto Quain, a fictional Irishman who has made Cuba his home and a nod to Borges. Throughout the collection, Menéndez adopts different styles and personas, each voice commenting on the mythology of Cubanness and undermining any notion that Cuban identity is fixed or that anyone has a monopoly on authenticity. The niece of celebrated Cuban poet, Dionisio Martinez, Menéndez began her writing career as a journalist for the *Miami Herald* before finding herself more at home writing fiction. She received her MFA from New York University and shortly after won a Pushcart Prize for "In Cuba I Was a German Shepherd." Publishing success followed with a lucrative multi-book deal from Grove Press, which included her story collection and the bestselling *Loving Che*, which traverses similar territory of nostalgia and a search for a past that can never be truly known. Menéndez continued her work as a journalist and wrote and spent extensive time in Afghanistan and India. This experience led to her third work of fiction, *The Last War*, which she describes as a breakthrough book in terms of exploring identity and other selves outside of being Cuban American. Menéndez spoke to us about her forthcoming novel *The Apartment*, her first book since 2011, following years where she wasn't sure she would write fiction again, and shared how reading led her back to telling her own stories. Menéndez teaches at Florida International University, where she divides her time between the English Department and the Wolfsonian Public Humanities Lab. She spoke to us from her home office in Surfside, Florida.

JAVIER: How has the pandemic impacted your writing? And can you speak more generally about your writing process?

ANA: My last book, which I feared was going to be the last book for a long time, came out in 2011, the same year that my son was born. Having a child changed my life drastically. I have a super involved husband, but even so it has been hard. My writing process for the last eleven years has been very slow. During shelter in place, we were fortunate that we didn't get sick. We didn't suffer any losses. We're in a small minority of people who were privileged to be able to shelter at home. We spent part of the time in Slovakia where my husband is from, and I taught online. Because of the time difference, I was able to get a lot of writing done before the East Coast woke up. There was nobody online, nobody could bother me, no questions, no emails, nothing, and I was able to do that final push on this new novel I've been working on for eleven years, which has changed drastically from draft to draft.

In the last couple of years, the writing process for me has been "I take it when I can." It's not a consistent practice, certainly not as consistent as I would like it to be. I need more than just a three-hour chunk in a day. I need a long calendar block. One of the things that really helped me last year is when we came back from Slovakia, my husband took my son and they went back to be with his parents, and so I had six weeks in the summer by myself. I just blocked that off, did the final edits, and that's when it was finished. I find that I need to block off weeks rather than hours.

Maceo: *Adios, Happy Homeland!* is framed as a personal anthology of an Irishman who has claimed Cuba as his home. There's a letter in the book by the many authors who write to the editor resenting the label "Cuban" and questioning the editor's authority. Can you speak to this issue of authority when it comes to Cubanness?

Ana: I started writing *Adios, Happy Homeland!* just to have fun, I wasn't planning to publish anything. That sense of playfulness animates the book. To the question about authenticity and who has the right to call themselves Cuban, as a hybrid writer—Cuban, American, every other identity that I claim—what are you allowed to write? Are you allowed, as a Latina writer in the United States, to write about non-Latina issues? Are you allowed to take inspiration from an Argentine old fuddy-duddy? These are all questions that animate me personally. The book came out at a time of intense frustration with the publishing industry, with being pigeonholed, with all sorts of nonproblems, but they're very personal problems when you're in them. The book was a way of saying, "Who gets to be Cuban?" In Cuba, critics were saying, "We can't call the Cuban American writers Cuban." Then there were debates in the States saying, "Cuban writers aren't Latino because they don't have the same concerns that the rest of us do," and so forth. So there's this question of, Where do you fit in? Where is the story? Where are your observations as a writer? Because really, for me, writing is more than personal experience, it's about what you are paying attention to and what do you want to highlight in your experience, and in the experience of others, and why? Why do these things grab you? The book was a way of working these things out. People have interpreted it in various ways. I did a reading at a college and someone said, "This Herberto Quain is a cultural appropriator." Sure, you can describe him that way, but I was trying to get at something deeper, and that is which identities we get to choose and wear like clothes, and which are we not allowed to ever take off, and why, and who gets to choose? A lot of it was my own personal push and pull through those questions.

Javier: Did you start out wanting to write a fictional anthology?

Ana: I had written another novel, which became the short story, "The Boy Who Was Rescued by Fish." It was a traditional novel. It had a plot, and it had character development, intention, all those things which we're taught, and it bored me to tears. I finished it, and I thought, "This story is so boring." I was just forcing myself to go in and write. I said, "This bores me, and I certainly can't inflict it on anybody else." I had a crisis, thinking this writing thing is not for me anymore. I've done it. I have no inspiration, and I'm not interested. But I did what I always do, which is I went back to reading. I went back to the reading that delighted me, and it doesn't tend to be plot-heavy books because after a while I can see all of the mechanisms underneath. I went back to Italo Calvino, who has always been a huge influence and favorite, and I picked up *Six Memos for the Next Millennium*. He has a chapter on each of the qualities which he thinks will animate literature in the next millennium; in our millennium. That book led me to Georges Perec's *Life: A User's Manual—La Vie mode d'emploi*. I love that book. It's just nuts. I felt reinvigorated about the possibilities of writing and what it can give us. The sort of magic that's inherent in constraints. All writing is problem-solving. In giving yourself a series of constraints, you're upping the stakes. You're making even more problems for yourself than writing already has. In that problem-solving, there's so much joy for me as a writer because the process itself becomes a joy, not just the outcome of what you're trying to produce. With Calvino in my head, I went back and read Borges's "An Examination of the Work of Herbert Quain." I thought, "I'm going to write one of the books that Herbert Quain wrote," and I wrote the story about the two men waiting on a train platform, "You Are the Heirs of All My Terrors," which became the foundational story for the book. From there, I developed the constraints—there had to be some kind of transportation, maybe trains, maybe some kind of flight. The last line of each story begins the line of the next story. Then it just grew. I wanted to repurpose that horrible novel that I had just written because the themes were similar. Then I had another story that had been published in *BOMB* magazine. I was like a magpie with my own things. "Oh, this is shiny. I'm going to put this in here, too, because this also fits with the theme." So I started with Herbert Quain, and as an homage and a thank you to Borges, I transformed "Herbert" into "Herberto," and I gave him the reigns of the entire anthology.

Maceo: If we could go back a little further, what have been the formative moments in your journey as a writer?

Ana: My uncle is Dionisio Martinez, a very well-known poet. He doesn't write anymore, tragically, but he was very celebrated when he was writing. Just a fabulous poet, and very eccentric. I grew up in Tampa at the bottom of a cul-de-sac, very middle-class suburbia. Two houses this way was my maternal grandparents' house, where my uncle lived. Two houses that way were my paternal grandparents. I grew up surrounded by them, by their stories. They're all storytellers and liars, mostly. My uncle, the poet, would give me poetry books all the time. I was in kindergarten when he gave me two books from Carl Sandburg that were meant for children. One of them was *Early Moon*. I still remember, "The fog comes / on little cat feet." They just delighted me. His best friend was Silvia Curbelo, another celebrated Cuban poet. They were in and out of my house all the time. Silvia Curbelo once said to somebody, "I've known Ana Menéndez since she was in diapers," and somebody responded, "Oh, that must have been quite a party." It was this moment where there were these great writers around me, and they were poets. I never grew up with this idea that poetry was inaccessible, or strange, or elitist. These were all middle-class, even lower-middle-class, neighborhoods, and poetry gave us life.

Reading was always part of my life. Because I read so much, whenever I would write anything for school, the teachers were like, "This is great." It wasn't, it was just I was reading a lot, but that kind of early praise makes you feel at least that you can do it, you can continue. I always knew that I wanted to tell stories. I was the class clown. My son now is exactly like me. My husband gets so mad because he doesn't pay attention in class and he's joking around. I was that person. Go to lunch and just tell funny stories about my family that were exaggerated. That power to make people laugh or to move them in some way was intoxicating. This is before I even put pen to paper, just the act of storytelling. I was the high school newspaper editor, worked on the college paper, and always knew that I wanted to study English literature, even in the '80s when nobody was doing it anymore and everybody was studying business and my family was freaking out. They wanted me to be a lawyer. I got a job when I was still in college at the *Miami Herald*, and that was a good education in writing, in editing, in paying attention, in not getting snowed, and not letting your preconceived notions get in the way of the story—all the things that are so important as a writer. I was a journalist for a couple of years and then I burned out. I have a habit of leaving jobs that start to bore me, just like novels. I got burned out and bored and applied to a couple of MFA programs, not really knowing what MFAs were. I was very lucky that I got accepted by NYU with a full ride because I wouldn't have paid for it. My first book was basically my master's thesis.

JAVIER: *Adios, Happy Homeland!* is concerned with poetry and poets. Your novel *Loving Che* is a narrative, but there are lyrical moments throughout. Can you speak about the influence of poetry on your work as a fiction writer?

ANA: I'm a completely frustrated poet. I didn't feel that I was good enough. I remember taking a poetry class in college and the professor was like, "Yeah, no." Little things like that can really change your trajectory. And not that I would be competing with my uncle, but I felt like I couldn't do what he was doing. I needed to hone my basic skills first. Not that short story or novel writing is more basic than poetry, but there's a compression in poetry that takes a long time to get right. Poetry is incredibly difficult. Not difficult to understand, but difficult to write, and the simpler it looks, the harder it is. To me, poetry is a kind of an altered consciousness. It's a way into magic. Poetry, like certain visual art, gets at the truth in a way that is not always possible, or maybe ever possible, through narrative. All these ways of communicating and looking at reality are necessary because we're limited by our senses. There's a kind of claustrophobia in how much we can know of the world and how much we can know of reality. I guess I have this voracious need to experience as much of it as possible. I think it's probably led to my doing all these jobs and living all over the world, this kind of hunger for—not "understanding," because I think that's hubris—but for experience and for burrowing under the surface of experience. Poetry does that for me. *Loving Che* is more of an extended prose poem that would get at this intoxication that we have with revolution, with beautiful people, and how it's all very similar, the feeling of transformation, of transport. That's poetry for me.

MACEO: In thinking about the more lyrical aspect of your writing, and your beginnings as a reporter, did you feel as if your fiction writing needed to be a departure from your work as a journalist? Were you conscious of the stylistic separation between the two?

ANA: I'm not sure because a lot of how we write is unconscious. It's below our will in a way. Another way to look at it is that I was ill-placed in journalism. One aspect of journalism that I never enjoyed was the facts. I was crazy about them, and I'd wake up in the middle of the night saying, "Oh, I misspelled this person's name." Real anxiety, which kind of spiraled out of control. This is one of the reasons I left: because I became so fixated on getting it right. It was almost like I understood that I wasn't interested in the facts, that they weren't the most important part of the story, and so I became obsessed with them. In daily journalism, it's all about the facts. You have to get the facts right. I think that tension created this enormous anxiety in me. I was so afraid of getting something wrong. When I was at the *Orange County Register*, I did a profile of this woman, an English-only activist in California who was Mexican American. She dyed her hair blonde and she wore blue contacts. This was interesting to me and I led with it. Then, as night began to fall, I was like, "How do I know they're blue contacts? Maybe they're her real eyes," even though I had asked her. "Maybe they're blue contacts, but her real eyes are also blue." It just spiraled into this madness where I was online, trying to find her DMV records to see what her real eye color was. I realized, okay, I need to get out, because it's driving me mad.

I got into journalism because I like to write and I needed a job. Journalism gave me all of that, and it gave me an excellent education in writing, but I was less interested in catching people. Every young reporter starts in the municipal beat, and when there are elections you have to do criminal background checks on everybody who's running. I would go down to the courthouse to look through stuff and I'd be praying that I wouldn't find a criminal record. "Oh, please let this person be okay." That's not a real journalist. A real journalist is dying to get some dirt on people and make it public. I was much more interested in the storytelling aspects of journalism, what makes people tick. Like why this Mexican American woman is an English-only advocate? What is she about? I'm much more interested in those aspects of being human that are powerfully explored in a lot of nonfiction work—sometimes even better than they are in fiction—but that aren't so important in the nuts-and-bolts reporting of every day.

MACEO: In *Loving Che*, the narrator writes "This endless pining for the past seemed to me a kind of madness; everyone living in an asylum, exiled from the living, and no one daring to say it plainly." In other stories, we often see Cuban exiles' relationship to Cuba as a form of hysteria. How did this idea crystalize for you and become a facet of your storytelling?

Ana: Both my parents consider themselves exiles. My father came in '61, and my mother came in '65. They met in Los Angeles, and I was born in 1970. As a kid, I didn't really appreciate the fact that they were in the States for not even a decade when I was born, and so of course they were completely discombobulated and young and waiting to go back. Just never able to accept this disaster that befell them, going through life in a state of shock. For us kids, it became a joke: "Everything was better in Cuba." My mom would say, "In Cuba, you would drop a seed in the ground and a tree would grow." The chocolate was better there, the American chocolate was horrible—which was probably true in 1970s Tampa. Everything was wanting. My dad was from Varadero, so he couldn't go to the freakin' beach anywhere without eye rolls about how horrible this beach was compared to Varadero, where the sand was so fine it was like powder. On and on, and on and on. They were living in a kind of state of suspended animation, like they could cryogenically freeze themselves and just transport back to Cuba when Fidel died. It became clear to me at some point that this was never going to happen. That even if it did happen, you can't visit the same island twice.

Then I went to Cuba for the first time in '97. I had always considered myself Cuban, but when I went to Cuba, I was like, "Oh wow, I'm not Cuban. What am I?" Yes, I spoke Spanish like a Cuban. I was indistinguishable from them outwardly, perhaps, and even linguistically, but completely different culturally. It was liberating in a way, because then I figured you really are what you want to be. You are what you rub up against. I wrote an essay recently, called "Traveling with My Selves," about this process of learning that identity is a fluid thing, that as we move through the world, we shed bits of it and we pick up other bits. I lived in India for three years, and in India, I was Western. In Miami, I'm Cuban. I go to LA, I'm Hispanic, or spic, or whatever else they called me. Then, in New York, I fit in. In New York, I'm not Jewish, but I get "Shabbat Shalom" everywhere I go. In Pakistan, I am a woman, and so forth. You see that who you are really is contingent on a bunch of different factors that go way beyond where your parents are from, what kind of culture you grew up in. It's the people you meet. It's how people see you, and all of those are important aspects of identity, which I think the

Cubans missed out on. The Cubans who left, my parents' generation, because they came to the States and didn't leave their own community, they didn't really have that contact with other cultures, with other people, with other stories. To them, they're the only ones who suffered in the whole world. There's a lot that you gain from listening to other people's stories, and you don't lose anything. I think the Cubans felt that they would lose, that they would lose those memories. Not all of them, I'm generalizing, but in my own family, I saw this play out, and I was determined not to be like that.

JAVIER: Could you share your experiences in getting your works published, either positive or negative?

ANA: I wasn't really interested in publishing; I was writing just for fun and for myself. There's been so much talk, MFA versus NYC, and is the MFA useful? Is the MFA useful to writers of color? For me, it was incredibly useful because it gave me time to read and it gave me time to write. It gave me a wonderful group of people to hang out with, go drinking after workshop, and just enjoy my life after years of working like a dog. Edna O'Brien led one of my first workshops. She loved "In Cuba I Was a German Shepherd," and she didn't like anything. She was fierce. She used to throw stuff across the conference table with "This isn't literature." But she told me, "Send this to *Zoetrope* magazine. Use my name." I sent it in, and they also rejected it. They said, "It doesn't have enough plot for us, but good luck with it." Then I went back to India where I was living part of the time. I went back to reporting and freelance photography. I forgot about the story. Then *Zoetrope* sent me an email a couple of months later and said, "We can't stop thinking about the story, and we'd like to publish it." It won a Pushcart Prize, and my first agent found me. I showed her some of the *Loving Che* stuff, and she had a two-book deal with Grove in two weeks, for a nice chunk of money—six figures. Back in those days, you could do that. Later, I met up with a friend of mine who also wrote for Grove. We were drinking, and I think he had had a few, and he said, "We're all poets now," because the publishing industry has changed tremendously.

For me, in terms of publishing, I haven't really had any horrible experiences. Part of it is because I approach writing in a very collaborative spirit, probably from my journalism days. I need a good editor, somebody who's smarter than me, somebody who can really see what I'm doing and make suggestions that make it better, which I'm not capable of. I think the best editor-writer relationship is one where the editor is smart and can't write or they're so smart that they don't know how to put into writing what they're thinking. The writer is a workaday writer who's a craftsperson who needs that extra magic. That's a perfect melding of minds.

MACEO: *The Last War* is about a disintegrating marriage between two journalists, most of it set in Istanbul. It's a thematic departure from your other books about Cuba and Cuban exile communities. At some point, your narrator, a Latina expat, says that people would say to her, "You should be with your own people. I had found it terribly condescending. . . . Why was someone always trying to shove you into last year's trendy bullshit about identity and belonging?" Was this a tension you experienced?

ANA: Yes, I was chafing under this very rigid sense of identity because I was beginning to experience just how fluid it really is. We've become much more attuned to the way gender is fluid, but we still haven't caught on to the way that all our other identities are also fluid. This was the first time that I really was deciding I don't want others to be defining me, and I don't want to be defining myself. Let me just experience the world and then see what comes of it. In a bit of frustration, I made the character Dominican just to not make her Cuban. That novel was very much influenced by things that happened in my own life. I was a reporter in Afghanistan in 1998 when the Taliban was at the height of their power and influence. I saw a live execution, saw a live amputation of a hand, and was really scared in a multiplicity of ways. Then, of course, the sense of what it means to be a woman there. That was a profoundly life-altering experience, and I could not return to writing about Cubans in the same way. And so *The Last War* was a necessary buffer for me in terms of how I approach my subject and how I approach the larger truth beneath everything that I'd been writing.

I was interested in ideas of displacement and exile and loss, and Afghanistan and South Asia just blew that up for me. Where did that leave me as a writer? Am I still going to be writing these bespoke little stories, or do I take what I've learned and expand on it? *The Last War* was a transitionary novel for me, and *Adios, Happy Homeland!* took that idea even further. *The Apartment*, which comes out next year, explores it even more through different stories that all come back to this question of violence, and not violence in the moment but the aftereffects of violent upheaval. That's what interested me about the Cuban story. My uncle on my father's side was a political prisoner in Cuba, and it destroyed his father—my grandfather. He was never the same emotionally after that. The revolution also destroyed my maternal grandmother, emotionally and psychologically. I've always been interested in how the fragile, solitary individual continues to live after violent upheaval. In that sense, *The Last War* was, for me, a break from one storytelling to another, but the underlying themes remained the same.

JAVIER: There are definitely a lot of political events, incidents, and references in the work, but do you perceive yourself and your work as political?

ANA: I think all writing is political. The act of observation, of paying attention, is political. What do you pay attention to? What do you not pay attention to? I think I've become more overtly political the older I've gotten, and part of it is because I feel more sure. In my earlier work especially, I wasn't sure and I was trying to find out through the writing. I was trying to understand, trying to solve problems, trying to get at some essence. There are many kinds of politics in art. There is the very overt politics, and there is the quieter politics of what it is that you pay attention to. My friend, the poet John Murillo, makes the point that when you're writing about Black suffering, there's also Black joy. There are many writers of the Black experience who want to focus on Black joy, and that's also political. That's something that we need in the conversation.

I don't see my work as wanting to change anybody's mind so much as invite them to look deeper and invite them to see the people behind the big politics that affect them. There's the big politics of Cuban exile and that's so huge that I don't feel adequate to discuss it straight on. I can only discuss it in the microcosm, as just one person within that maelstrom. To the extent that my work has any politics at all, it is a plea to look closer and to understand how we're connected. I believe that we move in systems and that those systems affect us, that we affect the systems, and that to look at politics with a big key misses the richness of how the world acts on us, and how the world deforms us, and how we're able to continue to live, and to thrive even, and to create thanks to our interconnectedness, thanks to art, thanks to those aspects which dig beneath the surface. That for me is the politics that I want to write about. My ambitions are more commensurate with my talents in that they're small; they are more animated by the microcosm, by the small moments that we observe and how those perhaps inform the bigger picture. I don't pretend to know what the answers are, I can only explore them by paying attention.

MACEO: You write about a contested history, and the Cuban exile community is uniquely sensitive to that history. Do you feel that pressure when you face the blank page? Is the fear of getting it wrong acute for the Cuban American author?

ANA: I felt it much more as a columnist for the *Herald*. You had to put on your flak jacket. The militant right wing of the Cuban exile community really drove me from Miami in 2008. I came as a columnist in 2005, and it made my life a living hell. I was not overtly political as a columnist necessarily, at least I didn't think I was, but even things like being against the embargo would get you into hot water. They boycotted the *Herald* over me. They circulated a petition to have me fired. I was going through a divorce at the time, and somebody dug up my divorce files and spread them all over the internet. There was a writing posted that said, "Ana Menéndez is a known Cuban agent," which was putting my life at risk. Some popular blog wrote, "It's time to take Ana Menéndez behind the woodshed and slap her around a bit." I was called a cunt on a regular basis. But ultimately, it wasn't a good fit for me because I think columnists who are good at what they do are very certain, they already know what they know, and they're not interested in finding out more. That's what makes a good columnist, and we need people like that. We need people with moral certainty, and I didn't really have that. A lot of times, I'd have a strong opinion and then I'd go out and talk to people and be like, "You all have a point." Once you do stake out a position, I was acutely aware that I was entering contested territory, contested history. It's a history war here, which is a theme that runs through so much of my work. What really happened in Cuba? I wasn't there—what really happened? I think once you decide on a narrative, you freeze it and you become rigid, and you're unable to see how really fluid it is and how it continues to change and change us.

When it comes to my fiction, I don't feel it as acutely because I go in with complete naivete and with a focus on simply the character and what the character is feeling. There are characters I don't agree with. In *The Apartment*, I have a character who's very anti the new Cubans, and she's screaming and yelling, and she comes off as a cartoon, but then we get another side of her at the end. I have these people in my family, and I know that they would rescue a lizard in their house. People are complex, and fiction allows you to be less certain. I think that's a gift. I think the world would improve a lot if we were less certain. Fiction has always given me that realm to be curious.

JAVIER: Can you talk about the use of humor and satire in your work as a form of resistance?

ANA: For Cubans, making fun of everything is a real survival mechanism, and I've always been interested in that. I recently put together a class on humor as resistance, and it was very timely because in the middle of the semester Russia invaded Ukraine. My students were able to find these instances of Ukrainian humorous resistance: "Russian warship, go fuck yourself." All of these wonderful moments. I thought it was a very important class for my students. I was a sophomore in college when the Berlin Wall fell. My college years were full of hope. It was a great symbolic new start. This generation has all the opposite. They have a global pandemic, followed by World War III, followed by inflation. They'll never be able to buy a house, their college is too expensive—on and on and on. As I told them during class, "You need to understand how people have coped with oppression. If you take nothing from this class, I want you to take from it this emotional and philosophical stance towards life, which is to approach it with lightness as much as possible. To have a kind of lightness, a kind of flexibility in the face of suffering, in the face of personal tragedy and disaster, that allows you to continue to make a contribution, to continue to be alive to the world." I think that's one of the most important things that we can teach our young people is to not lose hope. The way you don't lose hope is that you acknowledge what's going on, you acknowledge that it's horrible, and then you find the lightness that allows you to meet the challenge, and to work for a better world. Again, it sounds naive, but what else are we going to do? Are we going to join the destructors? Are you going to join the people who will destroy life and hate life? No, that's not an option.

JAVIER: In your story "In Cuba I Was a German Shepherd," Máximo makes jokes about Fidel Castro but that are also making fun of the Cuban exile community and their hopes. The joke is felt as longing, as in, "How much longer can we take this exile?" Is there a tension between lightheartedness or lightness and the seriousness of pain and suffering?

ANA: To the extent that I am political, it is in the ambiguities. What makes a work of art is that it can be read in multiple ways because life is complex. The truth is out there. I believe there is truth, but it's work to get it, it's hard work, and it's something that we have to get at together. It's something that we have to discover in community. It's not something that is the sole possession of one person, certainly not one writer. In a lot of ways, my work is an attempt to enter into the dialogic with my characters and with the reading audience to say, "I don't know the truth, but I'm interested in it and let's find it together. Let's closely observe the life that we have and come to some sense of order and sense of truth from it." In that particular story, yes, was he a German Shepherd? Was he a mutt? Was he something in between? It's all lost and it's very sad. The joke that I heard was from Tony López, one of the great Cuban American sculptors who lived here in Miami. I went to do a profile of him when I was a very young reporter. He told joke after joke. I couldn't get a word in because it was just one joke after another. "In Cuba I Was a German Shepherd" was a joke that he told, and I wasn't sufficiently skilled as a reporter at that time to use it, but the joke haunted me because I laughed and laughed, and then after I finished laughing, I was like, "But that's so sad." I couldn't describe that in a newspaper story, but I could attempt to describe it in a short story. The whole short story is my attempt to give the reader the feeling that I had instantaneously when I heard that joke. I think all my work has been that. That light, that heavy but light, the partial truth, the whole truth—hopefully, someday together, if we read enough and we write enough, and we observe with enough compassionate attention, that we're able to understand or approach understanding in a way that a single person cannot.

—June 2, 2022

5

LORRAINE LÓPEZ

Lorraine López has published seven books of fiction, including her first story collection, *Soy la Avon Lady and Other Stories*, which was selected by Sandra Cisneros for the 2002 Miguel Mármol Prize for Fiction and published by Curbstone Press, an important publisher of Latinx writers. López's early stories often feature characters estranged from their surroundings and loved ones, attempting, often to humorous effect, to find a way to close that distance. After publishing *Call Me Henri*, a young adult novel that won the 2007 Paterson Prize for Young Adult Literature, López made the leap to a mainstream publisher with *The Gifted Gabaldón Sisters* and *The Realm of Hungry Spirits*, an experience that left her disillusioned with the commercial publishing industry and the frustration of relinquishing creative control of her work. She returned to an independent publisher and achieved critical success for her second story collection, *Homicide Survivors Picnic*, which was a finalist for the PEN/Faulkner Award for Fiction. Many of her stories in that collection are set in the South and feature characters from diverse backgrounds. We know the stakes they're facing—often the aftereffects of violence, incarceration, and loss—but their Latinx identity is relegated to the periphery, if we're aware of it at all. This is part of López's project, to expand and challenge our understanding of the Latinx experience, and we see this most concretely in her coedited anthology, *The Other Latin@*, which sought to bring together writers explicitly resisting the limited range of subject and style imposed on Latinx writing. In addition to her fiction and edited anthologies, López was the Gertrude Conaway Professor of English, director of creative writing, and cofounder of Latino and Latina Studies at Vanderbilt University, from which she recently retired. She spoke to us from Nashville, Tennessee, but shared that she and her husband will soon be moving to Asheville, North Carolina, where she's looking forward to dedicating all of her time to writing.

JAVIER: How has the pandemic impacted your writing? And can you tell us more generally about your writing process?

LORRAINE: The pandemic clarified for me what I wanted to do with the rest of my time. Before COVID, for instance, I didn't see myself retiring this early. The pandemic gave me consecutive days at home to write without having to go to campus and deal with people or otherwise spend the psychic energy that should go into writing. My last year of teaching I taught online, which I enjoyed a lot. I had some of my best evaluations because I just took to teaching online. Staying at home also fed my writing. I was on leave when the pandemic started, and we had traveled to Spain and Portugal and Puerto Rico just before the pandemic hit. Almost immediately, things began shutting down. In about three months' time, I drafted a young adult novel—a work of speculative fiction that grapples with the pandemic. Having those contiguous days at home launched the book for me. It can take me ten years to write a novel. In three months, I had a draft that I was ready to send to my agent. That was one outcome. Now I'm writing another book. I know that restrictions have lifted, and I'm free to go about the country, but I'm not traveling. I'm staying home and writing, and I'm already 140 pages into a new manuscript.

As for my writing process, I get up early in the morning. This is something I learned from my mentor, Judith Ortiz Cofer, who has written essays about rising at 5:00 a.m. Now I think of rising at 5:00 a.m. as "sleeping in" because I often get up around four in the morning, and I begin writing. I write until my husband has to pull me away to have breakfast. For about half an hour after that, I'll do some physical exercise, and then I'm back writing until lunchtime. A brain fog descends on me in the afternoons. I reread what I've written, but I don't try to write anything new, because I know it will be stupid. That's pretty much what I do every single day. I don't care if it's Sunday or Tuesday. The fact that we're now moving [from Tennessee to North Carolina] is very upsetting to me because I know that I'll have to take time from writing to put things in boxes, and I don't want to do that.

MACEO: What was it like before, when you were juggling your responsibilities at Vanderbilt and still trying to carve out time for your writing?

LORRAINE: I was always stealing time to write—I also have children and grandchildren—and so I'd feel guilty about stealing time from them, too. That wasn't good. I had many administrative responsibilities. I was the interim chair of the English Department for a while, the director of the Creative Writing MFA program, and the faculty director of Latino and Latina Studies. Teaching and administrative responsibilities are a drain on the energy that I need for writing. Still, I've managed to be fairly prolific despite those responsibilities because writing's what I want to do. Sometimes I get asked, "How do you have the self-discipline to write?" and I say, "I actually need self-discipline to go to the gym and get on the treadmill." That's when I'm cracking the whip on myself. I don't need self-discipline to write. I *get* to write. That's what I love to do. It's a different approach from others. I see how my colleagues struggle with a blank page, and though I feel for them, I'm confused, because why would I want to do something that doesn't bring me joy?

MACEO: Your first collection of stories, *Soy la Avon Lady and Other Stories*, wasn't published until you were in your forties. I've heard you talk in other interviews about being introverted or preferring the role of quiet observer, which are good traits for a writer, but did you struggle to find the agency to use your voice as a writer?

LORRAINE: When my first book came out, I was already a grandmother. Publishing proved really challenging, and I had a very slow trajectory. I needed to develop my craft; I needed years for that. I published my first story, called "White Radio," as an undergrad at Cal State University, Northridge. I would cringe if I saw that story now. It took a long time for me to get from there to having a book of stories. And agency was part of it because I didn't believe that I had strong work. My mentor,

Judith Ortiz Cofer, pushed me to submit for the contest that ultimately led to the book's publication, after being chosen as the winner by Sandra Cisneros. I feel like I've had these two fairy godmothers who were kicking me forward when I doubted myself. I had a lot of self-doubt about my writing. I knew that I would write, but I didn't really believe that I would ever publish. Publication came as kind of a surprise to me.

JAVIER: Can you discuss the importance of literary sisterhood? Sandra Cisneros selected your first story collection as winner of the Miguel Mármol Prize, which resulted in its publication, and Judith was a close mentor and friend. How important was it to have these Latina writers guiding the way?

LORRAINE: I don't know that I would be the writer I am today if not for either of those women and more women writers who inspired me. Even if I didn't know them personally, they inspired me on the page. I did have the privilege of knowing Judith quite well and becoming her friend after I was her student. I have the pleasure of knowing Sandra, after meeting her through Macondo Workshops, and being treated beautifully by her. Long before I met Sandra, I read her story "Woman Hollering Creek" in a supplement in the *LA Times*. Reading that story changed my life, in that I saw that there was someone who was writing about characters in situations that I was deeply familiar with, and she was being published in this very mainstream way. I thought, "There's a door open now. Someone has opened a door that I can go through. I want to be writing stories like this." From a young age, I knew I would be an artist, but I wasn't sure how this would happen. Sandra's example was almost a roadmap for mc. I don't know that I would be a writer without having read that story. I don't know that I would have this career, the privilege of a writing life, without Sandra picking my book for publication and opening that door for me and without Judith pushing and shoving me through it with all her might. I don't trust that I could have done this on my own.

JAVIER: Overall, what have been your experiences getting your work published, either negative or positive?

LORRAINE: When *Soy la Avon Lady* was published, I had a terrific experience with Curbstone Press, which was run by Alexander "Sandy"

Taylor. He was a wonderful man, who passed away years ago. He was the kind of man I could pick up my phone and call and he would answer and be delighted to speak to me. It was a very singular experience. I think I was smart enough then to realize that this isn't very usual. This isn't how it happens at Random House. He not only published my book but set up so many readings for me that I practically had a cottage industry as a speaker with this book, and I've never had anything like that since. That was on him. Sandy had many connections, and he sent me all over the place. He nominated the book for prizes, a few of which it won. Then he also published my second book, *Call Me Henri*, a book that won the Paterson Prize for Young Adult Literature because Sandy submitted it for that award and everywhere under the sun. Again, that was a great experience.

Then for my third book, I wrote it for a specific purpose. To achieve tenure at a university, especially a research university, you must have a new publication, and at my university, this had to be through a major press. That's troubling to me because, in effect, administrators and colleagues were deferring an aesthetic decision, a value judgment, to a corporation. They were saying, "Let this corporation give you the stamp of approval." My first two books, *Soy la Avon Lady* and *Call Me Henri*, wouldn't count toward tenure because they'd been published by Curbstone, an independent press. I had to have a book out by a major press. I didn't want to lose my position, so I worked very hard to have my third book published by a commercial press. That was extremely difficult. The first firewall was finding an agent. For *The Gifted Gabaldón Sisters* I think I queried over twenty agents, and they sent me conflicting letters back, some saying, "Get rid of the interchapters," while others said, "We love the interchapters, but not anything else." I really didn't know what to do. Finally, I saw an ad from an editor at Grand Central, looking for Latinx authors with novels. I wrote directly to this editor. She asked me to send her my manuscript, and she loved it. She said, "Now you need to get an agent." Of course, if I'm going to take a book that's already accepted to an agent, I'm basically saying, "How would you like some free money for the work that I've done?" Even so, I consulted my friend Tayari Jones, author of *An American Marriage*, who had been in my program at the University of Georgia, and she told me about her agency. That's where I found my agent, who did want some free money, so she signed me up.

We made the deal with Grand Central, and then the process that

I call "divestiture" began, wherein you're an author and you think the book you've written is *your* book, but everything that the commercial publisher does is calculated to make you understand that this is *not* your book. They have bought it; now it's their book. Even though your name will appear on it, it's their book. There are so many things that they do that are similar to the way cults brainwash people. For example, they tell you, "You thought that was your title? That's not your title." My title for *The Gifted Gabaldón Sisters* was "Fermina's Gifts," which I believe to be more dignified and appropriate. But no, they said, "'Sisters' is the keyword. Everybody loves books with sisters." This was when *The Sisterhood of the Traveling Pants* was out and people were excited about the word "sisters." That's the first step. Then they come up with ridiculous cover art featuring women with no heads or wearing white dresses with butterflies floating around, supposedly to connect the story to magical realism when I'm a realistic fiction writer. That's the process, and it was challenging for me, very challenging. I think I noticed it all the more sharply because I had such a wonderful experience with Sandy Taylor. It was startling, too, working with people who were trying to cram me into the popular fiction/chica lit pigeonhole, when I am a literary writer.

MACEO: Where did that leave you afterwards? You had an agent, and you had this connection to a commercial press. How were you thinking about the next steps in your writing career?

LORRAINE: *The Gifted Gabaldón Sisters*, my first commercial book, did make the press money—not a lot, but it did earn out. Then a second book came out from that major publisher, and the press did not invest a lot in publicizing that book, nor did they give promoting it much thought. For example, they sent me to a book conference where I was on a panel for Southern belles. Southern belles? I appeared on that panel and said, "Frankly, I don't know why I'm here, but I'll tell you about my book." There's a brouhaha going on now and publishers are realizing that they weren't too supportive of Latinx writers. And they really weren't. My second book did not earn out and the publisher didn't make much of an effort to get it in front of readers. I suppose I could have done that, but I'll be honest with you, that's not what I do. I'm not a merchant. I am a writer and that's it. I'm not going to sell my books. I don't have a Twitter account. I'm not on Facebook or Instagram. I don't want to spend my time on social media, quite honestly. I just want to write my books.

MACEO: You were coeditor along with Blas Falconer of an anthology, *The Other Latin@: Writing Against a Singular Identity*, published in 2011, which really aims to dismantle narrow definitions of what it means to be Latinx. How did this essay collection come about?

LORRAINE: Blas also lived in Nashville and taught at Austin Peay University, which is in Clarksville, not too far from here. He had proposed to the University of Arizona Press a book about the "OtherRican"—Puerto Rican poets moving away from Nuyorican stereotypes—a collection of essays to show that they come from all parts of the country and aren't limited in terms of subject matter or form. Arizona bounced it back, saying, "We'd like the collection to include prose writers and writers from different Latinx backgrounds, not just Puerto Rican." He asked if I wanted to edit the book with him. I've had people invite me to work on projects before, and my litmus test is this: if you can answer email right away, I will work with you. I really can't be tortured by people who don't answer email right away. Blas is of the same mind, and so we found ourselves to be email-compatible, and we launched this project. We wanted to show the range of Latinx writing and some of the expectations people have labored under in producing this range of writing, how readers and publishers, and even educators and scholars, try to limit that range, and how resistance is manifest against such limitations. He looked for poets and I looked for prose writers who were doing something different, or who were identifying outside of the stereotypical ways in which Latinx identity is construed. That was our goal. We now feel the project was remiss in a big way because we didn't work hard enough to include Afro-Latinx voices. We really didn't. The book came out in 2011 and now it's 2022, and we missed the boat. I feel we screwed up.

JAVIER: Where do you think the demand for that singular identity comes from? Does it come from the publishers, what they view is marketable at certain times?

LORRAINE: I think it's very reductive and simplistic. It comes from a place of wanting to perform this weird synecdoche wherein the part represents the whole because a single part is easier to grasp than the complicated whole. This reflects a lack of respect for the intelligence of readers. The stereotype, in a very pervasive, even unshakeable way, has become so powerful that it negates empirical evidence. In this country, we talk about immigration so extensively that for many people, Latinx equals immigrant, but my family has been on this continent since before Jamestown, and genetic testing indicates my more distant ancestors entered North America from Beringia as early as fifteen thousand years ago. My people have been here for millennia. They're hardly immigrants. But in reviewing *The Gifted Gabaldón Sisters*, which is about native Hispanos like my own family, a critic wrote, "The book is another take on the immigrant experience." What? What immigrant experience? There are no immigrants in the book. It's very hard to eradicate that stereotype. This is just an image that the reader has, or the general public has, and if you write something that supports that image, they can more easily understand your work. We saw what happened with *American Dirt*, where the novel panders to stereotypic sentiments that portray this country as being a wonderful place for immigrants to come and start a new life and kiss the dirt, etcetera. That fits expectations and appeals to a lot of readers, and so even an offensive and poorly researched book becomes popular. On the flipside, I've also had a critic say of *Homicide Survivors Picnic*, "How is this Latinx literature?" In other words, because it did not meet this white person's criteria for Latinx identity, it should not count as Latinx literature, suggesting that I, as a Latina, should not have been allowed to write it.

MACEO: In your personal essay, "When We Were Spanish," in *The Other Latin@*, you write, "As a writer, I have found that the limitations imposed by my ethnic identity complicate artistic production." Can you elaborate on those limitations and how you've navigated them?

LORRAINE: I think it was truer when I was an emerging writer, just starting out. I felt like my first book should be about immigration. I actually did feel that. Then I got that creepy, appropriation-of-identity feeling because I didn't have that experience. Imaginatively, you should be able to write about anything, but I also feel that there are particular authors who have particular stories that are not mine to take. But it was there in my mind that I should be writing about this. It's only now that I can commit to writing about whatever I want to write about, stories that belong to me, because the best writing comes from writing I want to write. Now I'm looking for a fight. I'm ready for someone else to tell me I'm not writing Latinx literature and hoping to probe that question, probe that judgment more. Maybe if I had danced the dance I was expected to dance, I might have had a different career trajectory. I don't know if it would be for better or worse, but I wouldn't like myself, and I probably wouldn't like writing as much if I wrote to meet the expectations of others rather than my own.

MACEO: One common aspect of essays about identity is there's always acknowledgement of cultural ambivalence but then, by the end, there's a synthesis and a form of cultural understanding. My read on your essay is that, for you, the ambivalence never ends, that there's no synthesis to be had.

LORRAINE: It does feel like I come from a bifurcated cultural place. I want it both ways. I want to be free to write whatever I want, but I also want to not have to apologize for or explain about coming from a particular cultural place. I don't know that I can reconcile the two, and I don't know that I have to. I think it creates good tension, and tension is good for drama. I think of Joy Castro's ending to her essay in *The Other Latin@*, where she claims, "I write from a complicated space," as she's trying to pull disparate pieces of her identity together. I think there is resolution there, and synthesis, but I still have a chip on my shoulder about wanting to be free and also wanting to belong somewhere. Wanting to wander wherever I want, to wander unseen between the camps, as Gloria Anzaldúa might say, an act that speaks to a superpower I've always wanted: invisibility. This is the desire to be the unnoticed observer in the background, the chronicler.

JAVIER: Your novel *The Darling* tells the story of Caridad, whose reflections on love and relationships are intermixed and informed by her reading of classic novels featuring female heroines, such as *Anna Karenina*, *Madame Bovary*, *Portrait of a Lady*, and, of course, Chekhov's story "The Darling." Caridad reads these books for clues or answers to her own relationship woes, and yet all of the works are written by men. Much has been said against the canon of "dead white men." Why was it important for you to place Caridad's story, a Latina college student, within this literary context and lineage? And how did you feel, as a woman, that you were reinscribing the classic heroine?

LORRAINE: One of the joys of writing that book was I had the chance to read all those books again, from Chekhov, who's my favorite really, to Flaubert, to Nabokov—the many authors that I read as a young woman and, to a certain extent, inhaled, in terms of what being a young woman meant. These authors, through their characters, created for me this ideal. It wasn't until many years later that I realized, "Wait a minute, these are white men." Yet their voices are so powerful that they can have the effect of informing someone's idea of womanhood, or ideal womanhood. I think the short story "The Darling" by Anton Chekhov is one of the best examples of that because the main character, Olenka, is a vessel for any man that she's with, absorbing his interests until almost becoming a succubus to consume him. I wanted to play with that idea. I suspected that reading books would have a very negative effect on my main character in the same way, but books also benefit Caridad. For example, Henry James's advice to be kind, to be kind, to be kind informs her in a beneficial way at a critical moment. The books referenced in my novel are beautifully written books, which is why they're so powerful. I think my protagonist comes to a place where she understands that she's the one who's responsible for synthesizing what these books offer. She's responsible for separating the chaff from the grain and absorbing what is helpful and enriching and discarding what is limiting and blinding. That's what I hoped to do with the novel as it progressed. Moving from book to book with Caridad proved a helpful organizational way for me to think about each chapter and about how the character is interweaving her reading life with her lived experiences.

Javier: How do you perceive your role as a writer in relation to your community, as you see it, and US society?

Lorraine: To me, the role of the writer is to write and, in writing, to communicate and perhaps to open minds to some extent. To make known stories that deepen empathic imagination in others who will read them and subscribe to the humanity of people very different than they are. That, writ large, is what I think a writer is supposed to do. I think it's also important to represent the community as fully and honestly as possible. And within it, to be an honorable person, generous with other writers, whenever there's an opportunity to be generous, while protecting one's time to write. This is a tough one for me because I am that introverted person who doesn't know the neighbors because I don't talk much to them. I don't want to do that. I need to be writing.

Years ago, my husband and I both started a nonprofit, The Institute for Violence Prevention, and I feel very strongly about promulgating anti-violence messages. But that's separate from being a writer, though it does draw on the same energy. This is probably my worst answer, but that's where I am. I feel like I've done a lot of volunteer work. I've done a lot of community work and mentoring, and now I can just be a writer and hope my writing doesn't do any harm.

JAVIER: In the stories in *Homicide Survivors Picnic*, many of the protagonists are dealing with the consequences of having a close friend or family member incarcerated and institutionalized. What is central to these stories is not so much the violence, loss, and incarceration but the emotional and material support of those who have to step up. What is the value of emphasizing these efforts in the stories?

LORRAINE: A lot of the stories were drawn from my experience in the nonprofit that we had in Athens, Georgia, and which we brought to Nashville, where we actually had groups of batterers and programs in prisons. Those stories were holding a mirror up to that time and I wanted to create characters that I could respect and admire, even those who were egotistical enough to believe they could make things better for others. I remember the poet Philip Levine conducted a workshop I attended when I was a graduate student at the University of Georgia. He had read all our work and gave us feedback on it. One of my colleagues had written a story about a main character that she clearly had contempt for, and he said, "Let me stop you right there. If you have contempt for this character, why are you writing about him? Contempt for the character is contempt for the reader." That stayed with me. I want my characters to be respectable. I want to respect them and to respect the reader.

MACEO: Your most recent story collection, *Postcards from the Gerund State*, takes place on a fictionalized college campus. You lampoon institutional politics and patriarchal structures within academia and show just how damaging a place the university can be, especially for women of color. One of the ways you address difficult subjects in your work is through humor. How do you view the use of humor in your work?

LORRAINE: Humor erupts from incongruence. The reader, or the audience, thinks one thing is going on, and something totally absurd pops up, and it's funny. I'm really charmed by the idea of incongruence creating such ruptures. I'm very interested in exploring that, but that's only one part of my attraction to humor. I also like the idea of humor of invasion and humor of resistance. Humor of invasion is created by characters that emerge in new situations—say, immigrants. Everything seems incongruent to them, creating wonderful opportunities for misinterpretation, mistranslation. Humor of resistance comes from the expectation that everything should be a certain way, so of course, this is a perfect setup for all kinds of Murphy's Law events. But that's the analytic side; on an individual aesthetic plane, I just want to write the kind of book that I want to read, and the books that I like make me laugh. Humor is a powerful vehicle for getting across hard points. You can make very cutting observations in a less threatening way with humor. It's a good way to poke the bear.

JAVIER: This is related to humor, because if you think of the king's court, it was the jester that was allowed to openly criticize the king. Do you perceive yourself and your work, maybe the use of humor in your work, as political?

LORRAINE: Yes, I do. I'm very aware of how humor works in hierarchies. One thing that stung me is when a reviewer I respect wrote that stories in *Postcards from the Gerund State* "punch down." That's something I never want to do. I really don't believe I did. Jury's still out in my mind, but yes, humor is a great way to critique institutions because of their hierarchies. You can't punch down and be funny. You really can't. If you were, say, a white man, you can't mock or make fun of Lucinda, a Latina in *Postcards from the Gerund State*, and be funny. Well, you can do that, but it's not funny. Humor flows in a certain direction, and that's what I love about it. If you're at the bottom of the hierarchy, you can punch up, but those at the top cannot punch down. Humor's an equalizer because while those at the top have everything else, they can't have this. Some of the funniest conversations I've ever overheard are by people who are marginalized or disempowered. They can make fun of anything or anybody. And they have to, otherwise they'd become very angry or bitter or even lose their minds. To me, that's how humor works. It's a wonderful vehicle for critiquing institutions and systems that don't serve everybody and, in fact, remain strong, with resources intact, because they serve only a few.

JAVIER: When we think of Latinx literature, we think of New York, Florida, the Southwest, California. In much of your writing, especially in *Homicide Survivors Picnic*, your stories take place in the South, and specifically in Georgia. What place does the South have in the literary landscape of your fiction? And why is it important to also see Latinx stories set there?

LORRAINE: Many people don't realize that the Latinx population in the South is exploding. I believe awareness of this is building, but slowly, because many are firmly entrenched in construing race as a binary, as Black or white. So the Latinx presence is a little confusing to them. That was one of the walls I hit when I was developing the Latinx Studies program at Vanderbilt. The administration resisted this. As if to say, "Whoa, we're already dealing with the Black students and the Black Student Cultural Center, and now you want this?" It was just too much. A very careful argument had to be made, and we found that our strongest allies came from African American Studies and Diaspora Studies and the Black Cultural Center. We could not have gotten the program up and running without help from those allies who understood what we meant and understood easily why our program was important. No argument needed, they got it. I will say this, in the South, there are opportunities for amazing alliances among people of color. There are also tremendous barriers because the South can be a place of weird denial about the past, and the pretense that everything's fine now, along with unwillingness to grapple yet again with race and cultural differences. For a writer, though, that's heaven. All the conflict, that's some wonderful stuff, and I thought it was important to make known to readers outside of this region, that yes, there is a pervasive Latinx presence here and it's not limited to the person who's cleaning hotel rooms or cutting grass. There are writers from the South, there are academics, there are students, there are doctors, who are Latinx. My old dentist retired and a new dentist took over. When I met her, the hygienist said, "Dr. López, I'd like you to meet Dr. López." We were like, "What? In the South? In Nashville? What are the chances?" Well, now the chances are getting better. I'm thinking again of Judith. Though she passed away in 2016, she's often with me in my thoughts, and she told me about encountering the Nuyorican poet, Miguel Algarín. When they met at a conference, she was introduced to him as a Puerto Rican poet from Georgia. Miguel Algarín took one look at Judith and said, "There are no Puerto Rican poets in Georgia," and he turned his back on her, as if negating her existence. So I also feel I should take advantage of the opportunity to raise awareness of the Latinx presence in the South for Judith.

MACEO: What are the milestones of Latinx literature so far in the twenty-first century, and which directions do you see Latinx literature taking as we continue into this century?

LORRAINE: It seems in publishing there's now more receptivity to Latinx voices. I think that's an important milestone. There's also some awareness in publishing that the industry has not always done right by Latinx authors and hasn't always been supportive of careers entrusted to them by Latinx writers. The conversation about the discrepancies in advances on royalties, the difference between what authors of color are paid compared to what white authors receive, has offered opportunity to interrogate what kinds of materials get disseminated and what publishers will invest in and put into the hands of readers. This turning point has been crucial for forming ideas about culture and cultural groups. If we begin to understand how much influence publishers wield and we begin to be critical of such power and influence, then that's an important milestone.

Another great milestone in Latinx literature is related to race: the understanding that this is a cultural group that embodies all races. I think it hits me hard that *The Other Latin@* did not address this more because my grandchildren are Afro-Latinx and I would hate them to feel that I did not acknowledge them. It's important that we begin to say, "Yes, we constitute this cultural group, and we are very lucky ours is a multiracial cultural group. We are much more than our national imaginary has construed us to be for many years." Also we must open up more to LGBTQ+ voices, which was something that we did consciously go after in *The Other Latin@*. Another great milestone for us will be reached by stepping away from stereotypic notions and harmful cultural patterns because this gives the writers who come after us the freedom to write what they're driven to write and not to feel restricted. Stanley Kunitz says tradition is not "a cistern full of toads," and it's not. We should write with information about tradition but also with the intention of going forth from tradition to new places.

Maceo: You write very evocatively and humorously about siblings, and sisters in particular. How do you feel that your own family dynamic contributed to the way that you perceive stories and the way they unfold?

Lorraine: I have three sisters and a brother. With my sisters, it's almost like having three instant best friends. I can wear one out with complaining and go to the next one and then wear her out and move on. If you come up in a big family, you understand that in this organism that is the family, when one member is upset or experiencing anything difficult, this ripples out to everybody. Nobody exists independently. A functioning family is interlocked, a system like a machine in a way. That is what it is for me to be a sister, but there's also another tension going on, at least for me, and that is to be a writer, you need to be at a remove. You cannot write from the thick of the action. You need to be there, but not there. You need to step outside to have some distance; otherwise, you're myopic about what's going on. You can't see things when you're too close to them. You have no objectivity. It's almost like being a scientist who's involved in the experiment. Yes, it's a self-imposed marginalization. You're of this world, but not of it, and for family, this can be challenging. I think my sisters initially were a little wary. They'd read my stories and say, "Oh my God, is this me?" But now they see that my characters are characters and they're an amalgamation and a blur of things, not just that or the other. My sisters are now some of my earliest readers, and they give me good feedback. I feel very lucky to have been born into a family with great sisters who read and support my work. My brother supports it, too. When *Soy la Avon Lady* came out, my brother bought a copy, took it to my father, and read it to him. I do feel fortunate to have that support.

—February 25, 2022

6

RIGOBERTO GONZÁLEZ

Rigoberto González has published books in multiple genres, including poetry, fiction, memoir, YA, and children's literature, as well as a significant body of book reviews and essays. Since his first book, *So Often the Pitcher Goes to Water until It Breaks*, published in 1999, was chosen by poet Ai as part of the National Poetry Series, González has been awarded numerous prestigious literary prizes, including the American Book Award, the PEN/Voelcker Award for Poetry, the Lenore Marshall Poetry Prize from the Academy of American Poets, and the Shelley Memorial Award of the Poetry Society of America, as well as National Endowment for the Arts (NEA), Lannan Foundation, and Guggenheim Fellowships. His memoir *Butterfly Boy: Memories of a Chicano Mariposa* published by the University of Wisconsin Press in 2006, traces González's painful childhood mired in poverty and abuse and details his struggle to come to terms with his identity and sexuality. It has become a seminal work of queer Latinidad. The son of Mexican migrant farmworkers, González was born in Bakersfield, California, in 1970 but was raised in Michoacán, Mexico, before returning to California where he completed his education, becoming the first in his family to attend college. He graduated from the University of California, Riverside, and holds a master's degree in English from the University of California, Davis, and an MFA from

Arizona State University. He is now a distinguished professor and director of the MFA program at Rutgers University in Newark, New Jersey. González's influence has also come as a literary activist and champion of Latinx literature. In addition to hundreds of book reviews for publications such as the *El Paso Times*, *LA Times*, *San Francisco Chronicle*, *NBC Latino*, *Lambda Literary*, and *Los Angeles Review of Books*, he has also been a board member for the National Book Critics Circle, the Poetry Society of America, and the Association of Writers and Writing Programs (AWP), among others, where he has ensured that Latinx voices receive the attention they deserve. His work to increase the visibility of Latinx, queer, and other marginalized writers has been tireless, and a whole generation of Latinx writers is indebted to his advocacy.

JAVIER: In terms of your writing, has quarantine given you more time and space to write, or have you found it difficult to write during this time?

RIGOBERTO: In the beginning I kept getting the same suggestion from friends: "Oh, treat it like a residency." Of course, it's one thing when you choose to ensconce, another when you're forced into isolation. Fellow writers eventually admitted to me: "I can't even read." It was true. I don't think I read my first book until July. I spent the first couple of months of the pandemic feeling uncertain about whether I was going to survive and afraid of getting sick because I didn't have any relatives or friends on the East Coast that could simply come over and nurse me back to health. Living alone was my biggest anxiety. It's a benefit until it isn't, so that was hard to live through alone. I finally started to work because I had exhausted every other possibility—binge-watching TV shows, cooking, taking five-hour walks every other day. I didn't want to watch another stupid film. I didn't want to have another phone call. I didn't want to sit outside on the balcony and just stare out into space anymore. My resort then was to turn to creativity. I was able to work on three projects. The first, my "New and Selected Poems," was already under contract with Four Way Books.

I had to write new poems for the book, and many of them were informed by the times. Not that my work is ever cheery, but these came out particularly bleak. It was a combination of turning fifty and being anxious about what I was going to do with the rest of my journey here on this planet—if I survived. That's the one thing that COVID did to all of us: it made us reckon with what really mattered. While writing poems, I was also able to work on another memoir, which I'd been thinking about for five, six years. That's my creative process: I think about a book for years and years, always piecing it together in my head, and once I sit down, if I get to page two, then I know that it's going to get done. That's how I wrote this book about my abuela. I call it, "Abuela in Shadow, Abuela in Light." It's about trying to understand who this woman—a Purépecha from Michoacán—really was. She raised me, yet I knew very little about her. In the book I'm trying to understand why this woman who took care of me as an adolescent remained a stranger.

And for the hell of it, I started a novel as well. I'd been thinking of writing about these four middle-aged gay men, Latinos—Chicano, specifically. It's a story about trying to understand what it's like to become a middle-aged gay Chicano in this country. I survived the AIDS plague, but what does it mean to now contend with surviving, with growing old? I'm alone, estranged from family, never really found that partner to marry. Aging is a reality now. Who takes care of me? This community that I have with my other gay friends reassures me once in a while: "Oh, we'll take care of each other." But how much of that is wishful thinking? Is that really going to work? These are some of the big questions I tackle in the book. Also, I'm trying to present the different ways in which our experiences are very different compared to white gay men. What are the different cultural urgencies that are still with us? The whole notion of familia. What happens when they're not there? How do we preserve our connection to a childhood that we may not have loved but that's ours? How do we mature with our national identities, our sexualities? These are gay men who are professionals. Where are the gay men that lived to this point and had happy lives or partnerships and marriages, who went to college before us—where are they? The role models are few. I know they're out there, but their visibility is lacking.

Javier: You used the word "middle-age," and the other word that comes to mind is "midcareer," especially considering that your "new and selected" is coming out. Looking back on your writing career, what have been the formative moments in your journey?

Rigoberto: I don't think it's the publication of any of my books. Maybe the closest is *Butterfly Boy*, only because it announced to the world that I wasn't going to hide anything. I was going to reveal. So maybe that book in terms of its publication and only because it is so connected to my family and to my father. It's not necessarily a career marker for me but rather an emotional marker. All my books are an emotional step forward for me, but in terms of my career, one formative moment was in recognizing that people wanted to read what I wrote. The response to my first book allowed me to think, "Okay, there's something here. I'm being called to share." I did not expect any of it. In fact, I did not expect to publish a single book, or to receive a single award, which is a very different sensibility from what I see on social media nowadays. People finish their MFA degree and they start asking, "Where's my MacArthur 'Genius Grant'?"

The second milestone is in understanding that I could also be a book critic. I saw how our books were being ignored, which meant I didn't hold my breath that my book was ever going to get reviewed. Who could we turn to unless somebody stepped forward to do the job? When could we ever take for granted the things that white writers do—that their books are reviewed and talked about? I decided I was going to be the guy who reviews those books, and I've been doing it since 2002.

Thirdly, becoming an academic was formative, and it's something I fled for a very long time. I received my MFA in 1997, and the first thing I said was "I'm not going to be a teacher. There's just no way." All I heard was writers complain that their teaching duties didn't allow them time to write. So even after I got my first book prize and the Guggenheim and people were telling me, "Now you can get any job you want," I didn't do it. I didn't have my first full-time teaching job until eight years later. I had five books by that time, which made me very competitive on the market, so I was able to get a job that I really wanted, not just a job that I could get. For me, those are the moments that I look back and identify as key stages in my career—as a writer, as a critic, and then as an academic—that allowed me to see myself as part of the larger literary landscape.

JAVIER: What have been your experiences in getting your works published?

RIGOBERTO: Even after the first book received awards and recognitions, I didn't know what came next. You publish a book, and then what? Looking back at the Chicano writers before me, this was always a struggle. A book was published and then five or six years went by before the next one came out, if there was a next one. I never looked for an agent. Even though I was in New York City and writing prose, I just thought, "For what?" The only big-press presences out there, at that point, were mujeres like Sandra Cisneros and Denise Chávez, and I saw myself as a different kind of writer. Most of my Chicano ancestors were small-press authors, and I just followed that path. My novel *Crossing Vines* was published with Oklahoma Press's Chicana and Chicano Visions of the Américas. Then my memoir *Butterfly Boy* was published with an LGBT series at University of Wisconsin Press. I knew about the series because that's where Jaime Manrique published *Eminent Maricones*, a book that I loved, and I thought, "I belong there." I couldn't see myself in the big houses. Sandra Cisneros, Julia Alvarez, Denise Chávez, and Ana Castillo were still the exceptions. So I just continued my small-press life, which didn't affect the kind of rewards that I got. I continued getting book prizes, I continued getting job offers. We always look at those who came before us and note how many got lost in small-press invisibility. Well, I set out to be one of the success stories.

Maceo: You've done so much to promote the work of other Chicanx and Latinx writers. When was it that you first started to feel the responsibility to be a literary activist?

Rigoberto: I always credit my mentor, Francisco X. Alarcón. He was my teacher at UC Davis. His had this nervous energy, but it got people moving, it got people excited. I didn't have the kind of charisma that Francisco had. My own personal disposition was different, but I knew what I did have was discipline and versatility. One time I visited Francisco, and he said to me, "Tú sí sabes escribir memorias. I wish I had that gift. I hope that with everything you do that you continue doing that. We need those queer Chicano stories." It made me happy to be recognized as both a writer and a literary activist. So when I joined these national boards—the National Book Critics Circle, Poetry Society of America, AWP—I said to myself, "These folks probably haven't even read my books, but they know my name because of all the work that I do. What am I going to do with this? Am I just going to be a glorified board member, or am I going to try and do something while I'm in there?" That fire I learned from Francisco Alarcón. He always said, "Let's go in there and do something." Even if it was crashing a local radio station to read poems. I recall that he was part of a group that was advising the curation of a Mesoamerican exhibit at the de Young Museum in San Francisco. He told us, "That's how it's done. You get in there and you do something." That became my philosophy.

JAVIER: What are the milestones of Latinx literature so far in the twenty-first century? Which directions do you see Latinx literature taking as we continue into this century?

RIGOBERTO: The express train that we took to the big presses is an important milestone. We should be everywhere. It's not either-or. We should be in the small presses. We should be in the big presses. I also take heart that those writers who are being published in the big presses are communicating and interacting with writers who are not, because they understand that they are part of their community, their readers, and the people who are going to support them. We're finally being seen in a way that we saw ourselves: as good writers, as excellent storytellers, as great poets. The fact that these other folks are seeing us doesn't make us better, but it allows us entry into a whole other population of readers. Juan Felipe Herrera becoming the US poet laureate was another important milestone. It brought him national, and even international, recognition. When Juan Felipe won the NBCC Award for poetry—another great moment for Chicano/Latino letters—Roberto Bolaño also received a big award for fiction, and plenty of Latin American newspapers seized on that. They were like, "Oh, the Latin American writer *and* the Latino poet won!" Juan Felipe was in the headlines along with Bolaño. That was an important moment because our Latino visibility became vertical as well as horizontal.

In terms of where we're going next, I hope that these careers that are now receiving so much attention continue to receive that light. I also hope that young writers don't narrow their paths or don't narrow their visions of their future, because right now there seems to be this fervor, like, "Oh my God, I have to be a Ruth Lilly fellow and then I have to get an NEA, then I have to be a bestseller to be somebody." Whenever I have young writers come at me with that, I feel disrespected because I didn't do any of that and I turned out okay. That was the whole point of me doing what I did—to show that there's another path towards success and that it's just as valid and important. I hope there will be enough young writers who have their feet on the ground to understand that this is a long game. Getting a book out, getting a prize, getting recognition, getting likes and retweets—those are short-term. May they have all that, but I hope they're also looking to nurture a long career. That the goal is to exercise this passion for writing fifteen years from now, and then another fifteen after that. And that success is not dependent on whether they've published so many books or received so many awards or gotten this much attention. Some may think, "It's easy for you to say because you've got all those things." But there's a difference. Whenever I get anything, I'm still shocked, because I've never felt entitled to a single thing. I'm the first Latino to get the Academy of American Poets' Lenore Marshall Prize, for example. As much as I celebrate that I'm the first, it's also sad that somebody born in 1970, somebody published in the year 2000, is still the first one, when we have such a lineage of worthy writers who came before us. But I try to take advantage of these recognitions and do something good with them.

MACEO: In thinking about that lineage, what do you feel are the literary traditions that you've inherited?

RIGOBERTO: I've never read Chicano or even Latinx books where I didn't see a political energy. I say "energy" because sometimes it's language, sometimes it's sensibility, other times it's the context, or all of these elements woven together, but there's a political energy to the work that I've always felt a kinship with. Writing is a political act. The fact that we're writing, the fact that we're our own protagonists and our own narrators, that we are our own speakers—all those achievements are important political acts. That continues to be part of how I see and appreciate literature. Even now when people think, "Those fights are over," well, no, they're not over. There's an illusion of closure because we see some change, but it doesn't mean that the struggles are over. Just like when Obama became president and people declared, "Racism is over." No, not really. If anything, it's going to become more apparent.

The turn towards community is another sensibility that is important to me. When I wrote, I always looked around for my communities. It's always plural for me. It's never just one. Who are my communities and how am I serving my communities with what I'm producing, with what I'm writing, and with what I'm doing? I claimed the Chicano community, the Latinx community, the queer community, the immigrant community. Whatever I do, how is it that I'm serving each of them?

The third thing is the importance of mentorship, whether that's mentorship in the classroom or when I reach out to young writers at AWP or through email. Even my books out there are a form of mentorship. Because that's what I felt when I first read books by Chicano/ Latino authors. I grew up reading Ana Castillo and Dagoberto Gilb. They were important to me and I got to meet them, but there was also this set of writers that I never got to meet and I consider them my mentors. Tomás Rivera is a perfect example of that. *Crossing Vines* was inspired by his *. . . y no se la tragó la tierra*. With *Butterfly Boy*, I looked toward John Rechy, Michael Nava, Francisco X. Alarcón, and Gil Cuadros, who were the few visible gay Chicano writers in my youth. Cuadros is the only one I never got to meet. I decided I wanted to be part of what they were doing. I wanted to take that courage with me to write my truths down and share them.

MACEO: How do you perceive your role as a writer in relation to your community, US society, and then literature itself? You mentioned the importance of communities, so maybe you can address how you see yourself within, say, the queer community or the Chicanx/Latinx community.

RIGOBERTO: I've always seen myself as a champion for our Latinx experiences. By being very specific, I'm presenting one more vision of who we are. One more portrait of who we are, because people on the outside see just one thing. When I write I ask the following: How am I breaking that frozen image apart? How am I shattering that stereotypical perception of who we are? I have the same approach with representing the immigrant community. I'm the immigrant who grew up in Mexico, then comes and works in the grapevines of California, pursues an education, and eventually becomes a distinguished professor at Rutgers University. That's what this immigrant did. When I received the PEN/Voelcker, I read a poem about the children in cages, and said, "What happens to these young children who cross the border when they are very young? Well, you're looking at one now." As an individual, I am expanding the landscape of our experiences and understandings of who we are. Within our communities I hope I'm able to inspire another young person who's like me. That's always been my audience: youth trying to find themselves, looking for their experiences on the page. I want to write to that person and say, "Look, you are seen, your experiences are valid," but also, "Pick up a pen, get in front of a computer and write it down, because I did."

MACEO: In your memoir *Autobiography of My Hungers*, you explore psychological and emotional hunger in addition to actual hunger. I wonder to what degree literature has been a way of satisfying that hunger?

RIGOBERTO: So much of my own path, my own way of being in the world, comes from my immigrant ethic. Once when I was visiting Macalester College in Minnesota, a young Latina said to me, "How did you do it? How did you stay in college and not just run back home?" I asked her, "Have you ever heard of the string theory?" She says, "Like in science?" "No, no, it's this: go home, put up a map on the wall, and put a string to where your people come from." She came from Nicaragua. Then I told her to stretch the string all the way to where her family made a life inside the US. "Look at the length of that string," I said, "and you want to go back home, even though, unlike your ancestors, you speak the English language, you attend college, you have opportunities they'll never have? How much are you going to add to that string if you're not even going to leave home? This little bit. But your mom traveled this far. Did you not learn from her strength?" Not to say that everybody has to leave home, but our imagination, our courage, and our vision have to stretch beyond that. You don't have to leave your family, you don't have to cut them off, but reaching into places that are unfamiliar is important. It's a risk-taking that's part of our immigrant cultural heritage.

My grandparents and parents were semiliterate. My mother always hid the fact that she couldn't read or write. Yet look at how much they accomplished. I think about the time my poor father drove us to Disneyland. We had this map and a big clunky station wagon that broke down twice on the way. We left at five in the morning and got there at 1:00 p.m., even though it was only three hours away. None of that stopped my family. There were so many limitations out of their control, that they couldn't overcome, but they still managed to do something for themselves, including get this kid to think about the possibility of doing something larger, expanding the world that he was living in. Where does this courage come from? My poor mother was out there at the picket lines risking deportation. My grandmother was Purépecha, and there she is taking a leap of faith along with my grandfather. "Let's go, vamos al norte." There were serious dangers, with serious potential failures. So what are ours? You might fail a course, you might fail out of college. That seems so small. My family knew they wanted something. They did not imagine exactly what that looked like, but I'm going to figure that out on my own and help them fulfill this dream of what we all sacrificed to come to this country for. I think that's the hunger that fuels me.

The one thing I've always wanted of this literary journey, even from the very beginning, wasn't the money, or the awards, or the publications—it was respect. Only because I had seen my family be so disrespected. Even by other mexicanos because we were the newly-arrived farm workers. To see my abuela get looks of disdain at the market, having people comment on the kind of cake she bought or seeing my father always nervous when he crossed the border. Sometimes people saw that and they were empathetic; other times they jabbed at it, made it even worse just to see him sweat. In everything I do, I write for my younger self, but the respect I'm garnering is for my family, for my parents.

MACEO: When you look at your own writing, but then also the writing of other Chicanx and Latinx writers, what do you feel is our unique perspective on US society?

RIGOBERTO: As much as we look at ourselves through outsiders' eyes, we can see ourselves through our own eyes and we don't have to convince ourselves to love ourselves. We don't have to convince ourselves that we're worthy of respect. In our writings we are complicated. We understand that we're not perfect, but we can still love our flaws. Whenever I read any Latinx writer, besides the beauty of language or the beauty of storytelling there is a level of thinking, of understanding, of searching, of curiosity that writers don't have to prove exists in our community. We have it already. It's already with us. It's affirming to see that. We're seeing white writers freaking out that they can't write our stories anymore. They're like, "Why not? Writing is writing." The thing is they can still write them, they can still publish them, absolutely, but when I read an African American writer write about the African American community or experience, a Latinx writer write about the Latinx community or experience, I see a person who understands—or is looking to understand—so much about their own community without having to prove anything to anyone outside that community.

With the Trump administration, we were given another level of burden to prove that we're not this monolithic image. We're not thieves and rapists. All anyone has to do is look at our literature to understand that Trump's wall is there, but we can still live and thrive on both sides of the border. Even if they make that wall stronger, even if they make it higher, we're still going to be here. We can define ourselves apart from the damn wall. Our Latin American ancestry, our Latin American roots are still very much important to us. Whether or not a writer chooses to connect the writing to the rest of the Américas, the sensibility is still there. We're now embracing our identities so openly, and I think it's fantastic. Before, there was still a little bit of hesitancy. People thought that to make it in the industry, one had to "just be a writer." Once at AWP, I was on a panel with Luis J. Rodriguez, and this woman, an older Chicana, comes up to me and says, "I have a book that I want to publish. What do you think my chances are?" I told her, "It's an exciting time to be a Chicana writer." And she said, "I want to stop you there because I don't want to be a Chicana writer. I want to be a writer." I said, "Well, then you're speaking to the wrong person. You might want to go talk to all those white people out there, they know what it is to just be a writer. I don't know how to be that kind of writer." But that argument is moot now, because people love multiple identities, with our chosen gender pronouns. In 1998 or 1997, if you were trying to be like, "I'm this and I'm this," it was too complicated. "What? You're going to be a writer *and* you're going to be a gay writer? *And* you're going to be a gay Chicano writer? What are you trying to do? You're going to divide your audience. Only gay Chicanos will want to read your shit." That was the narrow thinking of the past.

MACEO: You've placed special emphasis on Chicano, Chicana, Chicanx writings, and not wanting the Chicanx tradition to disappear into a pan-Latinx identity. Why is that distinction important for you?

RIGOBERTO: Latinx has become the term now, and I have colleagues and friends who are feeling as if the work that we have done to assert and affirm and celebrate Chicano is going to be erased. Now Latinx is going to take over. I'm not sure that's a fight worth fighting because every generation has to define itself by its own terms. You don't have to surrender to it, but you have to engage with it. You don't have to adopt it, but you have to understand it. But to fight it or contest it, or to shout it down, you're going to be the person that we had to deal with when we were trying to affirm Chicano back in the day. There were people pushing against that identity. Let's not go there. Let's accept that the new generation has a very different way of being in the world. Same thing with nongender binaries. I remember one of my colleagues asked, "Can't they wear signs?" Are you serious? Remember back when the first question you got was "what's the difference between a Chicano and a Latino and a Hispanic?" You really want to go there with gender? Because that's exactly what that sounds like to me. I was educated with a '70s sensibility of literature because that's what I had. I was going to college in the late '80s and '90s. At that moment, MEChA was still very important. Now, I understand the critiques of Chicanismo. Even Gloria Anzaldúa is being questioned in terms of the racial Indigenousness. I think that's important. Otherwise, you freeze Anzaldúa. I think, if anything, it only affirms that Anzaldúa is still part of our conversations. Also, nobody's going to cancel Gloria Anzaldúa. I know they tried to do that with Sandra Cisneros, which is the stupidest thing I ever heard. The answer is to listen, not get on social media and rant and rave. There are moments when it's important to shout it out. There are moments when it's important to sit and protest silently. Those are the tones of being an activist. I always shirk activism that's monotone, only shouting, or behind-the-scenes back-channeling. "Are you listening?" That's another tone. Whether or not you agree with what's being said, it's important to listen.

In terms of my own work, I'm still going to continue to champion Chicano. The best advice I got about the term was from Pat Mora, who said, "Identity is situational. When I'm in a room and I feel like I have to be Chicana, I'm going to be Chicana. If I have to be Latina, I'm going to be Latina. That doesn't mean I don't know who I am or that I'm shifting. No, I'm still who I am. It's just that now, whom I'm speaking to matters. If this group over here has a problem with me being my Chicana self, then maybe I shouldn't speak to them. I have to know when I can stand up and affirm who I am and do so when it matters." Most of the time these preoccupations with labels are just a distraction. If we're getting stuck on a name, then we'll never get to the next level of thinking or doing.

I identify as a gay Chicano, but I adopted Latinx because I know it's here for a reason. When I took over the series at the University of Arizona I said, "It has to be Latinx literary series." Latinx because that's today—the nonbinary. I see it in my own students. They're embracing it, and I have to as well.

MACEO: You've written about how your grandmother's memory was triggered by place, and it was very literal—she had to go back to the place to be reminded. Yet for you, as someone who has left home in more ways than one, what is the trigger that you keep returning to?

RIGOBERTO: I've always identified with Gloria Anzaldúa's turtle that carries its home on its back because memory has to be home for many of us. I learned that from my own family. Home was Michoacán. Many could not go back. Many never did. My abuela, for example. So home had to be memory, that weight that you carry on your back. For me, homesickness has always been a trigger. Right now, my maternal grandparents are still alive, even though my mother isn't, and they're in Michoacán, and I haven't been able to visit them at all. They don't even know me anymore because they have dementia. As troubled as my childhood was, as bizarre as it was, there was also a kind of comfort in knowing that these people were within reach, and I think I need that again. Even though I just completed an entire book about my abuela, my paternal grandmother, she too remains unreachable. I'm still stretching out my hand, whether she can reach back or not. The triggers are homesickness and loneliness, too. I'm looking forward to the moment that I can go back to the Southwest. The Southwest still calls to me very much. I miss the sun, I miss the desert, because they remind me of those moments when, yes, we were going hungry, hiding from la migra, but I could still walk out and look at this beautiful mountain range, the Hershey mountains, and look at this beautiful sky, and *that* nobody can take away. I still have my memories of home, in both Michoacán and Califas. And yet I don't want to write about my family anymore because it's emotionally exhausting going back to that period in my life, my adolescence. I don't know if I can go back again to my own personal traumas and my own personal anxieties. Maybe that's why I'm turning to fiction. It offers me another, less painful way to reconnect to home.

JAVIER: We're in a global pandemic and we are also in a state of global mourning. What is the role of the poet in writing about that death? Mourning it, marking it, both as you see it in your own work but then also in the moment that we are now.

RIGOBERTO: I've always seen it as a practice of going back to the rubble, looking through it to see what happened. Let me go back, let me sift through the devastation again and try to make sense of it. I think that as writers and poets, it's important, because when I read the early works from the '70s, José Montoya, Lalo Delgado, and even Alurista, I saw that these writers were already looking at the shittiness around them. They were already questioning. That's an important connection to today. It's important to acknowledge that this activism, these urgencies, have been part of who we are. That's our legacy. That we are always going to turn toward these issues, because they continue to affect us. So we continue to challenge them. I think that if we don't do that today during the era of COVID, if we don't look at the turmoil around us, what message do we send then to writers thirty years from now when they look back and say, "What were those writers thinking about during the pandemic? In the age of Trump and COVID, what were they doing?" The thing is, we're doing exactly what people thirty years ago were doing: looking at the fucking mess, trying to make sense of it. Finding ways to express that grief but also our hope, and articulating our understanding of what's happening. There is a strange sort of solace in that.

When I was doing research on Tomás Rivera in the 1920s in Texas, I saw that the three big issues for this community of Chicanos were police brutality, wages, and schools. Someone might say, "Oh my God, we're still there," but I say, "No, no we're not still there." Those things are *still* important to us, that's what it is. Don't look at it as, "All of this, and nothing? No progress?" That's disrespecting everybody that brought those issues to the forefront and wrote about it and talked about it and marched and protested. You're not looking at it correctly. That fight continues, and that's critical. That's how I see the role of writers now. As we're writing about our experiences, how is it that our imaginations are speaking to the present but also dialoguing with the past? In the face of ugliness, to write something beautiful is resistance. In the face of shattered homes, to write about a home that's not getting put back together, that's resistance. But we have to continue creating, we have to continue imagining. It's an essential record. These are important documents that we have the privilege to shape and create. Let's do something with that power. If we're not running for office, if we're not taking to the streets, then what should we be doing? Writing.

—January 10, 2021

7

MANUEL MUÑOZ

Manuel Muñoz is the author of two short story collections, *Zigzagger*, which was published in 2003, followed by *The Faith Healer of Olive Avenue*, published by Algonquin Books in 2007. Both collections are largely set in California's Central Valley in small towns near Fresno among its Mexican American and Mexican immigrant communities. The stories often feature gay men struggling to find themselves and to find love in conservative small towns filled with even smaller mindsets. But the landscape and the people of the valley are also beautifully rendered, and its community members, despite poverty and limited opportunities, demonstrate persistence and desire, and as often as they hurt one another, they also show a deep capacity for love. Muñoz's novel, *What You See in the Dark*, is also set in the valley, but in 1960s Bakersfield, California, alternating between ill-fated characters with Hollywood dreams and a famous movie director and an actress who arrive in town for a film shoot. The novel is a treatise on filmmaking, showing a philosophical interest in what the medium can and can't do, and by extension, why literature remains so important in our technological age. Muñoz considers himself first and foremost a short story writer, and he returns to the form in his forthcoming collection, *The Consequences*. Muñoz spoke to us from Tucson, Arizona, where he has been since 2008 when he took his first academic job in the Creative Writing Department at the University of Arizona. A committed teacher and mentor, he spoke movingly about the impact of his own mentor in his MFA program at Cornell University, the renowned Chicana author Helena María Viramontes, who pushed him to advocate for his own work and ideas. She also cautioned him about a job in academia because of the time it takes away from writing, a struggle he acknowledged. "Four books in almost twenty years," he shared ruefully. But one author we interviewed predicted that in a hundred years it will be Muñoz's books that we'll still be reading.

Javier: What has been the impact of the pandemic on your writing? And can you speak more generally about your writing process?

Manuel: I was directing the Creative Writing program when lockdown happened. I won't get into the weeds, but the situation got really bad here at University of Arizona. Like a lot of places, especially public universities, and in a red state, things just went haywire, and it was really stressful. I was glad that when lockdown happened my story collection was more or less done. Lots of people who weren't used to being by themselves didn't know how to handle being by themselves. For me, it's a natural state. I'm single, I have no kids. I was weathering it pretty well for about three or four months. It became a way to get away from all the stresses of trying to manage directing the program, dealing with admin—not to mention individual student situations. So I had a little bit of quiet time, and basically from March to about July, I was able to look over the collection and determine that it was getting ready.

I harp on academia a lot because I recognize that there are lots of people who would want a tenure or tenure-track job, but I should have listened to the advice to stay within your nine-to-five and leave your mind open for your work, because when I was in New York, I wrote so quickly. I had a production editor job that finished at five, five thirty. I could think because I didn't bring anything home. I lived in Manhattan and I would walk across the neighborhood, a twenty-, twenty-five-minute walk home, ideas percolating in my head. I could write on the weekends. I finished *Faith Healer* in two years because there was nothing overwhelming me, but academia really robs your time. Or I should say it this way: if you're doing your job, it robs your time. It just isn't a job to half-ass. You have to be there for students. When people say, "I want a teaching job," I say, "Okay, well, you better be there to teach, because the students are expecting your time, they're expecting your expertise, your guidance, your mentorship, and you have to show up and place them first." That is a sacrifice. I watch some of my peers who are able to balance everything, but I've struggled. My next book, *The Consequences*, took me nine years to write. Just because I couldn't find space for myself. Something will have to change. I have to renegotiate how to think about writing, where I really do make it a priority in my life, the way it used to be.

MACEO: How much of the dedication that you feel toward teaching and toward your students comes from the influence of your own mentors, including Helena María Viramontes, who was one of your writing professors at Cornell? When I've seen you talk about her, her influence almost seems spiritual.

MANUEL: I remember the first time Helena and I did a presentation together, and she was just marveling at it. She said, "I couldn't get a word out of you in graduate school." Bien callado. Just the fear, the discomfort, the sense that I didn't know as much as everybody else, that I wasn't reading as widely, that my ideas weren't as complex. She knew all along that my hesitation was not well founded, but she gave me a lot of room to find the way to start expressing myself with more confidence. That's really all her. Going back to how I think of myself as a professor, I try to engage my students in a conversation that I hope they see is never-ending. Your work is the primary text. Tell me what you're doing in your work. I know some people don't like to do that. They might say, "Oh, my work speaks for itself." That's bullshit. Here's your one chance. You can say what your work is doing and to practice some of those ideas. That came from Helena. We would have lunch or go have coffee and she'd have my draft in front of her, and she was ready to cross out pages and say, "I think it starts here." Her constant challenge to me was, "What do you think, Manuel? It's your work. What do you think?" She wasn't training me to be combative or defensive. She was just encouraging me. She'd say, "You are the authority of your own work. Start speaking to it. Just speak." Sometimes I still hesitate to do that. She's famous for her big red *X* and always telling you, "Your draft starts on page five." "But Helena, I wrote all this great stuff." She'd say, "But it's not doing anything." Her challenge was "If you really think so, tell me why—defend it." I started learning to really speak up for some of my tactics or some of the strategies that I thought made for good storytelling. That was always her whole point. There's not *a* way to tell a story, there's *your* way to tell a story, but can you start talking about *your* way? I try to do that with my students, encourage them to own their work, own their confidence, and work toward their greater creativity.

JAVIER: What have been the formative moments in your journey as a writer?

MANUEL: Right now, I've been saying to myself that I'm a short story writer. The novel was a real pain in the ass. It taught me a lot over the five years that I wrote it and drafted it. It was basically one draft a year. My mind works in the micro, it really does. The first story I ever got accepted was "Campo" from *Zigzagger.* I drafted that story in Ithaca, at Collegetown Bagels, where I sat with a little pad and just started writing my story there. The reason it was formative is that I was not going to workshop it. I was already out of the workshop. I didn't have to show it to anybody, and I just thought, "I'll do this by myself and not show anyone." Drafted it and then got up the courage to mail it—mail because this was back in the late '90s—to *Glimmer Train*, and they took it, which was a huge validation. I thought I was real chingón. The other two drafts that I had going, I finished those and sent those out, thinking, "Oh yes, well, *Glimmer Train* took this one. They're going to take these." They got rejected quickly, but there was something there that made me realize that I knew a lot more about what I thought the short story form could do than I had given myself credit for. I just enjoyed the process. I enjoyed thinking about the micro, the various ways in which an arc can be an arc in a story. In *Zigzagger* you see all the little two-page stories versus a fifteen-page story. I had an openness to what it could be. I don't want to say that I was writing with confidence, because I was still struggling and circulating a lot of bad drafts that got rejected by journals, but that started teaching me: "Okay, don't be in a rush to send out. Think about this draft. Do you really think it's good? Why?" Back to Helena, her whole point of getting me to talk was so that I could have that conversation with myself. You've got to be your own editor as you start sending stuff out. Why is this story working? What are you defending about it? I was getting better when I was working on that book.

Maceo: Can you talk a little bit about your early trajectory? There's a man in your story "Anchorage," from *The Faith Healer of Olive Avenue*, who escaped the valley only to return and be trapped. You write, "Sooner or later the draw of home lulls everyone back." How did you experience your own escape from the Central Valley, and how did you navigate the draw of home? The physical draw but also in literary terms, because you write about it so extensively.

Manuel: I grew up in a very crowded house that I know is eight hundred square feet because of Zillow, and at one time it had eight people living in it between my grandmother, my parents, and my siblings. There was no privacy; it was loud, crowded. I longed for peace, quiet, no TV. No one turning the TV on at six thirty in the morning, and then turning it off at night at eleven. Just quiet. When I went off to college, it really felt like I got away from something. As much as I loved my family, I really needed my space. Did I have to go across the country? No, but I was eighteen, and also that decision wasn't a family decision. It was me. My parents had no idea what Harvard was. They couldn't have given a rat's ass what it was. All they said was, "Why are you going all the way over there? You can't go here to Fresno State?" I could, but I wanted to get away. Little did I know what I was getting into. I missed home a lot. I came home for Christmas when I could, and then I spent my first summer back home and I just started to have this perception of change. Meaning, things change. You go away, someone gets older, someone gets sick, someone moves houses. Nothing is stable, so you better start appreciating what you've got every time you get a chance to visit. In those early days of college, that's when I really started to pay attention. I'd always thought of myself as a writer, but that's really when my observational skills started to come into play. I went home, but couldn't go home that often, so when I was there, I was just absorbing and absorbing. "Remember what that vineyard looks like. Remember what that smell is like in late August when they're irrigating the fields and you can smell the dust. You're not getting that in Boston. You're not getting that in the big cities." As I stayed there longer and longer, I just became aware of—not a divide with my family, because I'm close with my family—but that I had something to cherish when I went back home. That it wasn't always going to be the same. As my mom calls it, "La bola de años"—just all of a sudden what was supposed to be four years, turns into eight, turns into twelve.

When I got into Cornell for grad school—again, no internet, just phone calls; this was around '95—they had been calling me to say, "Hey, we need an answer from you about this." I was debating between Columbia and NYU, but I didn't understand the tuition packages, all the financial aid packages, and Cornell was a free ride. What a pendejo I was. Anyway, Helena got frustrated because I wasn't answering, and so she took the application and called up my permanent home phone number. She talked to my mom. And my mom called me and said, "Hey, there's this profesora, you got to call her." That's how I knew. Whoever this woman is—because I wasn't aware of who Helena was in '95—but, boy, somebody is willing to call my house and explain to my mom, "Hey, I'll watch over him for two years." That made a huge impression on me.

JAVIER: You published first with Northwestern, then Algonquin, and your latest book will be published by Graywolf. What have been your experiences in getting your works published, either negative or positive?

MANUEL: I think my publishing experience follows what maybe is still the template. I'm not sure if it's true anymore, but I always feel that our writers, our community, get their feet wet in a small press before the bigger publishers take an interest. That started to change. Oscar Cásares was one of them with *Brownsville*, Alex Espinoza with *Still Water Saints*. But before, and still, it has been that we go to the small ones first. There's a lot to say about that, but as far as Northwestern was concerned, I felt very well supported. They published my book well and they still take care of it. This is almost twenty years later, and they're still doing a beautiful job with it.

Algonquin, to be honest, was not a great experience. *The Faith Healer of Olive Avenue* was published in 2007. You hear publishers talk a lot about wanting to support our communities, lots of different communities, but acquiring books and supporting them are two different things. They really let my books fall through the cracks, right down to the cover design. I hate the cover to *Faith Healer*, ay dios, the kind of arguments we had about images, approaches, ideal readerships, ways to just think more expansively and generously about who our stories could reach. To be honest, it's why I have been taking my time with the next book. I kept asking myself, "Why do this?" There's lots of good talk out there about how we want diverse readerships and diverse audiences, but it was mostly bullshit on the publishing end. It still is.

But the Graywolf experience has been fantastic so far. I'm hopeful. But four books in almost twenty years? I've just had a mixed bag. *Zigzagger* feels rock solid. I don't know about the fates of the next two books. They may go out of print, ni modo. But Graywolf is like a new start.

MACEO: Writers often thank their agents in their acknowledgments, but one of your books is dedicated to your agent, Stuart Bernstein. How did this agent-author relationship become so important?

MANUEL: Well, I had an agent before Stuart. I don't even remember her name. I was trying to sell *Zigzagger*, and I was going through the agent process, and she liked the work and said, "Hey, I'd be happy to send this out." She kept pushing for a novel. A story collection will always be more palatable to editors if you have a novel or a synopsis going. I was working on that and thinking she'd submitted the collection around, but after about six or seven months, I realized she was waiting for the novel so she could send both out. I told her, "That's not what I want to do, because I'm not sure what is up with this book for that matter, and *Zigzagger* is done." We parted ways amicably, but to myself, I thought, "Cabrona." But anyway, it was Rich Yañez who told me that Ilan Stavans was editing a new line at Northwestern—Latino Voices. He said, "You should send it in." I thought to myself, "They're not going to take a queer book." Remember, this was 2000, 2001, 2002. I'd been sending it out and that's what I was hearing from small presses. "Is the community really ready for some of these kinds of stories?" some editors asked. Look how far we have come in twenty years—incredible. Rich had a copy of it. Rigoberto González had it too. They passed it to Ilan, and Ilan said, "Hey, who is this guy? Do either of you have his email?" Rigoberto contacted me and said, "Hey, you're going to get an email from Ilan Stavans, dot, dot, dot, don't fuck it up." That's how that happened. That's how it moved out into the world.

Stuart, in the meantime, through Helena, was trying to get ahold of me to see my work. But I was thinking, "I'm done with agents. Give me a small press, I don't need an agent at a small press." Finally, he convinced me to go have a drink with him. What impressed me about him was—even though he knew that I had already signed with Northwestern, so there wasn't anything in it for him, with my measly thousand dollars that I got for signing—he still said, "I just think these are really great stories. I haven't read stuff like this." I told him about my previous agent experience, and this is what cemented it for me, he said, "I'll never tell you what to write. If you want to be a short story writer, go ahead." I was like, "An agent is really saying this?" Because I've never heard that before.

There was just a respect that he had for the love I had for the form. I thought, "Okay, I can trust this guy to push my work as far as short stories are concerned," and he remained true to that. He's a really good reader of my drafts. He gets what I'm doing, and he also knows my writing well enough that he knows my quirks and my patterns and then encourages me to break them, to tell me, "You did that already." There's a story in the new book called "Susto," which is a ghost story, and I was having real trouble with it. I remain accountable to Stuart, so I'll send him a draft just to show him I'm working. It was the fourth draft, and I was ready to give up on it. I said, "I don't know what the hell I'm doing writing a ghost story." He says, "Manuel, the first story in your first book has the devil in it?" And he was right! Because sometimes you just need a sounding board. He's been that for my short stories. He's been very good.

JAVIER: You've spoken in the plural when you said "our writers." I think you meant the Chicanx or Latinx literary community of readers and writers. Related to that, we wanted to ask you, what literary tradition or traditions do you feel you've inherited?

MANUEL: As I've gotten older, I've grown more appreciative of literature and different traditions being a slipstream. You're just one of many, the voices come together, if that makes sense. I just have a greater appreciation of where we come from as a group. Not how one writer opens the door for somebody else, but how the books over time, and the literature over time, open the doors for those who keep wanting to do it.

To me, that was at the heart of what Helena asked of me during one of my first meetings with her at Cornell. She asked me, "What did you study while at Harvard?" I said, "English literature." She asked if I had read this or read that, and she quickly realized that I basically had not read anything past 1920. I had one seminar on modern literature: Black Women and Their Fiction, with Henry Louis Gates. That was the only throughline I had into literature past 1920. She very famously told me, "What the fuck did Harvard do to you, Manuel?" She gave me a list. She said, "I need you to go look up these books. Some of these aren't going to sing to you, but you need to know where they come from." To be honest, half the books had me saying, "This feels old school. This is not what I'm down for." Now that I'm older, I can go back and trace what has gone on in a relatively short period of time, from the mid-seventies on, and feel part of that trajectory. Rather than following one or two writers like Arturo Islas and finding the throughline between him and me—that's only part of the story—really I now feel part of all Chicanx literature.

The other influence for me truly has been Black literature. Those have been the ones that have been much more formative for me, whether it was encountering Gayl Jones, or Edward P. Jones, or John Edgar Wideman. The impact that those books had on me. I'm not going to compare myself to Edward P. Jones, but he taught me how DC is his locale. As he writes stories about that community and shapes it, he's transporting you across time, across neighborhoods. I learned a lot in ways that I didn't necessarily always receive from Chicano literature, but our literature is very young. Fifty years. There's more, obviously, but I'm talking about books that started being published in fairly great numbers across presses of all sizes. We're a pretty young literature. It makes sense to me to look at the trajectory of other literatures in the country to see how we might start to diversify within ourselves. That's what I find so fascinating about African American writers: they don't sound alike at all. The depth and range of their production is astounding. We're still shaping our lit, and I'm really excited that we're shaping our lit together. Not one person does it—we all get to do it.

Maceo: I thought a lot about Arturo Islas's *The Rain God* and your work, particularly his preoccupation with death. So many of your stories, especially in *Faith Healer*, circle around tragedy. Sometimes it's direct, parents mourning the death of a child, sometimes it's indirect, some tragedy or loss in a character's past; but loss is somehow foundational to the character. How did tragedy become a starting point for you? Did it emerge from personal experience, your own losses?

Manuel: One biographical detail that maybe people don't know about me is that I never met my biological father. When I was a month old, my sister was a year older, my mom had five kids, and my dad took off to Mexico and didn't come back. My older siblings knew him and were old enough to remember him. So when my stepfather came into the picture, there was this tension over his role as the "real" father. "Why do I have to respect you?" My brothers were muy carajos, they were terrible with him. Whereas I was very respectful, and I acknowledged quickly and easily that he was my dad. That's how I have always thought of him. When I got older, I started to realize, "Holy shit, this man crossed the border multiple times, got deported multiple times, and kept coming back to five kids that were not his own." When I think about that, it's like, "Fuck, man, that's so much sacrifice and hard work." We were all working in the fields, with my dad working the hardest of all to feed five kids that weren't his.

So there's something in trying to understand the capacity for making such impactful decisions on the lives of others. Like my biological father: How do you take off when you have two bebitos and say, "I'm not going to come back?" Or my stepfather: How do you keep being so giving to people who are not your own flesh and blood? My stories aren't just about creating an arc; they're about trying to understand a character's motivation for doing something. Why are they doing that? Sometimes it's doing something terrible, or sometimes it's about why they have their particular ways of dealing with grief. These might be the only ways they know how. Those mysteries of human behavior have been at the core of so many of my stories.

JAVIER: In your stories a lot of the accidents and people leaving happen off-screen, and what the reader sees are the characters who are the caregivers, whether that's Connie who takes care of her son even though he's eventually going to die or Vero trying to take care of her younger brother, Nicky. What draws you to characters who are there to give care and support to others?

MANUEL: It's because there are two stories there. The first story is what everybody sees: so-and-so is taking care of so-and-so. The second story—and the heartbreaking one to me—is what the caregiver sees and hears on a daily basis: the look on someone's face when they regret or they wish they could say something to the rest of the family. I think of the intimacy of caregiving. Do I tell what I heard to the rest of the family, or do I keep the intimacy private?

I'm glad that you brought up Vero because I started to think about what it means for siblings to care for one another. Especially thinking of my younger queer self who was not out, and my older sister later telling me, "I knew all the time." Behind that story is why she didn't say anything about it. What kinds of circles was she spinning for herself about what she suspected? There's something really fascinating about that. I think I started getting even more attuned to caretakers because as *Zigzagger* came out and I got invitations to read in classes and have conversations with college students about the work, the question of point of view came up a lot: "When are you going to start writing more about women?" I found this very surprising, because it was, on the one hand, my first book and it's rooted in a queer experience. It makes sense to me that most of the POVs come from those characters. It wasn't criticism, but it kept being a question. What about the sisters? What about the mothers? What about the tías? I didn't say, "Oh, let me sit down and write a story about a tía," but it's more about that interaction. What role do they play in the family? Invariably with the women in my family, it has been caretaking that ends up being their responsibility. There's emotional work and burden that comes with it. They end up being the carrier of so many stories and so much pain, and that pain demands the release of those stories. I think a lot about the consequences of that role.

Maceo: There's a bleak repetition in your stories—I guess we would call it a cycle of poverty or generational trauma—but there's something beautiful about the relationships that are formed through this bleakness, even if it's just a single relationship. Your stories always feel redemptive and hopeful, and I'm curious how you struck this tone.

Manuel: I don't think of stories as needing to have redemptive qualities. That's not how I typically feel I must end a story. That's not to say I'm discounting the question. What I'm saying is no matter what story I've decided to enter into, I've come to an understanding of "story" that means it must always come as a kind of blessing. There's a really beautiful privilege in being able to see the interaction between two people at whatever levels of intimacy they share, to understand that something profound has happened between them. It is beautiful. It's a human interaction. What is it our literature has always suffered but the discounting and disregard of our lives? These lives don't matter as much, or they're not worth putting to page, or they're not worth thinking about, whereas in fact, wherever you look, there's a story.

I talk about this line from *Faith Healer* a lot, because the Gold Street locale is loosely based on a long street in Dinuba called Golden Way. I remember taking a drive on that street and I counted all the houses, and it was fifty-seven houses on one side of the street. I remember doing the math in my head. Every house on that street has a family; they have all these permutations. You could write novels just on that street alone. No matter how you look at what can appear to be bleakness or despair, there is human life. There is interaction. There's a possibility for change. There's awareness of one another. All that redemption can come in different forms. That's why I keep loving stories so much, and why I like reading them as well—because they keep telling me, over and over, this iteration: "No, you haven't seen every story in the world. You're about to see another one."

Javier: Thinking about place and community, you've created this world along Gold Street, which you're continuing into your third collection of short stories. The characters often appear in their own story, but then they appear in other stories. We see that just because we left that story doesn't mean that the characters stop existing in the world. Can you speak to the creation of that world, and then also about the privilege of being the storyteller for this community? How do you understand that role?

Manuel: I'm glad that you put it that way, that just because a character has disappeared from a story, it doesn't mean that their story is over. Once we encounter them, whether they're on the page or we receive them from someone while we're sitting at the kitchen table and hearing something, it's a part of that big slipstream—a continuation of life after life after life after life. It happens again in *The Consequences.* There are going to be lots of little crosscurrents. "Oh, yes, there's that character again." I like doing that, and some of that has to do with the sense that none of these characters ever exists in isolation when they're in a town that small.

To the second question, that's a hard one because I don't necessarily see my role as a storyteller as standing in for anyone. I don't speak for anyone. I just acknowledge that I have an ability to tell a story. I'm exercising that ability. I've seen people answer that question, I've seen it get asked a lot, and I keep dwelling on it because I don't know if anyone would want me to be speaking for them. As I'm getting older, I'm getting weary of pronouncements. It makes more sense to listen to everybody. When you have various artists speaking to our collective experience, that makes more sense to me. Our stories are so individual and so unique and we have so many unique ways in which we express ourselves that it doesn't make sense for any one of us to take a big prominent role, but instead to acknowledge the fact that it's our work together that creates the sense of what our literature is doing. And that's just literature; we also have visual artists and filmmakers. That kind of expansion and growth is really exciting to me, to see the directions that we're going to go. We don't even appear in films. That time is coming. It's going to come, and when it does, I think it'll be fantastic to start to see those artists, not only as actors but screenwriters, producers, cinematographers. I'm a big movie person, so I keep waiting for the day the big breakthrough happens.

MACEO: In many ways your novel *What You See in the Dark* feels like a dramatic departure from your short stories. It takes place in the distant past, it focuses on heterosexual desire—just to name two major differences. How did writing a novel feel different from your short story collections, and how conscious were you of going in a new direction? Did you feel any sort of insecurity about whatever responsibility you may have felt to write about the queer experience in the Central Valley?

MANUEL: I've gone as far to say I consider the novel a failure. Sometimes I have a feeling that I was too optimistic about where we were. It was the mid-aughts, and I just thought we were about to hit this big renaissance. Alex Espinoza had just got picked up by a big publisher. Oscar Cásares just had his collection in 2003. I thought there might be this shift coming. Not just what publishers are ready to look at it but maybe what we, as readers, are also looking at. Maybe the experimentation was going to start coming—different kinds of stories. I was interested in what I had learned about Hitchcock and the valley as a backdrop, a movie site, and that excited me because that was a new facet of the valley that nobody ever gave much license to. It was clear to me, especially once the novel came out, and I could sense a bewilderment from people: "What the fuck are you up to?" That question about being responsible to one's community also ends up being a big restraint because it's what the community thinks *you're* ready for. I was really resentful of that because if I had listened to that twenty years ago, trying to write the queer stories I was drafting, I would never have published. There has to be a letting go of what—I don't want to say, "What we permit our artists to do," because we go and do whatever the hell we want—but of our narrowness and, instead, embrace our artists with an openness and a curiosity about where they're willing to take us. Are there really only a handful of narratives or themes that we look at in our community? That's why, again, I go back to when I was trying to shop *Zigzagger* around and the answer I kept getting: "It's too queer." I look back at it now and it's like, "This is such a tame book," but twenty years ago, editors were clutching their pearls.

JAVIER: Two of the stories in your new collection take on migration, documents, and deportation: "The Happiest Girl in the Whole USA" and "Anyone Can Do It." What inspired you to take on this theme?

MANUEL: My parents. In recent years, they started to share their experiences as young people. I tell my students all the time, "Your parents are people." If you have a good relationship with your parents, ask them to tell you about how they fell in love. You'll get a great story. Transcribe that for yourself, for your draft. Sometimes the story is a reaction: "¡Ay! ¿Quién eres tú para estar preguntándome?" The shame or the humor might be enough to notice—something will come up, if you dare to ask.

I just started asking my dad lots of questions. My mom has always been very forthcoming. My dad talks about other people but wouldn't talk a whole lot about himself. To me, he was a mystery. I happened to ask my dad, "Didn't we have a '74 yellow Duster?" He said yes, and that's when my mom told me the story of how she'd gone down to the border in that car, and my dad showed up with this guy saying, "Oh, I just met him, we'll take him with us," and my mom says, "You're crazy. I'm just taking you." So they let this kid go along with them. He was young, and of course they got stopped, and my mom got arrested, they all got arrested, and they got thrown over the border. My mom was a US citizen, so she got locked up for two days, but they impounded the car, and she says, "That's how I lost the car, because you brought that fucking pinche huerco."

A lot of these stories come up when we're together and have to deal with everyone talking at the same time. My mom doesn't like cell phones at the table. If we're eating together, she hates the "text-mex," as she calls it. "Allí están con el pinche text-mex," and then she'll go on these rants about it—"You're all useless without these machines" and "No saben que hacer" and "You'd drown in a cup of water"—and that's when some of those stories will come out. She'll say, "I used to go get your father without any of that, I didn't even have a credit card." And we'd hear the story of how she would travel three hundred miles without plans in advance when we didn't have much money to begin with. That's how I learned the plan she and my dad had for meeting up when he was often deported. She said, "You know, we had a park that we met at in LA, and if he didn't show up there, I went to the park in San Diego, and he told me, 'If I don't show up there, que ya estuvo.'" I never know if that's actually a joke or not, but this is back in the '80s. It was hard to cross, but the border wasn't militarized the way it is now. My dad would tell me how he could literally sneak in on the side—they were watching him, but they didn't care. It was more about money and whether you had transportation to get where you're going, and as long as you didn't run into anybody asking questions.

They told me this great story. They had an old Pontiac Bonneville and this car was on its last legs, and she had taken it to pick up my dad. She tried to go the back way around Los Angeles so that the cops wouldn't stop her, and of course, the car breaks down. A cop stopped, un mexicano, and he started talking to them. He knew what they were doing, but he didn't care. Nowadays that wouldn't have happened, but he helped them fix the car and got them on their way. To me, that's an incredible story. That's where they come from. I only thought of those family histories in terms of myself—waiting for him to come back after being deported not understanding what it meant, wondering, "He's gone, is he coming back?" Never did it occur to me that my father actually had his own story about *how* he was coming back. *Ask*.

When my dad had his stroke a few years ago, I felt this urgency to start asking because I worried that one day he wouldn't be able to recollect. So that's a bit of my role right now, when I think of my parents and my family and the valley and my community and my writing: not to remember *for* them but to make sure that they're remembered. That we're remembered. All of us.

—January 14, 2022

8

OSCAR CÁSARES

Ever since his debut short story collection, *Brownsville,* Oscar Cásares has written about Texas's Lower Rio Grande Valley. Born in Brownsville, Texas, in 1964, Cásares uses fiction to push back against the ways that the US-Mexico border is distilled into political sound bites and stereotypes or altogether ignored. In his most recent novel, *Where We Come From,* Cásares tackles the subject of immigration and its impact on the lives of people who live on the border, but mostly the book is about the metaphorical walls we construct to protect ourselves that only increase our isolation and insularity. The same condition can be seen in his first novel, *Amigoland,* about two elderly brothers, Don Fidencio and Don Celestino, who must overcome their estrangement and dismantle the barriers between them to become whole. Many of Cásares's characters are stubborn or stuck in their ways, trying unsuccessfully to weather a changing world, but despite their foibles, Cásares imbues their stories with dignity, humor, and affection. In the short story "Charro," Cásares describes a man who feels "as if he were standing in the middle of a river trying to stretch his arms and touch both sides. No matter what he did, he'd never reach far enough." However tortured his characters might feel about their liminal existence, it is this condition that Cásares considers his inheritance as son of the border region. Cásares has received fellowships from the Guggenheim Foundation, the Copernicus Society of America, the Texas Institute of Letters, and the National Endowment for the Arts, and he teaches creative writing at the University of Texas at Austin, where he first attended as an undergraduate. He told us he has no recollection of even applying. He came home for lunch one day and an acceptance letter was awaiting him. "To me, it was like I'd been drafted," he shared. "Like I didn't have a choice. It wasn't like I had applied anywhere else. The letter showed up, and so I thought, 'Well, I guess I got to go.'" With a few exceptions, including graduate school at the Iowa Writers' Workshop, he has been in Austin since 1985. Cásares spoke to us from his home office.

JAVIER: How has the pandemic impacted your writing?

OSCAR: Right at the beginning of the pandemic, I was notified that I'd won a Guggenheim, but I delayed the whole process because I knew I had a ton of research to do, and it allowed me to get all that research out of the way. For writers, the continued lockdown—and you don't want to admit it too much—means you get to stay home and that's not altogether a loss. Personally, it affected my family. One of my cousins got COVID, and he and his wife died within forty-eight hours of each other. The funeral was live streamed. The news itself knocked me on my ass, but the grieving process happened in a really weird way.

MACEO: For your novel *Where We Come From*, you spent time researching smuggling and safe houses. How important is research to your writing process?

OSCAR: I'm always a little wary of research because it can go on and on and become a form of procrastination. In *Where We Come From*, I had the majority of the story already written, and then I met this former INS agent, Hipolito Acosta, who for years had crossed into Mexico and posed undercover as an immigrant so he could be smuggled across and then bring down the smuggling rings. In general, I walk into the research tentatively or just very cautiously. I want to know what to include and what is extraneous, so that I can then write with some sense of what's actually relevant. What I'm trying to avoid is an information dump—for the reader to be asking, "Do I really need to know this? Is this pertinent to what the story is about?" When I'm including those details, that specificity, I want to make sure that they're adding to the reader's understanding of the story.

JAVIER: In *Brownsville*, whenever Domingo speaks, it's in Spanish, and it's Spanish that's local to Brownsville or northern Mexico. In earlier Chicanx and Latinx books, especially those published by mainstream publishers, there would usually be a translation that comes right after, and your books don't have that. What have been your experiences weaving Spanish into your writing and working with publishers?

OSCAR: Writing an early draft can get complicated for me because I'm essentially working in two languages. People are reading the novel in English, but the characters are not speaking to me in English. As they're thinking, as they're processing, as they're seeing the world, it's generally in Spanish. So I'm balancing what the character has said in Spanish and how it may sound in English. For me, it's not a literal translation; or I should say, it's not an adaptation. There are times where I want it to feel a little stilted. For Domingo, I was having a tough time because I was essentially learning to write with that book, and one of the things that I was struggling with was writing about this immigrant man living in a bilingual world, when he spoke only Spanish. I felt like there was a disconnect for me any time I had a character who was clearly speaking in a different language but we're reading the words in English. It felt less authentic. I struggled to figure out how to write that character, and what I ended up doing was writing the entire story in Spanish. I put my pocho Spanish to work, and I wrote the whole thing, the first draft, in Spanish. The sentence structure was totally crude, but for me, it tapped into the way he was seeing the world. When I went back through, I literally translated what I had written. For instance, Domingo is cleaning some woman's yard and she brings him lunch. As he's sitting out by the pool by himself eating the sandwich that the woman brought him, he imagines that this is the way wealthy people eat. In his mind, as I had written it, and as I had always heard my parents refer to wealthy people, it was "gente de dinero." When it comes out on the page, the literal translation is, "This is how he imagined people of money eating," as if the people emerged from the money. It helped me get that much closer to him, to try to see the world the way he was seeing it. Part of the labor for me is finding the way that I'm going to tell this story that, in many cases, is being communicated to me, that I'm hearing and imagining, in Spanish, yet it's coming out in English. Where do I find the balance?

I work really hard for the Spanish to feel as natural as possible, particularly when there's code-switching. I work hard on it because just as I had an issue with hearing characters speak English when clearly they weren't speaking English, if you're someone from a bilingual world who has been around code-switching, you know where those breaks are, where the shift is and where the shift back is, and you know when somebody is not doing it well. There's also the very real possibility that I'm going to hear from an editor, "I don't understand what this means. Clarify, or explain, or do we need a glossary?" I've never had that issue, I think in part because I'm aware of not wanting to interrupt the flow to explain something. I want a reader to have an immersive experience. I'm not your tour guide. I'm not here to teach you Spanish. I'm not here to teach you about what's happened with our people. I'm not here to educate you. Now, that doesn't mean I won't make references, but I think that's up to you to go do that research if that interests you. To me, the Spanish when I include it needs to work contextually. What has led up to that moment? What is happening? How are they saying it? Is it a tense moment? What would happen if I took that line out and I put it in a different language? Would you still get it? I'm constantly asking myself that question.

MACEO: What have been the formative moments in your journey as a writer?

OSCAR: My personal story as a writer doesn't get told without the fact that I grew up in a house with no books, and in school, while they encouraged reading, it didn't take. I essentially did not start reading until I started writing. Now, the only thing that makes up for that, the only saving grace, is that I had these tíos who came over to the house and held court, telling stories. The stories dated back to the mid-1800s and went through the early 1900s with the Texas Rangers and into the Depression. It was the whole history laid out for me in this narrative of how our family intersected with these events, how our lives were affected by them. I was just fascinated when they would tell these stories. It was the thing that brought me inside; it was the thing that turned the TV off.

As is usually the case with these family stories, they're ones that get told over and over again. You don't just get one shot at it. They show up, and people request, "Tell the one about"—órale, and they launch into it. Well, if you hear the same story multiple times, and you're as interested as I was, then you're going to have some working memory of how they told it last time. You understand that they changed something this time, or you understand that when they get to this part, they lean forward, or they wait for a reaction, or they wait to drop that one line that is going to bring out the laugh.

As a kid, having no idea about books, no idea about storytelling other than what I was immersed in at that moment, I began to—not even knowing what the term meant—deconstructing the way they were telling stories. I'm going, "Okay, he's saying this because this is going to come up later, and he's planting this little seed there." The tíos did not talk about foreshadowing, they just knew how to whet your appetite a little bit and bring you in a little bit more. I think it's one of the things that has most informed me as a writer, and one of my early challenges was how to bridge the gap from the oral to the literary. It's not the same. In the very beginning, I thought, "How difficult can it be?" Well, it's a lot more difficult. You can't gesture with your hands, you can't raise your voice, you can't bark if the story involves a rabid dog, as one of my tío Nico's stories did. You have to figure out how to do that on the page to a similar effect.

When I started writing, it was a fluke. I was around thirty-two. I'd been in a bar telling some friends a story about one of my tíos. The next day, I was at a coffee shop, and I thought, "Let me see if I can write that. It was a funny story, let me see if I can get it on paper and see if it translates." And I thought it wasn't half-bad and I had fun writing it, trying to figure out this new way of communicating. So I wrote another one, and another one. These are all stories that I knew backwards and forwards. I didn't have to create them, I didn't have to imagine them; I just had to figure out how to get them on the page. I went through all the stories my tíos had told me and some of my own, and then I started on new stuff. It took all of five months to convince me that this is what I was going to do. In the summer of '96, I walked into my boss's office and quit the advertising job I had at the time. You can do anything when you don't realize how really difficult it is. I just said, "Well, if it doesn't work out, I'll just come back, y ni modo." I gave it a shot. Thankfully, things started happening.

Another formative moment happened at one of the first readings I ever gave. I had been taking classes at the community college, and I was going to read a short story, maybe four pages, at a festival organized by the college. I had worked in advertising where I was always presenting to people, trying to sell my ideas. At first, the idea of doing a reading was like, "Well, I used to do that all the time." But suddenly, it was like, "Oh, shit, this is my stuff. It's not pretend, it's not some client, it's my stuff." My heart started racing and I thought I was having a panic attack, that I wasn't going to be able to get the words out and my voice was going to crack. But then I just took a deep breath, and I was like, "I've lived this. This story is mine." I remember just telling myself that this was as real as it got, and nobody could tell me it wasn't real. Once I accepted that, that what I was writing had happened, that the people that I was writing about were real people, real lives, real hearts broken, a real narrative that stretched out for generations, that was indisputable, and then all I had to do was get up and do the next part.

I can say that about everything that I've written—that there's some part of me in it. There's some part of my family's experience in it.

Maceo: Your stories and novels are almost entirely set in Brownsville, Texas, in the Lower Rio Grande Valley, which is also the terrain of the Chicano author Rolando Hinojosa. He describes in his essay "The Sense of Place" how he had to learn that the people, places, history, and language of the Valley could be the subject of his writing. What was the process like for you?

Oscar: When I finally started reading, I tried to read as much Chicano literature that I could. Most of these stories were about people living on the margins. Whether it was *. . . y no se lo tragó la tierra* or *Bless Me, Ultima*, it was either rural or there was some downtrodden aspect to it. Usually, there was a white antagonist of some sort, or just a larger world excluding the characters. But that was my parents' experience, not mine. So I had to ask myself, "Where am I writing from? What is my vantage point in this story? How do I contribute to this narrative of writing about a minority?" And that's when the light bulb just popped. It was like, "What minority are you talking about?" I grew up in Brownsville, Texas, demographically 93 percent Mexican, Mexican American, Mexican of some descent. Really, it's 100 percent. Even the O'Malleys are Mexican, at a certain point. If you're in Brownsville, that's just what you know. Sure, there are people living on the margins, but it's more about class, it's more about when they arrived in the country.

I was blessed to be born into a very old family. My dad was born in 1914, which means he was raised by a man from the 1800s. The stories that my tíos were telling had been handed down to them from the previous generation. For them, these weren't legends or myths. Some of the people in them were still alive, at least when they were growing up.

So that was a paradigm shift for me, when I looked at our experience from the vantage point of where I had grown up. I was writing about the mainstream. And when I was in graduate school, so far from the actual border, writing my first book, I approached it from the inside out, as though I were living in Brownsville. What that meant was, well, if I'm in Brownsville, and I'm telling this to somebody else who's in Brownsville, then there's stuff that I'm not going to say because it'd be like, "Why are you telling me that? We both know that." That takes away that didactic, "I'm going to hold your hand as I take you through this." No, no, you're going to come with me, and I'm going to show you what it was like, or what it is like, but I'm not going to pander in that way because this is our world, and this is the world now. With *Where We Come From*, it strays a little bit off that immediate world because there's a bit of Houston involved. In *Amigoland*, it strays southward into interior Mexico, but it's still pretty much defined by the experience of growing up in Brownsville.

I can remember moving to Austin in '85 and feeling on the outside looking in, of not being part of the conversation, being on the periphery. But in Brownsville, it's very different. The guy that gets caught at the bridge trying to smuggle whatever he's trying to smuggle is Mexican or Mexican American. The guy that arrested him at the bridge is Mexican or Mexican American, the lawyer is Mexican or Mexican American, the federal court judge is Mexican, and so you develop a very different way of looking at the world.

I worked in advertising for eight to ten years and got a lot of my cues as to communicating and writing from that experience. Not in the sense of literary fiction, but as far as telling a larger story compressed in a shorter amount of space. I think having grown up in this very insular world in Brownsville and then radically moving outside of that into this larger corporate world, and then reversing course and going if not literally back, then emotionally back, I think there was always this feeling that I was trying to live my truest self, but there were cues that indicated to me that I could only bring in part of myself, that culturally, some part of me needed to stay outside the door. That part of me didn't have a place in the corporate environment. It was disappointing, it pissed me off, it stirred a lot of things in me, but also, to a large degree, I thought, "Well, I just don't think you know our story, I don't think you've heard our story quite yet, and I think that there's room for that story."

I wanted to be aware of how the material might be received, and for me, in creating the world of Brownsville, I never wanted my reader to forget that the characters are mexicanos or Mexican Americans or Chicanos or whatever label. The idea was for them not to forget that identity, but also at a certain point they probably do forget it, because they ideally begin to see them more as just people, and they begin to see the conflicts that they're immersed in. For me, if I could get somebody invested in the emotional part of the conflict, then I had done my job, because now they were seeing that, yes, we are different, we do speak a little differently, we do eat a little differently, we do certain things a little differently, but when it comes down to it, when you get down to the core, we're all the same. We have different influences. You can parse out the values that we have versus other people, but I think at the end of the day, we more or less want the same things. That has become a huge part of the stories I tell. Now, I don't begin writing with this in mind, but I think it's a byproduct of the canvas that I've chosen to work on.

MACEO: You attended the prestigious Iowa Writers' Workshop. It's the same program that Sandra Cisneros went through in the '80s. I read an interview with her where she talked about how she found her voice almost in opposition to her mainly white teachers and peers. When you attended in the late '90s, was the environment supportive of your stories or did you feel a similar disconnect?

OSCAR: We attended the same school, but we attended under pretty different circumstances. If I'm not mistaken, she was in her twenties, so fairly young. When I started at Iowa, I was thirty-five, so I was one of the older students, and I had had a career. I didn't know my way around that literary environment, but I knew my way around an equally challenging corporate environment. I'd applied in '98 and started in '99, and the environment was on my mind because I'd heard some of those stories, particularly about Sandra. I even debated whether to delay it even further, to defer for another year or two, but again, I had worked in a very brutal environment.

Sure, there were things that people didn't get about my stories, or the experience did not register with them. I remember there was one woman who couldn't understand in the first story in Brownsville, where the kid is working at the fireworks stand, why the kid would want to work at his age. This idea of the pride in seeing your father work and wanting to emulate that just did not register. There were other points where they didn't know if I had made up this place called Brownsville. They thought it was a place with brown people that I called Brownsville and it's a Macondo or something, that it was more of the imagination than a real place at the very tip of the border. It just seemed odd to them.

But in general, I arrived with a different mindset. I pretty much knew what my job was. I had written what would become two of the stories in Brownsville and ended up writing, I think, probably another four or five of the others there, some of them that didn't land well and others that were more successful. In a way, I'd come out of a war already. It wasn't anything all that new to me. There were a lot of people that were older and there were people that had left law careers and medical practices. I always feel like I should have had a worse experience. I had a few dustups, but they weren't anything that I walked out with later saying, "That was horrible."

JAVIER: Your most recent novel, *Where We Come From*, was published in 2019, the same year that there was the controversy around *American Dirt* and Oprah's selection of it for her book club. The controversy raised an important question about who gets to tell certain stories. Who gets to tell stories of undocumented migration? How does your book inform this conversation?

OSCAR: That particular incident is obviously not a new phenomenon, and it does a disservice to a story that has not been told or been told very sparingly. For me, I understood that I could tell part of the story. I never walk into a story assuming that I know it all. In fact, I take the opposite approach. I assume I know little to nothing.

The idea for the novel sat with me for several years, way before things heated up with immigration. Immigration has always been out there, but not the way it has been the last five, six years. In the end, I felt like I was close enough and I was going to do the research, the homework, to get myself closer to the story. Immigration is obviously central to the story, but even something like writing from a woman's perspective required some time. I grew up around women, I know women, I'm married to a woman, but for me to presume that I know what their experience is like—I walk into that very cautiously. In a commercial sense, you can make the argument that anyone can tell the story, but when it comes to realism, being able to identify those nuances is such a critical piece of telling the story because those little details are essentially what distinguishes the story from it being simply genre or commercial fiction, from it being a story that anyone could tell. It's when you get closer to understanding the mindset, the fear, the terror, the heartbreak, everything that's going on in that character, that you move a step closer to making them real people others can relate to.

Admittedly, I didn't spend time reading that novel, but I very much enjoyed reading the essay by Myriam Gurba that exposed everything. Oh my God, what a voice. Like a grenade, calling out all of these writers who had gotten behind it and calling out what happens in those rooms. She gave everyone a sense of how these decisions are made. I was teaching a course this past semester called A Sense of Race. One of the last books we read was called *The Other Black Girl*, which is a really candid look at how the publishing industry works and how they make decisions about what books they decide to go with and how much support they're going to put behind them. Personally, I've heard comments such as, "We already have somebody writing about Mexicans." Only one per house. Comments like that are just—until you hear them, you think, "You don't really think that way, do you?" They do. Some of them anyway.

MACEO: *Where We Come From* centers on the relationship between Nina, an older woman, and her godson, Orly, and how they end up hiding Daniel, a stranded immigrant boy who escapes his smugglers and la migra. Throughout the novel, in italics, you share backstory of characters, many of them minor, who enter into the story and have some sort of connection to immigration and being undocumented. How did you develop the idea to include these passages?

OSCAR: The idea of including the immigrants' stories felt as important as anything else that was going into the novel. We are constantly around immigrants, but in most cases, we're oblivious to these other lives. They're going about their business, and that is just somebody serving us, bussing our tables, sweeping the floors, mowing our lawns, caring for our babies—whatever they may be doing. While they're a part of practically everyone's life, their lives are not seen, and yet they're there—and they're always there—and in many ways they're holding this country together as we've seen, particularly during the pandemic.

How to include their stories was a struggle early on and was an issue of narration: How do I create this world, and how do I make these things happen simultaneously without it being a chapter unto itself but actually immersive in what's happening? I had seen and was taken by the narration in the film *Y tu mamá también*. Suddenly this omniscient voice comes in and tells you this story. In the novel, none of the characters—whether it's Orly or his godmother, Nina, or the father or whomever—no one outside of the italics knows the immigrant stories. These are very intimate stories about these people. The main characters are rubbing up against the immigrants and yet know *nothing* about them. Even Orly who is very close to his teacher knows nothing about the man's private life. This is even more the case with the characters who see the room service guy come in and that's their only interaction.

MACEO: Do you perceive yourself and your work as political?

OSCAR: I grew up in a very political family: hard-leaning Democrat, no questions about it, straight ticket, "Don't even think, step in there, pull the thing and get out." That's just the way that it was hammered into me. On the other hand, South Texas is fairly conservative. It always has been. My brother-in-law and my sister once came back to Brownsville from UT Austin and my brother-in-law happened to mention to my father that he was now identifying as a Chicano, and the top of my father's head came off. He was of a generation where that was a loaded term, and it's a very regional thing, because you find the same people of that generation in California or even El Paso and it's not as loaded as it is in South Texas.

There's another story, of Reynaldo Garza, the first federally appointed judge that Kennedy appointed in '60, '61. Someone came into his court and the lawyer happened to describe him as a Chicano, and Garza just about threw them out of the court. He said something like, "You will not use that term in my court." Now, everything else that you read about the guy, complete activist, complete left-leaning, but you utter that word in front of him and he goes ballistic on you.

I didn't have any attachment to the word *Chicano*, but it was funny because I started writing and people would come up to me and they'd say, "Oh, you're writing Chicano stories." And I'd go, "Yeah, I guess. I'm just writing stories for people from Brownsville. You want to call them Chicanos, you can call them whatever."

As far as the politics, I realized it was going to be impossible to avoid this with *Where We Come From*. There was also this question whether in tying it to politics it would date the novel in some way. Would it be a novel about that specific issue at that specific time? Maybe that's not a bad thing, I don't know, but it was a discussion that I was having with my book editor when I got an email from an opinions editor at the *Washington Post* asking, "Did you hear these kids are being separated from their families? Would you be willing to write an editorial, an op-ed piece for it?" The stories had been leaking out that week, and I said, "Well, when do you need something?" They said, "Now." I'm like, "I don't work that fast." They said, "It's happening right now. We need a response." I said, "I need time to think about it," and so they said, "Okay, think about it and get back to us in the morning."

I knew where I stood but I also knew that venturing into the fray and getting into that discussion generally leads to a lot of people yelling at each other. I've written stuff that you wouldn't think would stir anything up. I published something with the *New York Times* about traveling to Matamoros when I was a kid, and still people got all stirred up and started throwing around some harsh words, and then somebody else throws it back, and they throw it back, and by the end it's just yelling and nobody hears anything. If that's your game, if you like to yell and you like to do that, then go for it. But if I'm going to do something, I want it to be heard and processed, and then maybe you think I'm full of shit or whatever but at least you've heard me. At the same time, I don't want to just put something out there so that you can agree with me because you already agreed with me. I want to find that place, if I can access it, where I might be able to shift the way you feel. Even if you're already inclined to my position, I want to be able to see if that's possible.

So I thought about the family separation issue overnight and I was just scrambling trying to figure out what, if anything, I would send this editor. At the same time, someone had recorded and leaked this audio of the kids being pulled from their parents and put in the cages, and they're just screaming and crying. It's almost unbearable to hear it. I thought, "There's something in this," and so in the morning I sent the editor a note and all it said was, "What language are these kids crying in?" and she was like, "Write that. Go with it." For me, if I had an agenda, it was to strip the politics from the issue because it's not a fucking political issue, it's a humanitarian issue.

That's what I was hoping the novel would do. That it would get to that point where you're no longer talking about left or right, red or blue. You're talking simply about lives, you're talking about a child wanting to be with his parent, you're talking about the fallout of that, you're talking about all the other immigrants that got their italicized sections and what they're struggling with. In each of those cases, there's a human side to that story. I guess to answer your question, I couldn't give a shit about politics, but yes, I understand that politics is what makes things happen or not happen. I was just trying my damnedest to move this beyond the politics.

MACEO: You talk about your work on this continuum, from the oral tradition to the Chicano tradition to you as a writer just telling the stories you know best. What are the directions that you see Latinx literature going?

OSCAR: My work has been centered almost entirely in Brownsville, but I'm excited about work that's coming out that is expanding the idea of what it means to be Latino in this country, stories that venture into more experimental writing that give us more diversity within that experience. I think it is crucial because it goes back to the idea of seeing us in all our facets. One of the parts of *Where We Come From* that I enjoyed was the challenge of writing Beto's conservative views on immigration. That sort of diversity of a counterview, of someone pushing up against the party line, to me, is fascinating. We have this old myth that we all think the same, we all vote the same. It couldn't be any further from the truth.

MACEO: I really was struck by the image and the character Marcelo in the story "Charro" from *Brownsville*. Marcelo says he felt as if he were standing in the middle of a river trying to stretch his arms and touch both sides. I also understood that this feeling was tearing Marcelo up inside. You've talked about your work and your experience in similar terms. You're standing in the middle of a river trying to stretch your arms and touch both sides, but for you, this has been a well of richness and your entire body of work has flowed from that feeling. I wonder if you could speak to what it's like to be in the middle of that river and to understand the anxiety that it causes, but then also how rich that space can be.

OSCAR: That pretty much nails it, in the sense of it's the feeling of responsibility, one that I accepted, I pursued, and I find myself wrestling with daily. Also, most of the time, I feel incredibly privileged and blessed to be able to mine this part of my family, my culture, to be able to find those things that have in some cases caused me pain, in other cases brought me great joy. These are things that I want my kids, when they're old enough, to be able to look at and understand as part of our journey, of how they got here. They have very different lives from their grandparents and, to a large degree, from the life that I had growing up on the border, but it's still all connected.

To be able to enter certain narratives and find those things to write about, and when I get close to it, when I understand that I've tapped into something, there's no better feeling because it's the real stuff, it's how it happened, it's how it happens. Yes, I'm a fiction writer, essayist, but a good part of what I'm doing is documenting. I'm getting those narratives on the page as well as I can. That comes with a huge responsibility but also a wonderful payoff. Most of the days, when I'm not banging my head on the desk trying to think of the next thing, I feel like I've got the best job in the world. Even if things had been more difficult in the beginning and I was having difficulty getting published, I want to believe that I'd still be doing it today.

—December 16, 2021

9

TIM Z. HERNANDEZ

Tim Z. Hernandez has published and received critical acclaim in multiple genres, including poetry, fiction, and nonfiction, as well as for his work as a performance artist. His debut poetry collection *Skin Tax*, an exploration of masculinity and vulnerability, won the American Book Award in 2006, which he followed in 2010 with his first novel, *Breathing, In Dust*. Through loosely connected poetic vignettes, Hernandez depicts the arduous road to manhood for a boy growing up in the suffocating atmosphere of poverty, violence, and sickness in a small Central Valley town, a setting that appears in much of his work. Born in 1974 in Dinuba, California, and raised in Visalia, Hernandez utilizes the many tools at his disposal to resurrect, unearth, and preserve the lives and landscapes of the San Joaquin Valley. This vision is perhaps best represented by Hernandez's two restorative history projects, which resulted in his second novel, *Mañana Means Heaven*, and his first book of nonfiction, *All They Will Call You*. In these yearslong efforts, he accomplished what trained historians and journalists couldn't or wouldn't attempt to do for over half a century: locate Bea Franco, Jack Kerouac's "Mexican girl" from *On the Road*, and both name and humanize the anonymous "deportees" of the 1948 Los Gatos Canyon plane crash first made famous in Woody Guthrie's protest song. In *All They Will Call You*, Hernandez moves seamlessly between voices, utilizing eyewitness accounts and his own research and analysis as well as his own instincts as a storyteller to recount the plane crash and the stories of the men and women whose identities and histories were assumed lost in the wreckage. Hernandez's extensive research was grounded in interviews with family members in the interior of Mexico, where he forged a community of survivors, many of whom had never had the chance to process decades of grief. Since the publication of the book, more family members have reached out to him, leading Hernandez to believe that the story of the Los Gatos Canyon plane wreck could be a lifelong effort. Hernandez spoke to us from El Paso, Texas, where he teaches in the MFA program at the University of Texas at El Paso. He shared that he was in "dad mode" at home with his two teenage children.

JAVIER: How has the pandemic impacted your writing? And can you speak more generally about your writing process?

TIM: I've been working primarily online at the University of Texas, El Paso, so the transition for my job was very minimal. But as a single dad, I didn't realize how much I relied on schools to take my kids for the bulk of the day and give me space to work. At first, there was a lot of resistance. I've had a strong meditation practice for years, so my first instinct, once I recognized the challenge, was not to try and escape it or run away from it but rather to sit with the discomfort that I was feeling and acknowledge it. Stare it in the eye. Then figure out how to work with it and see what opportunities it posed for me. What that meant for me as a writer was I had a lot of projects that I had accumulated, a poem here, the start of a screenplay, a novel idea. Over the years, you never really manifest any of those because you just keep moving forward. But during COVID, I found myself at a place where I was able to think about all that work. So I've been productive with a lot of ideas and the creative juices have been flowing.

Aside from the writing, going back to being a single father, it has really provided me time to focus on my kids. Outside of the parenthesis that is COVID, we just start spinning our wheels every day, making ends meet and taking care of what we need to take care of, but in the parenthesis, I suddenly was able to look at my relationship with my children differently and how I could be more present. We spend a lot of time together. We even meditate together. I've been able to find a way to balance my writing and my job with my time and my kids. Because of that, our relationship has really grown deeper.

MACEO: What have been the formative moments in your journey as a writer?

TIM: The project I'm working on right now is the follow up to *All They Will Call You*—the plane crash series. When I published that book in 2017, I genuinely thought that I was done, that I was moving on, but the stories and the people around that story called me back. I realized this might be an ongoing series for as long as I'm alive. Before that book I was searching for Bea Franco, which became my novel *Mañana Means Heaven*. So for the last ten, eleven years, I've been searching for people. To do that, I've had to reflect a lot. When I ask questions of others, the people I'm interviewing, the subjects, I'm having to turn that mirror back on myself and ask myself those same questions, and I've learned that any strides or major shifts in my writing have very much to do with how I am evolving as a person.

Once I stopped writing stories and poems from my own experiences and I started to write about others, not just people who had passed on or historical stories but those who are still alive today, I felt accountable to others in the community. It changed my perspective of what I was doing as a writer. In fact, it felt like the writing and the production of a book wasn't the purpose anymore. It wasn't even the point of writing. The book is almost, for lack of a better word, an afterthought. It's the documentation of where the real conversation is, the real subject, and that is going out and sharing stories with communities. How can we open up that exchange to encompass more conversation, more dialogue, and more perspectives around issues and topics? Now, more than thinking of what kind of book I can write, I often find myself thinking, "What kind of conversations can I have in the world? Where can I have them? Where will they lead me? What might that open up?" When I do that, I realize that as much as the communities say I'm bringing and offering something to them, that's only half the truth. I'm growing, and it's changing me and how I think about the world and myself and my place in it.

JAVIER: How do you perceive your role as a writer in relation to your community, to the US, and then to literature itself?

Tim: I often get invited to do Latinx-centric anthologies, but I've been declining them for years now. My concern is that if we continue to write for ourselves and continue to be our own audience, we'll always be put on the barrio bookshelves—yet our names like Hernandez should stand side by side with Hemingway. As an American writer, that's where we should be. At the same time, I'm not trying to turn my back on the Latinx community. We're all players on a team, and we're all after a common goal, which is to share our own narratives, to write our own stories, to share them with the world, and to say these stories are of equal value to any stories out there. But we each have our own strengths. Some of us are more politically active, others prefer to do experimental avant-garde writing, and others want to do more traditional, straight narratives. There's room for all of it. For me, I feel my place on the team is as outrider: the one who treks ahead into the unknown and reports back to the community what lies beyond the horizon. I'm originally from the San Joaquin Valley, and a lot of times I'm asked why I left the valley, why am I not still there, writing from that place? Well, because the rest of the world needs to know about the San Joaquin Valley, too. It works both ways, a kind of cross-pollination.

One of the big misconceptions about my work is that I'm the guy who goes looking for immigrant stories. But that's not how I approach a subject. I'm not looking so much as paying attention to where in humanity people have had their dignity stripped away. Where are the voids, where are the gaps, which stories speak to me, and which stories call me to them? When I wrote *All They Will Call You* about twenty-eight Mexican passengers killed in a plane crash and buried anonymously while the four American crew members were given their names and funerals and headstones, it would've been easy for me, and probably expected of me, to write only about the twenty-eight missing narratives, the twenty-eight anonymous mexicanos. But that would've been a disservice to my purpose, which is to highlight the shared humanity, the things we have in common with one another, more than the differences. That's why I felt it equally important to talk about the pilot and World War II hero, Frank Atkinson, side by side with the anonymous passenger Ramón Paredes and his family.

As a writer, and this is probably the poet in me, I feel very strongly about coming up with language that is inclusive and yet can get across the point I'm trying to make. How do I make language inclusive versus language that continues to create disparities and polarities, language that divides us, because that's very easy to do. It's very easy for any of us to write about an injustice and use language that divides us, that says it's us versus them. I'm not interested in that. I try and use language that includes everyone in the conversation, that says we are all accountable to one another, that we are, in a very real sense, all brothers and sisters.

MACEO: What literary traditions have you inherited?

TIM: In the most direct way, Juan Felipe Herrera was a mentor of mine and is probably the reason I set off on this writing path in the first place. He was the first person to point at what I wrote and say, "That's poetry, you're a poet!" The door had never opened until that moment. One of the first books of poetry Juan Felipe gave me was Benjamin Alire Sáenz's *Calendar Of Dust*. It was in his house that I started to learn about José Antonio Burciaga and others from the Floricanto generation. Lorna Dee Cervantes's poetry just blew my mind; so did Jimmy Santiago Baca's *The Crying Poem* where he says that as men we should cry, let us cry, cry all the rivers for all the generations, cry. I never knew I had permission to feel that, much less to say that out loud. It inspired me to write *Skin Tax*, poetry that explored male identity and machismo. Those were some of the original influences, and I still think about them a lot. I hear their voices and pay homage to them in my own writing.

If Juan Felipe was the mentor I had for poetry, Victor Martinez was my mentor in prose and novels. He gave me a lot of one-on-one feedback. He was from Fresno, too, and so we spent a lot of time talking about novels and writing and what that meant. He wouldn't pull punches. Juan Felipe was very generous and gentle with me, but Victor Martinez wasn't. He was like, "I would not be wasting my damn time with you, but I am, because I have a novel to write and you should be doing this or don't even write at all." Rest in peace, Victor, but that's how he was, and I needed that. Juan Felipe was always, and still is, somebody who encouraged, inspired, and even incited me. He knew when I first came in that I was a painter. He knew I was collaborating with musicians. He knew I did a lot of acting. He encouraged all those forms of experimentation in me, and because of that I was able to open up to different kinds of disciplines and lineages.

His wife, Margarita Luna Robles, was the first one to talk to me about meditation and yoga. I never knew that had a role in what I was doing. I'm just this brown kid from Visalia in the streets hanging out, and it was like, "Yoga?" But because of conversations with her and Juan Felipe, I ended up attending Naropa, the Buddhist university in Colorado. Meditation plays a vital role in my life, just as important and powerful and foundational to what I write and who I am as the Chicano/Latinx literary canon. If there's one overarching theme that I have in my writing, it's interconnectedness. How do I demonstrate that we're all interconnected—nature, people, everything? There's actually an organic intersection between these eastern contemplative practices and the Floricanto generation of Chicano writers. Alurista and Juan Felipe and others were looking to Hinduism and meditation back in the '60s as much as they were to ancestral traditions and ritual. They were looking at what Ginsberg and Kerouac were doing. Oscar Zeta Acosta also writes about the Beats. I did it in reverse. I started off with the Chicano literary canon and went backwards to meditation. For me, those are two intersecting lineages of several that I often find myself pulling from.

JAVIER: The San Joaquin Valley is central to your poetry and prose. How have you drawn inspiration from the landscape, its towns and cities, and its people?

TIM: I think of the San Joaquin Valley less as a landscape and more like a family member. The sentiment I feel toward the land is the same way I feel when I look at the altar of my grandmother and grandfather. By that I mean, there's such reverence I have for the landscape, for the history it holds, for the pain and the suffering it holds, for the possibility it holds. Yet, for me personally, because of circumstances and events that happened in my life, I don't feel like I can breathe when I'm in the San Joaquin Valley. But I would feel the same if I tried living in my parents' home today, because obviously I'm a different person. When I live outside of the San Joaquin Valley, it allows me to look back and to consider and reconsider it over time. Whereas living there, I'm looking outward, and it just doesn't offer me the same vantage point or perspective or the distance that I need to put it into writing. But I still feel affection toward it. It's a beautiful and important place to be from, and it's where so many of my stories originate. Focusing on a sense of "place" is a heavy theme in my writing because I'm constantly contemplating what environment means to the ones who inhabit it.

Since I moved to El Paso eight years ago, this has become my second home. This landscape here, this frontera, a trifecta of Mexico, Texas, and New Mexico, is my family's homeland as well. It's where my grandparents are from on my mother's side. My grandmother died at an early age, leaving my grandfather here in this landscape to raise six children on his own. It was a very traumatic situation, and my grandfather could not overcome it. All the kids ended up being orphaned. As a single dad, in the same landscape, I look back at my grandparents' story and I know their wounds still haunt me. I was raised by those wounds, and so it is in this same landscape I must overcome them in order for my family to move forward. I will not let this landscape swallow me. So, I'm not just a single dad trying to raise my kids here, but I'm also trying to end generational trauma. I take that with honor and pride. For me, this landscape is as vital and integral to who I am as the San Joaquin Valley, if not more so. In surrendering to this landscape, I'm able to look back at the San Joaquin Valley through a different perspective, see what I was struggling through there and what raised me there that I wasn't even aware of at the time. Again, I look at these landscapes like a relative, or more like an ancestor, with so much to teach me about who I am if I pay attention.

MACEO: Both *All They Will Call You* and *Mañana Means Heaven* are powerful works of restorative history. No one had taken the time to dig deeper, to really unearth the history, whether of Bea Franco, the "Mexican girl" in Kerouac's *On the Road*, or the names of the passengers in the Los Gatos plane wreck. How does the act of naming inform your work?

TIM: The historian in me says names are important. The Buddhist in me says names are identity and therefore ego and less important than we think. What we name things is not necessarily essential to who we are and how we live. We have to recognize that we are energy. That spiritual aspect of me battles with the historian in me that says, "Yes, but our people—" By that I mean Indigenous, Latinx, marginalized communities here in this country have not had our stories told, have been stripped of our names and our dignity, have been buried anonymously for years now. In order for us to correct that historical wrong, which is to say, to correct the age-old documentation that stands, we have to use names. We have to give it all a name. My mission as a writer is to reconcile the balance between the historical and the spiritual.

The book I'm working on now is very much historical. It's about the new families from the Los Gatos plane crash who have found me, and it's about naming that history, but then I include an epigraph by Eckhart Tolle that says, "Die to the past every moment." That's me trying to figure out the balance between the two. The writer-historian in me finds the naming necessary, but the man who needs to live in the present moment in order to be happy and to find joy needs to let go of the past and live in the present. Those two can exist at the same time. They do exist. It doesn't have to be either-or. It's no secret that the value of names is for our own family lineage. If we lose a name, we lose a link in the chain to who we are, and it's important to know where we've come from. I don't mean that in a general "don't forget where you come from" cliché, but in a very particular way we need to know where we come from. We should ask questions. If we have our elders alive, we should find out and we should document; we should record them and say, "Tell me your earliest stories of childhood, how you were raised." And we should document our own voices. Journaling is a part of my practice, and I don't even journal big things that happen to me. I'll often journal the mundane, things like, "Today I'm sitting here at my desk, it's seventy-five degrees. I have a purple bandana sitting on my desk and my cell phone is here, I'm talking to Maceo and Javier." Just very basic particulars, because when you do enough archival research, you understand how important it is that somebody documented those particulars a hundred years ago and why it's important to telling the story of who we are.

In *All They Will Call You*, the names of the plane crash victims were omitted, so I wanted to find the names, but once I found them, it wasn't enough. Names are just a symbol. They're our logo, our emblem of who we are and maybe who we descend from, but that does not substitute who we are today or how we live. A name in fact tells me very little about a person. When I found the names, we put them on a big headstone, but the work had just begun. Names are an invitation to find out who we are, which is why in systems like prison and in the deportation process, people are relegated to numbers. Because in those systems, the less they know about a person, the easier it is to treat them as less than human. They don't want the invitation to learn more about people. So names are an invitation, an open door.

Maceo: Do you perceive yourself and your work as political?

Tim: My goal is to find my own freedom. I'm after my own liberation as a human being. In order for me to do that, I utilize stories and writing. I learn, I read, I listen, I hear, I gather stories, and they help situate me and position me in my life. In the writing process, I start to figure out the issue and how I filter it through who I am. Once I've written it out and thought through it in writing, then I can ask myself, "What action will that enable me to take? What's the next step for me to take as a human being who's seeking his own liberation?" Anytime there's somebody seeking liberation, it's political. You have to cross through the political barbed wire to find liberation, because in this society, and in this country especially, it's not set up for liberation. It sells you the idea of it, but it's not what they want. It's a capitalistic society. Heaven forbid you have people running around free. That's just how it is, unfortunately. But for me, the mantra is not "be political." The mantra is "cultivate liberation." And it's also to leave a trail of breadcrumbs for those behind me, starting with my children and anybody else who reads my books. Here are the breadcrumbs down my own path toward liberation.

JAVIER: When you say liberation, I'm thinking of what you said about conversations with the community: it's not just finding the names, it's going to converse with those people who know those names, and give more life to the names. You found and interviewed Bea Franco as well as her son, then also family members of those who died in the Los Gatos plane crash. You had to ask them about events from long ago that were difficult or maybe even painful to talk about. How do you approach these interviews?

TIM: When I'm approaching these families, I know that I'm talking to them about grief that, in some cases, they've had unresolved for seven decades. Some of them are ninety-two, ninety-three years old, and they've been living with it since they were twenty years old when the plane crash happened. The grief of not just a death in their family—their father, their uncle, or grandfather—but not knowing what happened is part of that unresolved grief. If they knew, they probably would've healed that grief by now, or it would've been less daunting by now, but they've never known, so it remains an open wound. All of this has been a learning curve for me. My formal education is in poetry and literature. I never took a journalism class. But poetry has its own process of investigation. We're curious souls as poets. We want to get to the root of things. I went about all this instinctually at the beginning, following my curiosity. Bea Franco is written about in over twenty-two biographies about Jack Kerouac in different languages around the world over the last fifty years, and I wondered if anyone had ever even bothered to interview her. And then I wondered if she was still alive. These were just questions that came to me, and I followed them until I hit a wall or made a discovery. It was Bea Franco's story that led me to the story of the plane crash. I was looking for the labor camp she worked at in Selma in 1947, when in the search engine, the newspaper article of this plane crash came up. It seemed like a parallel story. Here are people who had no names and no voices, and I'm writing about this woman who has been left out of the greater story of Jack Kerouac's *On the Road*.

In the beginning, I was very naive. I knew a little bit about how to conduct interviews because I'd been working with the California Council for Humanities and part of my job was to record oral testimonies. That was definitely influential, but it was from a very safe position that I was asking questions. That was more like, "You're writing a grant, tell me what the story is about." Sometimes those interviews would slide over into the personal, and at the time I found myself very uncomfortable when that happened. But I'm at a point now where I know my role. It's not just as a writer who's coming to gather a story and write a book. In fact, it's hardly that. When I walk into a home to speak with someone who is going to tell me the story of their grief, I come in as an opportunity, an invitation for them to find closure. That's my job there. So I bring offerings with me. It can be anything from a little dessert, a pie, pan dulce, or flowers. I bring them a copy of my book. Then, most importantly, I bring them all the articles of the plane crash that happened in 1948. I bring them photographs of the memorial headstone. I'm able to sit down with them and hold space through their grief. That's the biggest thing I've learned in the last eleven years of doing this kind of research, work, and interviews with people. I've learned how to sit with people in their various emotions during interviews and not be removed emotionally. It's important that I remain compassionate and empathetic while they're talking to me about these wounds but, at the same time, remain objective in order to see as clearly as possible.

Javier: What have been your experiences in getting your works published, either negative or positive?

Tim: My first book *Skin Tax* was submitted as a hybrid of poems and stories back around 2003. It was combined with what later became my novel *Breathing, In Dust.* I sent it to the University of Arizona Press and they rejected it. Their response was that there's no bookshelf for hybrids of poetry and prose. These days I have so much love for the University of Arizona Press, but for the first ten years of my publishing career I sent them every manuscript I wrote and they rejected every single one. Finally, in 2013, they published two of my books back-to-back. And ever since then, they've been like family to me. I understood later why they rejected my manuscript when it was poetry and prose. I don't think it was so much that there wasn't a bookshelf for it but that I wasn't at a place yet where I could articulate why the two belonged in one manuscript, why they were one concept rather than two disparate pieces. These days a lot of my work is hybrid. I'm combining poetry, prose, imagery, and I'm able to articulate why they belong together and that there's no other way it can be published. But for that reason, publishing was difficult in the beginning. Even with *All They Will Call You* there were opportunities that the book had, but because it crossed genres and blurred lines, it didn't qualify. Even though it is cataloged in the Library of Congress as a nonfiction book, some of these committees would see it and go, "Well, there's fiction here, and then there's even poetry." But that doesn't stop me from writing the way I need to write. I tell the story the way it needs to be told, and whatever happens afterward, that's beyond my control.

MACEO: *Mañana Means Heaven* and *All They Will Call You* were both published by an academic press, which has a limited reach compared to a commercial publisher. At any point, did you try to find an agent and publish with a bigger press?

TIM: With *Mañana Means Heaven*, I tried hard to "sell out." I was like, "Let's get this one to the big publishers. Let's go all the way!" We sent it to thirty-two publishers and they all rejected it. My agent at the time asked each one if they wouldn't mind writing a brief statement as to why they rejected the work. That was probably the best thing she ever did for me because I got thirty-two responses, and I could then see how big publishers were thinking, what they were looking for in a story, and I had to ask myself, "Am I that kind of writer? Do I want to be that kind of writer?" Some of them were not flat-out rejections. Some said, "If he changes it, or uses the third person in this way, etcetera, we would reconsider it." All of them seemed to unanimously agree that my writing was "too lyrical," or "too literary," or "too poetic." I was like, "Well, shit, that's just the kind of writer I am!" At the end of the day, that's how I write. I'm a poet after all. I decided I was happy with who I am and made the decision not to change anything.

With *All They Will Call You*, I initially had the same agent from *Mañana Means Heaven*. So again we started figuring out a strategy for getting the book to big publishers, but I often left those conversations feeling deflated, the same way I felt after *Mañana Means Heaven*. Plus, with *All They Will Call You*, I wanted more control because I felt personally indebted to the families. And I worried that if I went with a big publisher, I was going to lose control of all of that. So I made a very deliberate move to not go with a big publisher, and when that decision was made, it no longer made sense for me to have an agent. For a moment there was a friendly tug-of-war between City Lights and the University of Arizona Press for the rights to publish *All They Will Call You*, but in the end, I opted to go with the University of Arizona Press because I liked how they handled *Mañana Means Heaven*. They supported me in every way. They gave me control, and more importantly, they got my vision for the larger scope of the project. *Mañana Means Heaven* had two production companies that were considering optioning the book, but they never manifested, and because it was going through the agency that represented me at the time, I was removed from that process. It was discouraging because I'm a mover and like to have my hands in the work as much as possible. But I would just get a phone call from my agent saying, "It didn't work out. Sorry." I felt distrusting of the whole thing. So when *All They Will Call You* came out and several producers expressed interest, it was me they contacted directly, and it was me they had to talk with.

I believed in my heart and in my spirit that *All They Will Call You* would reach the audience it needed to reach, and for me that was enough. It would get to where it needed to get. I remind myself that each book has its own spiritual or karmic path. And I have to trust that it will reach the hands and hearts it is meant to.

Javier: In your books you describe yourself as third-generation and even, in quotation marks, as pocho. You also write about being uncomfortable speaking in Spanish, but it seems like you were still able to make connections with these families. Can you talk more about your connection to Mexico?

Tim: The first time I went to Mexico to search for the families was in January 2015. I had never been to the interior of Mexico, only to the frontera—as far down as South Texas, all the way to San Diego, all the different towns along the frontera where my family lived. By then I had been researching for five years, and I was literally going, "All right, Tim, you got to go into Mexico now. There's just no other way. You have to go into the mouth of the lion and face whatever insecurities you have about yourself. There's no way around it. You're going to have to go through it." I journaled a lot about it, processed emotionally what that was doing to me, psychologically where this was coming from, and I found myself writing a lot about my relationship with my grandmother. As a child, when my parents would work, my grandmother Estela took care of me, and she only spoke to me in Spanish and I only spoke to her in English. My grandmother was born and raised in Corpus Christi, Texas, but she only spoke Spanish. We had an arrangement where she understood everything I said in English, and I understood everything she said in Spanish, and we never forced the other to talk in the other's language. It was a beautiful and practical arrangement.

When I was in Mexico, I could ask questions in Spanish. I'd have to look at my notes and ask them, but I understood everything. But I think, early on, it got to the point where the families were frustrated because I kept glancing at my notes. Finally, as I was writing *All They Will Call You*, I was traveling with Guillermo Ramírez, who is one of the descendants of the passengers. He was part of my research team, and after the first couple of interviews, he became familiar with the routine and my questions. So he started talking with the families before I even opened my mouth. He would just start chatting with them, and it organically got to the point where I sat back and realized, "This is powerful. I have one descendant interviewing the other descendants. They're interviewing each other." So I was now in a position of being a total witness, a fly on the wall. I talked to Guillermo afterward and said, "Are you okay continuing these conversations with the families? If there's something you miss, I'll chime in, but I think this is pretty special." Every family we'd go to, I would talk a little bit, niceties, we'd exchange these things, and then Guillermo would get into his flow, and I would just sit back and listen to the conversations and write and record what was happening. It was a powerful dynamic, and I ran with it.

I quickly learned that whatever I came with was enough, and all of my insecurities started to dissolve. When we weren't doing interviews, I was practicing my Spanish—talking to more of the families informally, ordering food, going to the hotels, whatever. I started to shed away some of the insecurities that were put on me by my family's past. I started to realize, as a third and fourth generation Mexican American born and raised here, that a lot of those ideals of what Mexico is like were placed on me by my own family. Without realizing it, I had inherited the insecurities that they carried. Once I started to see that, I was able to shed them more and more. I got to the point where I was comfortable even screwing up certain words in Spanish, which I often did and still do, and no one was ever impolite to me. They would correct me very nicely or they wouldn't correct me at all. Nobody put me down for being a pocho, nobody said anything bad about it. They recognized that I was an author there to gather and write their story, so they were generous with me; but even in places where they didn't know who I was or have that context, they were still very kind.

It started to change my perspective about why we'd been away from Mexico for so long. Why had my family never tried to find those connections we'd lost? We don't know any relatives in Mexico. It was an invitation for me to dig back and find where the link in the chain was broken. The last couple of years, I've been doing a lot of ancestry work, finding out who our relatives are. I've come to find out that the family I was staying with in Guanajuato, that maybe it felt so comfortable there because that's where my great-grandfather was from. He was from Guanajuato, an hour away from where I was staying. My family here in the United States was blown away because we never knew our connection to Mexico. Since then, I've gone further back to identify our Indigenous roots, and I learned recently that on my mother's side, it is likely we originated from the Coahuiltecas. I'm still researching this, but it feels like it's opening me up to who I am originally, perhaps even instinctually, and to who I am as a human being in general. Before I thought I was just a brown kid who grew up in the '90s listening to Nirvana. And I'm just now integrating these new discoveries, which are a part of me that I didn't know existed, that I've been lost to for so long. It's important work, and it feels good. And I owe all of this to the work around *Mañana Means Heaven* and *All They Will Call You* and to the people and communities who've invited me into their homes and have trusted me to tell their stories.

—December 5, 2021

10

DANIEL ALARCÓN

Daniel Alarcón is the author of four works of fiction, a journalist for some of the most prominent publications in the country including the *New Yorker*, and the cofounder and host of *Radio Ambulante*, a Spanish-language podcast distributed by NPR and dedicated to stories about Latin America. Born in Lima, Peru, in 1977 and raised in a suburb of Birmingham, Alabama, Alarcón maintains a strong connection to his birth country, including a Fulbright Fellowship there in 2001 where he studied literature, and much of his fiction is set in Peru or a fictionalized version of it. In fact, despite writing in English and publishing in the United States, Alarcón was named one of the Bogotá39, a list of the thirty-nine best Latin American novelists. In a 2013 *New York Times* article, Alarcón accepts straddling multiple literary identities: "I think I'm an American writer writing about Latin America, and I'm a Latin American writer who happens to write in English." The war in Peru between the government and the Shining Path looms large in his story collection *War by Candlelight* and his first novel, *Lost City Radio*, which is dedicated to his uncle Javier Alarcón, a professor and labor activist who was one of thousands of disappeared dissidents. The reverberations of the political violence are inextricable from his characters' lives, and while their stories are often solitary, they are weighted by the history of a country unwilling or unable to face its past. A graduate of Columbia University and the Iowa Writers' Workshop, Alarcón found success early, publishing his first short story, "City of Clowns" in the *New Yorker* in 2003. Since then, he has become one of the most decorated Latinx authors, including a Whiting Award, a Guggenheim Fellowship, a Lannan Foundation Fellowship, and the MacArthur "Genius Grant." His books have been widely acclaimed, and his 2019 story collection, *The King Is Always Above the People*, was a finalist for the National Book Award. After years in the California Bay Area, he now lives in New York with his wife and children and teaches at the Columbia School of Journalism. He told us that since his youngest son was born, he has almost completely transitioned from writing fiction to nonfiction.

JAVIER: How has the pandemic impacted your writing? And can you talk about your writing process more generally?

DANIEL: I flew to Chile on March 4, 2020, to write a story for the *New Yorker*. I was there for about ten days, until I was afraid they were going to close the border and I came back. We didn't leave the apartment for a couple of months, except to walk the dog and buy groceries. It was awful. New York was a mess. Now we're all used to it, but it was a very scary time. We were locked in the apartment with little access to the outdoors, with a moody teenager and a really bored seven-year-old who didn't understand why he couldn't go to school to see his friends. My wife and I were trying to not lose our sanity. This is hardly a unique experience, I think everybody went through a version of this. But New York at the time was the epicenter. The people who had places to go outside the city left. We didn't see anybody. Under those circumstances, I wrote relatively little. I read a lot. I read a lot with my kid—my youngest. Since he was doing school on Zoom, we started walking the dog together. As the weather got nicer, we would walk the dog and stay in the park. I'd bring the dog a bone, tie her to a tree, and we would read books together. Honestly, that was the most joyful thing about those months: the memories that I have. We didn't leave the city until June when a friend lent us her house upstate for the weekend. Just being outside was a revelation for us. It was weird, scary, and bizarre. I think writing was the last thing on my mind.

I have this thing where I always feel that I'm being really unproductive, then I look at my progress and I'm like, "Oh, I wrote six hundred words today." The most recent work that I've done has all been nonfiction, but I remember this from writing fiction as well. I have very few memories of writing these books that I wrote, except that I know that I did write them because the drafts are on my computer. I do remember the feeling of being immersed in a book. To a certain extent, I miss that, even though I feel like that feeling can't be replicated again because when I wrote those books, I was relatively young. I didn't have kids, I didn't have many obligations. My life was pretty simple. Wake up, breakfast, write until I got hungry, write some more, stop, go get a coffee. I had certain techniques. A teacher told me once, and I think this is a great bit of advice, that you should end your day when you know what your first sentence is going to be the next day. Discipline is required to not completely twist everything out of the sponge but to leave a little bit of energy in the tank for the next day, so that you begin and end each day on a high. That's a piece of advice that I took to heart.

The other thing that I would do is write on a computer, and then in the afternoon after writing, I would take a bike ride to the Grand Lake area in Oakland and have a coffee there. I would take a notebook, I wouldn't take a computer, and I would try to write out by hand, by memory, the scenes that I was working on that day because I sometimes felt that my writing would be too florid. What I would find in the revision by hand is that it would be simpler or a little more controlled because it was physically harder to write—just the different medium would help. And then at some point the next day when I was back at my computer, I would compare the two and I would see, oh, maybe this extra adjective that I had in the computer version wasn't necessary because it didn't show up in my notebook. Those were just a few of the techniques that I used.

The biggest part of the process—and one of the reasons why I don't write fiction anymore—is just showing up, just doing it every day. That's the hard part. My approach to writing has changed because my life circumstances have changed. I have kids and I have a wife, a family, a crazy dog, a mortgage, all this other shit that is just life. And I do find it hard, and I end up writing in these fugue states where I don't even know that I'm writing, and in a state of absolute panic because there's a deadline, that it's got to get done. That's slightly different from the relaxed, "Let's take a bike ride to the coffee shop and the sunny afternoon in Oakland," kind of way.

Maceo: Both of your novels involved extensive research. How has your work as a journalist impacted or informed your work as a fiction writer?

Daniel: I've always been doing journalism even when I was writing fiction. There was a lot of investigative work to write *Lost City Radio*. Even if I didn't realize what I was doing, I wanted to understand the life of my uncle and godfather, Javier. To create a version of his life in fiction that felt believable and nuanced and rich required a certain amount of research, even if I didn't call it that, and journalistic work, even if I didn't call it that. That was important to me. When I wrote my first piece of nonfiction for *Harper's*, my editor told me, "You're going to go into a room, you're going to talk to people and write down everything you see." And I'd do this thing where I'd go into a room and talk to people, and I was always keenly aware of power dynamics, who was in charge in the room, who were people being deferential to and how, and the small gestures of the way that power was manifested. I realize that I'd been entering a lot of fictional rooms in my head for years and asking my characters the same questions. It strikes me that there's a real similarity in my process of writing fiction and nonfiction. It's just that sometimes I'm going to real places and sometimes I'm going to imaginary places. Sometimes I'm talking to real people and sometimes I'm interrogating imaginary characters, but they're not that different. I think the things that are interesting about any story are always, Who's in charge? Who thinks they're in charge but actually isn't? What's happening behind the scenes? What is the emotional truth at this moment? I think that's interesting in literary nonfiction as well as novels and short stories. It's part of what attracts me to nonfiction. If I was doing a stenography of reality as a career instead of writing novels, I think that would be unsatisfying. The reason I don't feel like a frustrated fiction writer is because the stuff that I've been doing in nonfiction, the longer, more literary stuff that I write for *Radio Ambulante* and the *New Yorker*, they feel narratively ambitious in the same way my short stories did, and that makes it easy to have quote, unquote given up on fiction. I don't feel I'm making a sacrifice, because I'm still working in narrative and doing work that excites me.

Javier: What have been the formative moments in your journey as a writer?

Daniel: I've been fortunate to have great mentors and teachers, fortunate to have received good feedback early on so that I didn't have to wonder whether people were responding to my work, because people were. I remember a creative writing workshop where someone wrote a comment on a story that was something absurdly nice, to the effect of, "One day I'm going to tell people I was in a workshop with you"—that kind of thing. That was freaky and really kind. I think a lot of my early work is inspired by this deep desire to understand the country where I was born but not raised and, by extension, I think forming an identity in opposition to the kind of white American suburb where I was growing up. Not in any kind of rancorous way, but in a sort of, "This is all fine, but this is not who I am," and a real interest in carving out an identity for myself that didn't carry with it an obligation to be submerged in the Anglo mainstream. This was a big thing for me because I'm the lightest skinned of my siblings. My two sisters look much more, and I say this in air quotes, "Latin," but I was the one who was born in Peru. They were born in Baltimore. On paper, I was the Peruvian one, but in reality, I was the lightest skinned one who spoke the worst Spanish. My path was toward assimilation because there was no language or visible ethnic markers to hold me back if that's what I wanted to do, but I didn't want to do that, I wanted to be something else.

The central animating question of my adolescence was, "If I'm not this, then what am I?" That led me to really want to figure out what happened in Peru while I was growing up in a quiet American suburb, and who might I have been if we hadn't immigrated. Without romanticism, without this kind of idyllic view of what that might have been, but with an open eye view. A lot of those questions are worked out in my first book of stories, *War by Candlelight*. What if I'd grown up there? What if I'd grown up in New York? To a certain extent, *Lost City Radio* was about the defining story of my adolescence, which was the disappearance of my uncle Javier. That was the point at which it was impossible for us to ignore Peru anymore, that I couldn't hide in my American suburban experience but actually had to confront that stuff, because I was seeing the worry and concern and fear play out on the faces of my parents. I would say that if there was any defining experience, it was that.

There are lots of smaller moments, a lot of good fortune and privilege. I happen to have been in a writing class in high school with the novelist John Green, who's a friend of mine. Having someone who was just as nerdy and obsessed with literature and the possibilities of literature as I was at age sixteen was huge. To have someone to bounce ideas off of when I was aspiring to be a writer was just a great bit of fortune. I'm not sure that you can account for luck like that.

MACEO: You maintain a very strong connection to Peru, and most of your work is set in Peru or a fictionalized version of it, yet your work is written in English and your first audience is the United States, most of whom will know little about Peru or Latin America in general. I also know that your work has been translated into Spanish and read in Peru. How do you navigate the complexity of these multiple audiences that span continents and languages?

DANIEL: I think most writers, if you ask them, and if they're honest, they'll have to admit they don't think much about their audience. They don't because it's very difficult to do. It can be paralyzing to think too much about who might be reading you. I think you have to think about what inspires you and begin there. Now, this is something that's on my mind because I write about Latin America for the *New Yorker,* and every time I do a piece about a place in Latin America, knowing that my audience is *New Yorker* readers who are not necessarily from there, I feel an immense amount of pressure. I just wrote a big piece about the pandemic in Ecuador and the collapse of the public health system in Guayaquil, and it was devastating to report on. I'm proud of the way the piece came out. I also know that the *New Yorker* is not going to write another story about Ecuador for five years. There are very few magazines—and they're all American and European basically—that have the resources to have a reporter spend time there, write the piece, get the fact checking, have the research, really dedicate yourself to it so that it's something that is a historical document as well as a piece of literature. It's pressure that, honestly, feels suffocating at times. I don't feel that with *Radio Ambulante* because I know *Radio Ambulante,* first of all, is a collaborative team project, and second, I know we're going to do a story about Ecuador every year. Ecuador is us. We have two Ecuadorian staff members. There's just a completely different vibe. Also, we're telling it for ourselves because it's in Spanish, it's for Latin America and Latino communities here in the United States, it's for people who are learning the language, who are interested in the culture, so there's a completely different vibe to it. It's no less vigorous, but the pressure isn't the same.

At the *New Yorker*, certainly the pressure of being the cultural, political, social as well as the linguistic translator of a Latin America reality is immense.

When I was writing fiction, I didn't feel that because, one, I thought no one would read it. Two, I felt just a real sense of exploration, of adventure. I didn't have time to think about an imaginary audience. In a way, I was blissfully unaware of what it means to publish a book like this. When you're writing a book of fiction about a country that is not the United States in English, a large percentage of people who read you are going to be going on vacation there. This has never been more explicit than seeing my book recommended in the front of the Lonely Planet guidebook. Then literally having someone write to me after *War by Candlelight* came out asking for hotel recommendations in Cusco. I don't get offended by this at all because there's no point, but it's useful to remember, whatever your pretensions about art and the power of literature might be, you can never account for the reasons why people are reading you or how they approach your work.

JAVIER: What literary traditions have you inherited or what literary traditions do you see yourself writing in?

DANIEL: The Latin American literary canon and the US Latino literary canon are important to me. The style and inventiveness of Junot Díaz, for example, and Francisco Goldman as someone who wrote about Latin America in English and without sacrificing authenticity or gritty realism. I think Toni Morrison was important for her unabashed embrace of the sweep of history without getting lost in it, the particulars of people's lives against the background of these gigantic events. When I moved to Lima in 2001, I started reading Latin American writers in Spanish in a more serious way. I started reading Latin American writers of my generation as well. The Chilean writer Alejandro Zambra has been a huge influence on me, and he's a good friend of mine. Then I also started translating. I translated early stories by Samanta Schweblin, the Argentine writer. That was a huge privilege as well, because there's no more intimate reading than that.

I've just had a diverse array of readings. It would be impossible to list them all in a way that felt comprehensive. There are the books that you read before you were conscious that you were gathering influences. I remember vividly *The Firm* by John Grisham, these beach-read thriller-type books that I just devoured. I loved them. Before that, I loved history books. I loved these coffee table books about the Civil War, the history of the World Cup. I knew all kinds of arcane facts. I read Dostoevsky, Tolstoy, Chekhov, Turgenev, and Pushkin when I was seventeen. Just spent that year in Russia. I still think of Chekhov as one of my favorite writers. I feel fortunate to have discovered books at the exact right moment. I remember not knowing quite who the narrator was of *At Night We Walk in Circles*, and going to a used bookstore in Oakland with a friend of mine and finding *Group Portrait with Lady* by Heinrich Böll, and being like, "Oh, here's a path. Here's a way to do it." I also found George Faludy's *My Happy Days in Hell* just totally by accident. I bought the book because I liked the first line and the title. I never heard of it, never heard of him, but loved it.

I miss a bit of that. The same way that I used to go to Amoeba Records and buy old two-dollar records, not really knowing what was on them but just picking them for the pleasure of discovery. Last night we were in our apartment. I did something that I do, which is grab a record that I haven't heard and just put it on. To be fair, it wasn't very good. I used to listen to lots of music that wasn't very good just because I wanted to hear it. But now I have a family, and this record was essentially unlistenable. My wife was like, "Apágase esta mierda." I'm like, "Okay, sure. It's a Sunday afternoon, no one wants to hear this chalkboard scratching music." When you're living alone and you have this bent of discovery, everything is an influence; every shady, weird, experimental record from like Nigeria in 1970 is a potential discovery; every used book with no dust jacket cover but just the title and a good opening sentence is something that might inspire you. You're young and you're hungry and you just have this narrative ambition that you can't express to anybody because people will think you're weird if you say it, but you find one or two friends who also share it and you just devour the world. The world is books, and film, and poetry, and music, and music, and music. That's just how you recharge your batteries day in and day out, so that the next morning you can write your book.

As far as traditions I would place myself in, I do think I've become more Latin American and less American in some ways. I think because of my work at *Radio Ambulante*, because of my journalism, because that's just the region and the stories that I'm drawn to. Often people will talk about my work in conversations with Alejandro Zambra and with other Latin American writers of that generation, and it's just like a weird asterisk that I happen to write in English. I admire Alejandro and his work immensely. I was a teacher at Mills College, and a student of mine, Caro De Robertis, told me they were looking for something to translate and I'd just read *Bonsai*, Zambra's first novel. I gave it to them, and they translated it. Some of his first translations into English came indirectly via me. I would say I've taken seriously my role as an interlocutor for Latin American writers in the United States and someone who can help open doors for those writers, and maybe I've been incorporated into the Latin American literary conversation because of that. I'm sure it doesn't hurt.

JAVIER: Do you think it would benefit both Latin American writers and US Latinx writers if there was more conversation happening between them?

DANIEL: I think it would, but literature everywhere in every country can have a very elitist tinge to it. You take Carlos Fuentes and these giant Mexican literary icons and then you take these exceptional Chicano writers and you put them on the same panel, what ends up playing out often, unfortunately, is a great deal of classism and colorism and anti-pochoism and "Your Spanish isn't perfect, what are you doing?" The kind of bullshit that you see all the time. There are certain writers, like Junot for example, who've transcended that and in the Caribbean are respected and thought of as "real writers." Then there are other writers, like Sandra Cisneros for example, who are not thought of in the same way in Mexico. I remember having a conversation with her where she was complaining about the Mexican literary world looking down on some of her work. I think that's one of the real sticking points between Latin American and US Latino letters—how to have a conversation among equals.

MACEO: Throughout your work there's a strong distinction drawn between the capital city and the provinces. Both provide your characters a glimpse, and often the hope, of a different life—the capital is full of possibility, often upward mobility, but the provinces reflect a return to what's fundamental, a romantic possibility of returning to the earth. Can you speak to the reality of this dichotomy between the capital and the provinces, and also its metaphoric significance?

Daniel: Here in the United States, we have multiple centers—multiple cities, and even within states, smaller cities that feel like miniature centers. In Peru and in many Latin American countries, it's the capital or nothing. I think the question for me was always, where is the country? If you had to locate it, where is it? Is it in the hinterland, where there is some authentic, or more authentic, pure version of our national culture, or is the country itself an arbitrary agglomeration of cultures, such that you could only find the essence of that country in the vibrant mix of a city. When I was living in Lima, I was living in a district called San Juan de Lurigancho, which was on the outskirts of the city. Entire towns and villages had moved in response to the violence of the war, and had moved together and settled in San Juan de Lurigancho. There were also people from the jungle, people from the north, from the south, from different parts of the interior with different cultures. They were creating a new Andean culture on the coast. Which one of those is the realest version of modern Peru? There's a Peru that we put in the guidebooks, which is a postcard. It's not unreal, it exists. There's also the Peru, the cultural mix of those places, which has access to technology—they're walking the same streets and riding the same buses as traditional limeños, but they're remaking the city at every turn. And I'm really interested in those places because hybridity has always been interesting to me.

I remember living in San Juan de Lurigancho and seeing that there was the indoor language and the outside language and finding parallels to my own life. For example, in my house, we spoke Spanish, and we walked out the door and spoke English. There are houses in San Juan de Lurigancho where, for example, they would speak Quechua inside and then speak Spanish outside. Just seeing those linguistic parallels to my own situation, I found it very recognizable. Because the kids are also struggling too, like I was, trying to figure out where they're from. Are they from the inside of the house where grandma speaks Quechua? Or are they from the streets with kids their age who understand Quechua but are speaking Spanish and remaking themselves in a new vision of what the city is? That, to me, was a very recognizable and relatable experience.

Maceo: Do you perceive yourself and your work as political?

Daniel: I spend a lot of time worrying about politics and the political trends in the United States, the corrosive effects of disinformation, the abject failure of the Democrats to translate their power into a message. I worry about the Republican assault on our democracy, the "big lie." I worry about all that stuff. I worry about the country that my kids are going to grow up in and are going to become adults in. I think there's some political component to my fiction. Some of it is just who I am. In the context of all the anti-immigrant rhetoric that is continuously spouted by lots of people on the right, to be a successful writer whose English is a second language is in itself a statement. I think it's a reminder that this country has always made room and made space, sometimes against its will, for people. I feel like this is my country too. I completely understand and support people who take the knee. I also think about the way my parents, my dad, specifically, sings the national anthem and what it means to him. Nobody knows the country that I'm imagining when I'm singing the national anthem. It certainly isn't the country that exists right now. I'm a real sucker, and singing the national anthem of both Peru and the United States can make me tear up—not out of national pride but out of heartbreak. The United States is a heartbreaking country with so much to offer and so many betrayals of our best ideals. It crushes me, honestly. I wouldn't want anyone to see me singing the national anthem and interpret my singing the anthem as blind patriotism, because it isn't. It's more an act of when I sing it, I want people to know that this is my country, too. I know in my heart what I'm singing for.

Some of my journalism is political, but I don't see it as being the core thing that I am. In my writing, I always want someone to stay up all night reading my book, and in the same way, I want someone to hear a *Radio Ambulante* story and not be able to turn it off and miss their stop on the train or stay in the driveway to listen to it. In the same way that I want someone to pick up my *New Yorker* pieces and just read them until the end. I think being entertaining is really important—being gripping, compelling. There are so many ways to seduce a reader, whether it's the sheer beauty of your language, or humor, or motion, or just quirkiness and idiosyncrasies. More than politics, I worry about that. Politics will come out in your work. The worst thing, I think—the stuff that I find unreadable—is when the politics is so blatant that it feels like I'm not reading human beings but reading characters in a pamphlet.

JAVIER: What have been the milestones so far in the twenty-first century in US Latinx literature? What directions do you think it will take or do you hope it will take?

Daniel: A big milestone was when Junot won the Pulitzer. When Juan Felipe Herrera became US poet laureate was another. I also think the increased diversity in Latin voices in young adult literature is huge. It's huge for my nieces and nephews. It's huge for the next generation of writers. My youngest, who's nine, is a big reader, and he read a book by Carlos Hernandez called *Sal and Gabi Break the Universe*, and he noticed that the author's last name is Hernandez. He notices that the kids are Latin. When he was first starting to read, there was a great series of books about three Latino science nerds who were mentored by a mad scientist character. They all had Latin names. They were all like Javier, Maceo, and Daniel, names like that. Again, my kid noticed. I think that's a huge thing. I wouldn't know when that turn came, because I only became aware of it as my kids started reading. We're far beyond *The Hardy Boys* and *The Baby-Sitters Club*. We're in a more diverse moment.

Maceo: In thinking about the trajectory of your work—which has spanned the twenty-first century—from the reception of your first story collection to how your work is received now or understood, do you feel like there has been a shift?

Daniel: I had a friend who would always joke, "99 percent of my audience doesn't exist." In certain ways, I'm a successful writer. In other ways, everything that I do around *Radio Ambulante* has a bigger audience than my books. Right before I won the MacArthur, I got a royalty check. It was literally under ten cents. It cost more to mail the check to me than the value of the check itself. I've never made a living from my writing. I make more of a living now from teaching at Columbia and from *Radio Ambulante* than from writing for the *New Yorke*r. Even though the *New Yorker* is this wonderful opportunity and has prestige, I'm not supporting my family with that. I don't know what people think about my writing. I think mostly they *don't* think about my writing. I'm very aware of that, and I'm fine with that. People have other things to worry about. All I can do as a writer is do my best. As a reporter, report the shit out of a story and then do my best to convey what I saw as accurately and with as much emotional truth as I can. That's very important to me. The things that I've seen and experienced as a result of the career choices that I stumbled into—it's just overwhelming. I feel so fortunate. I know there are more talented writers than me, who work just as hard as me, who haven't had the success that I've had, and I don't have any way to explain it except luck.

MACEO: The ending of *At Night We Walk in Circles* suggests that the narrator "robs" his subjects' stories. What seems to motivate the narrator most of all is curiosity, but you seem to be saying that curiosity—following the story, getting to the truth—doesn't seem commensurate when compared to someone's life. Is the journalist's or writer's so-called dispassionate objectivity something that concerns you?

DANIEL: Absolutely. I don't believe in journalistic objectivity. I believe that we all have a subjective point of view and that I'm just one guy trying to figure out the story. The journalist doesn't have skin in the game in the same way that the protagonists do. I think the scene that you're describing has Nelson confronting the narrator with that reality. It's like, "This is just a story to you. To me, it's something else. To me, it's my life." That's just a fact. There was a character I met in my reporting in Ecuador, and this guy lost his mom in the pandemic. She was at a public hospital. He was fortunate in certain ways, because in the chaos of the hospital's collapse, he was able to sneak in, and he was with her when she passed away, which is very different from most people. He was holding her hand when she passed. They told him to come back the next day. When he did, they said her body had been moved to another hospital and then they never found her body. He told me the whole story of trying to find her and giving up eventually. He'd bought a coffin and he had the coffin in the corner of his house, and it was just resting in the corner. Every day he'd see it and be reminded that he didn't have a body to put in there. He was looking for his mom, and finally he gave up and put the coffin back in his car, drove back to the hospital where he last saw his mom, and sold it. As soon as he opened the trunk, dozens of people came to him and said, "I'm looking for a coffin." That moment that he described was so devastating. What happened next is that his mom was due a pension payment at her passing. It's not a lot, it's like $2,000, but it would've helped. The state social security office that owes him this money was unwilling to pay because the body hadn't been buried, because there was no proof of burial. Even though he had a death certificate, he didn't have proof of burial. On top of the pain of not having a body to mourn, it was this kind of Kafkaesque bureaucratic cruelty being inflicted upon him.

If there was no impact from my article except to tell that story in the hope that someone read that and he was able to get that money, that would be enough. Because it was so awful for him. It was the state that lost her body and was now refusing to acknowledge that she was dead, and it wasn't his fault. Maybe it's not the fault of anybody. Maybe it would've happened in any country. Maybe the chaos was such that nothing could've controlled this. I think about that a lot. What's the point of journalism? What's the point of telling these stories? Sometimes the point is just as concrete as the fact that I called the Social Security Office and made them go on the record saying that they were going to look into it or acknowledging that this was true. If nothing else, just to make someone uncomfortable, and hopefully they'll do something about it, respond to this one injustice, this bureaucratic cruelty, and solve that wound. I can't say that this happened. I can only say that something like that would be a worthwhile outcome. But the truth is, as hard as it was to report that story, when it was done I came back to New York and this is where I live and that's not my life. I saw a lot of people who suffered a great deal and they told me their stories and they trusted me with their stories and I did the best I could, but I live in immense privilege, teach at Columbia University, and live in Manhattan, and this is my life and that's theirs. If they want to tell me to go fuck myself, then they're well within their rights.

—May 2, 2022

11

URAYOÁN NOEL

Urayoán Noel's work has always blended poetry and performance, including his first published collection, *Kool Logic / La lógica kool*, which featured a supplemental DVD of Noel utilizing a whole repertoire of voices and personas reminiscent of stand-up, which he also did early in his career. His most recent collection, *Transversal*, features Noel's "wokitokiteki" poems along with links to Noel's website where we see videos of him walking and responding to the landscape as he generates his poems. At the heart of Noel's poetry is the play of mixtures between languages and vernaculars, cultures, influences, and literary traditions. Born in San Juan, Puerto Rico, in 1976, Noel cites his immersion in not just two languages but the different destandardized registers that were used, including his Anglo father who spoke Spanish inhibited by a heavy English accent and the Spanish jokes and traditional music he heard at home. The author of five poetry collections, Noel is also a scholar and translator. Noel's *In Visible Movement: Nuyorican Poetry from the Sixties to Slam* is the first book-length study of Nuyorican poetry. Like his own poetics, the book centers on performance in the poetry of the foundational Nuyorican poets of the 1960s and '70s, including Pedro Pietri, all the way up to the slam scene at the Nuyorican Poets Café in the 1990s and early 2000s. He also translated the Chilean poet Pablo de Rokha in *Architecture of Dispersed Life: Selected Poetry*, which was a finalist for the 2019 National Translation Award in Poetry, and spoke to us about his recent translation of Wingston González, a Garifuna Afro-Indigenous poet from Guatemala, whose work also mixes languages and registers. Noel teaches at New York University as well as at Stetson University's MFA of the Americas. He spoke to us from his home in the South Bronx, where he also has deep roots. His poem "Bronx, Piedras" speaks to the fluidity with which he moves between his current home and his hometown of Río Piedras in Puerto Rico, one always reminding him of the other.

JAVIER: How has the pandemic impacted your writing? In your most recent book, *Transversal*, we noticed there are several pandemic poems.

URAYOÁN: I'm right under the Bruckner Expressway, so we heard sirens for weeks and weeks. In the Bronx, it's largely working class and migrants and a lot of first responders, so we were disproportionately hit here. We lost elders in the community. I was looking for ways to cope, and poetic form helped me. I was trying to make sense of the SARS-COVID-II sequence, thinking maybe I could turn that into a form. The whole sequence ends in something like twenty or thirty *A*s, and it's all four-letter sequences. I was fascinated by that and tried to reclaim it for poetry. I also do these walking improvisations called "wokitokiteki" poems. Walking, talking, and "tech-ing." The last one that appears in *Transversal* was done here in my backyard in the South Bronx and was partly a response to lockdown. I'd been doing these walks on Randall's Island, which is nearby, but that was where the trucks with the bodies were, so it was too heavy to go there. In that context, my backyard became a solace, which coincided with the return of the birds early in the pandemic. It felt like this rare moment of nature speaking to us. As a city boy, I've always been ashamed that I can't rock the nature poems more. I ended up getting some binoculars and getting into bird-watching. That was also a way of coping with the heaviness.

Elsewhere in *Transversal* I was exploring what to do with these inherited European forms. I had this back-and-forth over Facebook with the poet Vincent Toro, very lovingly because I admire his work, where he was saying that no sonnet could ever be decolonial. The form itself is the courtliest—I will write to the state, I will write to the king and the queen—but I thought, "No, sonnets can do all kinds of things." Forms are just forms; it's whatever we do with them. I wanted to return to that sequence and see if I could make the sonnet do a different kind of work in a pandemic context. Thinking of a corona sonnet crown—because bad puns are central to my poetics—I wanted to do a different kind of shout-out, defining the Bronx voices within the sonnet crown and shouting them out, as opposed to crowning the corona and giving it the power to define us.

MACEO: You've cited Allen Ginsberg's influence and the idea that poetry is total—that it encompasses or engages everything. Nothing is off limits. How does this inform your work overall, your experimentation with different forms, your performances, and how does it relate to your walking improvisations?

URAYOÁN: I'm not a natural performer. I don't have the best posture. I stutter. If you told me when I was starting out that I'd be this over-the-top performer, I wouldn't have believed you. I was finding my power through poetry. I had teachers along the way like Pedro Pietri, iconic Nuyorican poet, who was a mentor to many of us. I remember being new on the New York scene and Pedro asking me to open for him when he was in residency at New Dramatists. The poets making room for me and showing me the way were poets working in this vernacular tradition and outside of the institution. I wanted to align my work with that influence. I had read "Puerto Rican Obituary," but when I saw Pedro read it, I thought, "How do I reconcile what's on the page with what this person shared?" That kind of duality fascinated me, and I wrote a book on the Nuyorican poets largely asking that question.

Pedro Pietri was, of course, a great reader of Ginsberg. There's an ambivalence and a critical edge in my recovery of Ginsberg. *The Fall of America*, which is the book where Ginsberg's experimenting with tape recordings and transcription, is one of the places I got . . . not the idea but more like the program for the wokitokitekis. Of course, the title, *The Fall of America*, comes from Whitman, and it's a super Whitmanesque—celebratory?—vision of America, even though it's dark and critical. As a Boricua, that's really hard. I don't want to be part of your America-with-an-uppercase-*A*-and-no-accent fantasy. Sorry. *Poems of These States, 1965–1971* is the Whitmanesque subtitle to Ginsberg's book. Well, Puerto Rico is not one of "these states," so I play with the poetics of the out-of-state—the title of one of *Transversal*'s sections. Ginsberg's there, as a poetics of queer accretion, and I was certainly influenced by the largely white postwar New American poetry—there's an elegy in *Transversal* for the late gay Boston/Gloucester poet Gerrit Lansing, a friend of Charles Olson's—and the idea of projective verse and open form, but as a lover of remixing classic forms and experimenting with rhyme, I always wonder, Who does open form serve? Corridos aren't open form, décimas and blues stanzas aren't open form—but they are how our communities tell stories. I want to complicate the idea that every vernacular poetry must be open form. It's going to be riffs on Ginsberg but it's also going to be décimas. That's all part of the mix of vernaculars. I want to see what happens when we don't privilege one over the other.

Javier: What are the literary traditions you've inherited or that you would situate yourself within?

Urayoán: It's a loaded question because I'm a professor with a PhD in Latin American literature. By virtue of that PhD, I'm at least institutionally indebted to a lot of stuff that doesn't fully align with my personal journey as a poet, but as raw material, it finds a way into it. For instance, during grad school I discovered Brazilian concrete poetry and Brazilian modernismo reading Mário de Andrade's *Paulicéia Desvairada*. That's a case where I have no community investment in Brazilian poetry, it's just something that I picked up in the classroom. I've traveled to Brazil, but it's not part of my activism or part of my community work. It has still been an influence. In terms of my own community identification and journey, obviously the Nuyoricans are paramount. Also, the '70s generation in Puerto Rico. A lot of those folks were connected to Pietri and the Nuyoricans. One of the poets I shout out in *Transversal*, who just passed, is Esteban Valdés, a Mexican Nuyorican concrete poet and visual artist. Within the Nuyorican poets, there are conversations with folks like Umbra and Black Arts. I think of my reading of Nuyorican poetry not as an end in itself but as part of a broader constellation and conversation among poets.

Maceo: What have been the formative moments in your journey as a writer?

Urayoán: I was lucky to grow up in a house with books of poetry in English and Spanish. I also got a lot of the oral tradition, the songs, the boleros, the proverbs, the jokes largely from my abuelos. I had that duality. I saw cool things happen with language in this space on the page but in this space off the page as well. How could I imagine a language practice that honors all those things? It's a conciencia that I had early on, and part of what fueled my poetry was the song, the jokes, but other times it was geeking out on a poem and going like, "Wow, what did Poe just do there? What did Rubén Darío just do there?" It was the blurring of the baroque function of language in an art context and the vernacular function of it in everyday language. I'm always trying to do both in my poetry.

In terms of discrete moments, I remember going to an outdoor party in Puerto Rico for the writer Mayra Santos-Febres—a longtime champion of poetry off the page—when I was around twenty-one. There were two stages: a stage for the poets and a stage for the rock bands. I told my friends, "I want to read a décima, but I want to read it on the rock band stage, not the poet stage." Basically, I did my thing and the rock band, El Manjar de los Dioses, jammed with me, and then their promoter came up to me afterwards and said, "That was really good, do you want to do this festival in Vieques?" I'm like, "I guess I got a gig now." Then, soon after that, some of my poems were published and I was described as "Urayoán Noel, poeta y performero." I'm like, "I guess I'm a performero." It just gained its own momentum. I hadn't thought of myself as a performer before that time. Then there was the Pedro Pietri moment, which I mentioned before, where I watched him at the Nuyorican Poets Café and realized you could combine all these things. Reading with Pedro opened up a lot for me.

Javier: You were raised in San Juan, Puerto Rico, but you have been based in New York for quite some time. How do you navigate artistically moving between both places? What is your relation to the city of New York? To use a phrase you've used before, what are the cities you walk and that walk inside you?

Urayoán: I have to be the cliché Boricua and add Central Florida now. In about a week, I'm going to visit my mom there. Wikipedia says that she lives in the least walkable city in the US—even less walkable than regular Central Florida. I have definitely done some wokitokitekis about walking the unwalkable. Still, for my conciencia, the Bronx is important. I have family connections to the South Bronx on both sides. In the middle of last century, a lot of my mom's family moved to the Bronx, and my great-grandmother moved a couple of blocks from where I now live in the South Bronx. It's meaningful to go to the post office she went to and see the community garden that used to be the building where she lived. The building no longer exists: it's one of the many places that was lost during the days of disinvestment in the South Bronx that's now gentrifying.

There are a lot of ghosts in general in the South Bronx, including the industrial neighborhood where I live, on the border of Port Morris and Mott Haven. The Bruckner Expressway, one of Robert Moses's final projects, is the border, and I cross it almost every day. It's a racialized and classed border for sure, as are so many in our barrios and literatures. On weekends when it's warm out, the viejitos do a block party called El Polvorín around the corner from my house where they dance and play and relive their salsa glory days. It's really beautiful, but you just think of who's not here, all who died or were displaced—and the pandemic only accentuated that. La Lupe is from here. There's actually a street sign for La Lupe Way nearby. There's El Teatro Puerto Rico, the iconic theater. I remember the stories of my great-grandmother going to watch all the great bands back in the glory days of Latin music in the South Bronx. My great-uncle, who's eighty-eight and used to live with my great-grandmother in the South Bronx, now lives in Florida, so when I go visit my mom, we go visit him as well. There's a lot of history that travels, too, and it feels strangely mediated with an intimacy and geographic distance that is emotionally complicated.

In terms of Puerto Rico, I feel the same mix of deep intimacy but also emotional and geographic distance. My neighborhood in Río Piedras is historically working-class, far enough from the beach, far enough from the tourist areas. It has fallen into disinvestment. It's very strange to see the place where my mom got her hair done back in the day in ruins—literally rubble where it used to be. It's not lost on me that the stereotypical vision of the South Bronx is rubble but there are so many stories beyond that. There's a poem from my book *Los días porosos* called "You Are Now Entering Bronx Piedras." It's about walking through the South Bronx and channeling Río Piedras and vice versa. That's one thing that has happened in my wokitokitekis: I walk and I translate the other place in my walking. The sensoria of the other place seeps into whatever it is that I'm responding to. In Río Piedras I'll channel the Bronx. The place I grew up in doesn't exist in the same way; at least big parts of it don't exist. In a real sense, when we come back, our places don't exist. They are different places now and we move on, but we carry the old place with us, and the weight of that for me is magnified post-María, post-austerity, even in my New York City privilege.

The number of ghosts kept multiplying and multiplying, and the pandemic got grafted onto that. It has been a journey to name those ghosts. My dad also joined the ancestors. He lived in Río Piedras right up to the end. My dad was a white gringo from Pasadena. I told him, "Why didn't you move somewhere else, some place 'nicer' or more touristy, or move back to California?" But he was hardcore that way. He liked it there, and I always admire him for that. So I go back and stay in the apartment where I grew up because all my dad's stuff is there. I don't want to get into the trendy bad Latinx cliché that we're all brujos now channeling the spirits, but I think the context of *Transversal* was very much that. First, the dead of María, then my dad, and the dead of austerity more generally, plus the dead of the pandemic. There are a lot of ghosts, folks who transitioned but who are still here with me. I still hear a voice. It's there somewhere. Poetry has to hold onto that and do the work of channeling those spirits.

MACEO: You've touched upon this, but your work straddles different mediums, moving between poetry, performance, even stand-up comedy. For you, what is the nexus of these different forms?

URAYOÁN: In my brief Bay Area days, I would hang out at the queer cabarets and do my bad attempt at Andy Kaufman experimental/durational performance and people didn't get it at all. I would even include poetry. It was all too geeky. Little did I know what I needed I would find through the Nuyorican Poets Café. I think it was less about straight up trying to be funny, which I have zero interest in as an end in itself, and more about using the humor and the absurdity in everyday life to dig deeper. In terms of what the connection is, as a queer person and as someone who's epileptic, there has always been the question of how to make sense of my own body. I've always had this strange feeling of not belonging to my own body. Initially, *Buzzing Hemisphere / Rumor Hemisférico* was meant to be a book that delved deeply into that, and I chickened out because I didn't know how to write about what happens in my brain, the disconnect between the brain and the body. Maybe I'm perceived as virtuosically wacky or something, but that's not the way I experience it. My life as a performer has been very slow. Coming to know my body has been painstaking and, in a sense, painful, especially for someone who initially saw poetry as a way to get beyond that. If I never performed again, I would still work through embodiment in my writing. That conciencia has helped me not try to be all things to all people, as I was sometimes trying to be when I was a younger poet.

From a more scholarly perspective, I've always been interested in the relationship between form and politics. What relationship is there between how we write, what we write, and what our work can become in the world? Again, you don't have to be radically open form if you want to have a radically open politics. You could be Robert Hayden or Gwendolyn Brooks and do stuff in a much more elegant literary style, and still have it connect to different kinds of political imaginaries. Thinking also of Latinx communities, whether Nuyorican poetry performances or Floricanto festivals, what's the relationship between the political movements and the particular kinds of embodied poetic practices that came to be important in shaping them? As someone who cares about politics and wants to understand how art can matter not just individually or in an atomized way but for movements of people organizing together, I pay attention to how our formal and embodied practices are, of course, individual but how they constellate with other people's practices and maybe build something larger than ourselves.

I would also throw in translation, because that's something that I've been doing more of recently. I had no inkling that I would become a literary translator, but translation, like scholarship, was a way for me to understand what was happening in other people's work and, therefore, to understand myself better. I'm at NYU as a scholar. I was not hired to be a creative writer or translator; I was hired to teach Latinx literature. So I have an incentive to do this critical work institutionally. But even if I got hired for the biggest creative writing gig tomorrow, I wouldn't stop thinking like a critic and literature professor. I can't imagine not learning from other people's work and trying to break it down and understand it as well as thinking: How can I teach this? How can I make this a resource for someone else? Teaching doesn't just have to be inside academia; as a community, how can we learn from the work of those who came before us or across borders? What's the classic line I get from some of my creative writing students—"I don't read other people because I don't want to be influenced." What's the point? If I weren't influenced, I wouldn't be here.

People have commented that my work is very citational—that I'm just oozing influences. I don't think I know any other way. In really dark moments, other people's work has sustained me. When I couldn't believe in my own work, I could always connect to somebody else's. For me, being a lit geek—not even just literature but also an art or music geek—has been sustaining in difficult times. Of course, I'm aware that lit and art apparatuses are sustained by the evilest of systems, and there's a need to think critically about the dangers in surrendering ourselves to that, but I draw meaning and sustenance from others' work. Aside from a few poems, I struggled for so long to write about being epileptic, but when I read *Kindling* by Aurora Levins Morales—which engages her epilepsy and broader disability journey from a queer Boricua perspective—I cried so hard, and I gave it to my mom because my mom is also disabled and epileptic but was not diagnosed as the latter until fairly recently. It reminded me of the power of literature: that something that I had struggled to do for so long, Aurora's work was able to open up for me, changing me in the process.

MACEO: How do you perceive your role as a writer in relation to your community, US society, and then literature itself?

URAYOÁN: There are two ways of thinking about it. The Pedro Pietri disciple in me is like pa'l carajo with your roles. That's not how my writing works, I'm going to do whatever the heck I want, and folks can just suck it up! Pedro would say stuff like that, but of course he did so much for the community. There's an institutional imperative, and that feels particularly acute to me as someone in a tenured position at an elite research university where there are so few Boricuas. I'm struck by the fact that after all this time, our demographic doesn't necessarily translate into institutional visibility. So I definitely have the sense that I need to show up institutionally. I've been doing La Treintena for the Latinx Project at NYU. For National Poetry Month, I do write-ups of Latinx poetry. I try to include folks on my syllabi, get folks to visit my class, including folks who don't have a tenure-track job, who don't have access, or who do the work that isn't going to find its way into the institution. I'm working with Raquel Salas Rivera, Ricardo Alberto Maldonado, and other brilliant folks for the Puerto Rican Literature Project, where we're trying to translate in both directions—English–Spanish and Spanish–English—so we can have the translocal Boricua conversations that we need to be having now more than ever.

As someone doing this work on the East Coast and in New York, issues of Afro-Latinidad are super important to me. More generally, for Latinidad to mean anything, it has to be situated. If it isn't, it's going to default toward whatever the mainstream hegemonic interests are—meaning the white, the straight, the cis, the documented, the able-bodied and neurotypical, and so on. We need to be deliberate in opting out of that and in naming our differences. I also feel a sense of responsibility as someone who got to benefit from elders who are no longer with us. What can I do to share all that I learned from them? I'm trying to write scholarly work that's coming from that conciencia, to support upstart editorial projects, to uplift folks who were forgotten within the tradition and find room for them within these conversations. One of the most exciting aspects of publishing my critical study of Nuyorican poetry, *In Visible Movement*, was being able to write about Lorraine Sutton's *Saycred Laydy*, published in 1975, a book that has been totally forgotten but that was crucial for Nuyorican feminist poetics. These little things, like bringing attention to a book that has been overlooked or experimenting with pedagogies that center the situated nature of our identities, don't make a big difference individually, but I think if enough of us do it, it can change the conversations we have.

In terms of the space of writing, it needs to be an autonomous space, which doesn't mean that autonomy isn't framed by our commitment to each other and our responsibilities. It's just that there's going to be tension there. Sometimes to write the work that you want to write, you have to betray what you hold dearest. That can be part of the urgency and self-knowledge of our writing practice.

JAVIER: In your role as teacher, critic, reviewer, and editor, what do you think the milestones have been so far for Latinx literature in the twenty-first century? What directions do you see this literature headed as we continue into this century?

URAYOÁN: In the past decade, there has been a welcome and hard-fought emphasis on honoring the differences between our Latinidades. For a long time it was important to get everyone under the coalitional umbrella so that we could get a *Norton Anthology* out and exist as a field, but that happened already. Institutional inclusion is not enough now. It never was. From a decolonial perspective, folks were never just mobilizing for inclusion. You can be included and be trivialized and disrespected. So more and more in the past decade, the differences that maybe got steamrolled in the name of inclusion have started to become more central. Black Latinidades, Indigenous Latinidades, undocumented Latinidades, trans Latinidades, disabled Latinidades—those identities also happen to represent many of the most vulnerable among us. If we can work from those differences, as opposed to an essentializing vision of Latinidad that flattens us, I think it'll be a much more sustaining conversation and also truer to the diversity of our communities.

As someone who is light-skinned, half-gringo, and grew up with plenty of cultural capital, I know the spaces that I occupy and the privileges I am afforded. Those privileges help grant me access to institutional space, so I need to show up and do the work, and that work is within the institution but also thinking critically about the limits of the institution. I want to make room for stories that haven't been told, to see what we can learn from them together. There's also a need for alternative institutional spaces, in the spirit of Afro-Boricua Arturo Schomburg: we need to get our hands dirty—akin to what Schomburg called "the dust of digging"—creating and supporting spaces of and for difference that aren't just reproducing the hegemonic institutions and all their violences.

MACEO: It seems clear that you view your work in these different roles—as a scholar, a teacher, and a poet—as political, but how do you understand or define that term?

URAYOÁN: If you call yourself Latina, Latino, Latinx, it's a political identity, whether or not you intend it that way. What differences animate the names we call ourselves and are called by others? The work of naming these differences becomes essential. Following Audre Lorde, I would say that diversity work can often feel managerial and cosmetic, like something done from above. The bosses can just make sure there's one of us to occupy this space, but the really transformative work, the really difficult work, is the work of difference, and that comes from below. It's painful, and it's in-group. I'm thinking of how Lorde had to navigate heteromasculinist strands of Black nationalism to find common cause, just as Anzaldúa had to find her way within heteropatriarchal Chicano Movement politics. We owe it to those who come after us to have the difficult conversations that are essential to any coalitional politics; working through this is a way to ensure we don't just reproduce the powers that be.

JAVIER: One of the key features of your work from *Kool Logic* to *Transversal* is the play of languages, the bilingual, and in many cases, the multilingual. Can you speak to the multilingual aspect of your work?

URAYOÁN: It's largely biographical. I grew up with mixed parents who swapped languages at home. "Mi papaw jablabaw españole con acento" like this, "an' my mom tok Inglich wid an accen'." I use those personae in my performances, but they're not gimmicks, they're profoundly, affectively charged to me. Destandardizing English and Spanish feels like home, like my parents. I have this lived experience of what Evelyn Nien-Ming Ch'ien calls—in analyzing works by multilingual writers—"weird English" plus "weird Spanish." I also understand the colonial imposition of these languages, and my Gen X cynicism always leans toward "Imperial language is bad, bad, bad," but I am inspired by Raquel Salas Rivera, a poet and translator whose work empowers me to tell myself: "Yes, these were imposed, but we turned them into this other thing. We embody them and subvert their hegemony." Raquel writes from a particular trans conciencia, with an intimately loaded sense of Puerto Rican Spanish being its own thing. Still, I embrace a range of poetics that can help us unsettle English and Spanish as languages of empire and reclaim all kinds of marked Englishes and Spanishes.

Over the past several years, I have really enjoyed translating Wingston González, the great Guatemalan and Garifuna poet and performer who mixes Spanish, English, and Garifuna in his poems. More generally, I'm excited by how Garifuna—for example, Pablo José López Oro—and Central American poets and scholars in the US are helping us have different, more nuanced conversations about Indigeneity and Blackness, about borders and diasporas. It's also great that in US Latinx poetry contexts we're also finally starting to take creoles and Indigenous languages seriously, realizing that Latinx life and literature are not limited to Iberian languages, and that our translingual Américas are much more complex than that. I also love that so many of these conversations are transnational and hemispheric.

As I've become more invested in translation over the past five years,

I realize how crucial it is, not just in decentering a US nation-state imagined as monolingual but also in the sense of building and sustaining networks across the Américas. It's very hard to do that if poets aren't reading translations and translators aren't reading poets. I hope that those conversations become more and more enmeshed. How many poets actually translate? I give a shout-out to folks like Sheila Maldonado, a Honduran poet from Coney Island living in Washington Heights, who has been working hard to build bridges with Honduras—and whose latest poetry book memorably invites us to "decentral America"—but conversations like these are happening largely outside of official recognition and institutional support. I would hope that the spaces that take Latinx poetry seriously in the US also take seriously the transnational and hemispheric conversations that are happening across many borders and diasporas and trying to think through some of these differences and give a fuller sense of our language histories, practices, and communities.

Maceo: You're comfortable moving between mediums, between poetries; there's a fluidity and confidence in the way you move from Spanish to English; you're as rooted in Puerto Rico as you are in the United States; you've absorbed Latin American art and culture as well as American pop culture. You're also comfortable as a scholar and critic of these cultural forms. Are there spaces where you find yourself uncomfortable, and how do you approach that discomfort creatively?

Urayoán: To say comfortable makes it sound easy, but it has been a lot of work, getting the institutional training in hemispheric literatures and figuring out how to connect that to the poetry, the translation, and the performance without many points of reference. That's where a playful term like "diasporoso"—thinking of myself and my poetics as "dias-porous" rather than diasporic in a familiar sense—is actually doing some serious work in thinking about my own journey. One of my struggles was getting to a place where I could even do a dissertation on Nuyorican poetry. I didn't feel that it should be me. I didn't know if I could do it. I was taking my graduate classes at NYU while reading and performing at places like the Nuyorican Poets Café. It took me a while to figure out the institutional code-switching involved. I wouldn't say it's merely comfort, although I'm very lucky to be in the position I'm in—I'd say you get emboldened partly because you get angry. You realize all the stuff that isn't happening and you get frustrated being in these institutions. It gives you greater clarity and conviction. I'm a proud product of NYU, having done my PhD there and then returned to teach, but NYU epitomizes the neoliberal university. I don't think the institution is made for people's comfort—at least our peoples. So part of the answer is building bridges to the community within the institution and making the latter's resources available to the former. I remember as a graduate student being so impressed by how the late Juan Flores would show up to all these community poetry readings, and now I watch in awe at how my colleague Arlene Dávila seems to show up to every community art exhibit in the South Bronx, Loisaida, and El Barrio. That's not part of the institutional labor of being a professor, but it's central to the work that we do. In its own small way, it's community work, which isn't always comfortable. Actually, I was pretty awkward doing community work. I'm not your smoothest activist, but you get better at it just knowing others showed up for you so you just have to do your part. I was comfortable analyzing poetry but intimidated by interview and oral histories as something outside my training. I look back on my interviews with Nuyorican poets like Tato Laviera and Louis Reyes Rivera for *In Visible Movement*, and I was young and kind of clueless, but they were so generous and I learned so much.

Sometimes I think, "I'm 80 percent of a poet, and maybe 80 percent of a scholar, 80 percent of a translator," and because I do so many things and feel like I can't give up on any of them—not to mention teaching—I'll notice a typo in one of my books and say to myself, "Maybe if I weren't trying to do five things at a time, I'd have better quality control." Should I just pick one of these things for a while? Surely there was a time when I was doing the Nuyorican book that I didn't write or publish that much poetry. My books *Hi-Density Politics*, published in 2010, and *Los días porosos*, published in 2012, had so much found stuff and early wokitokiteki improvisations, partly because I didn't have time to write, edit, and revise as I would have liked. That's probably one reason I'm writing sonnets again in *Transversal*—because I have tenure and less pressure to publish. For years, it was about academic publication, and my creative work took a bit of a backseat. I think the question of comfort is relative, since the many strains of what I do don't fit comfortably together, and perhaps it's best that they not do so.

The work I do doesn't necessarily fit into institutional categories and that gives me a certain freedom. I rarely have writer's block. There's always something else to do. But it has also been less intuitive than it needs to be, with a lot of siloed conversations. In translation spaces, I'll tell myself, "Wow, nada que ver with the kind of things that poets are talking about"—and the same thing with scholars. I feel like a double agent, or maybe a quadruple agent, because I try to be inside and outside these different spaces. In terms of the ease of moving back and forth between things, I guess that's my temperament. I'd rather do that than get stuck on one thing.

—December 12, 2021

12

REYNA GRANDE

Since her award-winning 2006 debut novel, *Across a Hundred Mountains*, Reyna Grande has published numerous works about the immigrant experience. Born in Iguala, Mexico, in 1975, Reyna followed her father to the United States when she was nine years old. Her best-selling 2012 memoir, *The Distance Between Us*, details her turbulent childhood in Iguala followed by the numerous travails she faced as an undocumented immigrant in California. It has become a landmark work taught in classrooms across the country. Her fiction and nonfiction works move between Mexico and the United States and tell raw and unflinching stories about extreme poverty and hardship, about loss, and about families torn apart. But her books also offer hope. They give voice to strong women who persevere despite the many obstacles in their path. Her 2018 memoir, *A Dream Called Home*, picks up where her first memoir left off and shows how the scars of childhood trauma continue to reverberate throughout her life, even when she has found success—first as a university graduate and then as a published author. Much of Grande's work focuses on the power of stories and literature to transform lives, and she has taken that ethos into her work as a speaker and educator. Both of us have taught Grande's work in our classes and have invited her to speak to our students. We've seen firsthand the impact her work has had, particularly on Latinas and young first-generation immigrants. In our interview, Grande refers to herself as a "little immigrant girl from Mexico" and speaks candidly about her traumas—her self-effacing nature is part of her power, both in person and on the page. When we spoke to Grande, she was rushing to meet a deadline for her latest novel, *A Ballad of Love and Glory*, which is set during the time of the Mexican-American War. She was generous enough to share a few chapters.

MACEO: What impact has the pandemic had on your writing?

REYNA: It has been a blessing in disguise for me because it has forced me to stay home and focus on my writing. Before the pandemic, I was traveling all over the country, giving lots of speeches and book talks, which didn't leave me much time for my writing. Then when the quarantine happened, all my events got canceled and I found myself at home with nothing much to do besides write. I started working on a novel that I'd been trying to write since 2014. I decided this was going to be the year I finally finished it. I threw myself into that project, and luckily I was able to sell the novel in both English and Spanish based on a proposal and sample chapters. I also got two more book projects lined up. I closed up the year 2020 with four book contracts, so I can't complain!

This novel has been difficult because it's my first time writing historical fiction, and also because I'm not just switching genres, I'm also switching genders because I'm writing from a male perspective. That was also a struggle for me. Mostly, the research kept turning me off, so for the last six years I kept putting the book away. Every time it got really hard, I put it away and put it away, but last year, with the pandemic hanging over me, I felt an urgency to get it done. So, I just about finished the book.

JAVIER: The male perspective you mention is an Irish immigrant named John Riley fighting in the Mexican-American War. Can you tell us more about the research that went into the novel?

REYNA: The first time I heard about the Saint Patrick's Battalion was six years ago—somebody told me about it. I went home and googled it. I was intrigued by John Riley and the San Patricios—immigrant soldiers, most of them Irish, who deserted the US Army and switched sides to fight for Mexico. I was fascinated by their story, so I ordered some history books and read them. I was really intrigued, but I was also scared of taking it on because it would be a story about soldiers, about war, and I would have to write battle scenes. I didn't feel that was my kind of writing and it would be too difficult. So, I put it away, but John Riley wouldn't let me go. Then I started reading other novels about the US-Mexico War, and that pushed me to start writing mine because a lot of war novels are written by men and I didn't really like their take on the war. I wanted to see if I could offer something different.

I started to read more and more books about the war itself. Mostly I read history books in English. I tried to read some in Spanish, but they were hard for me to read. The language was a little too elevated for my reading level. I read firsthand accounts, too—a lot of soldier diaries and letters that they wrote to their families. That's how I was able to get deeper into the details of the war. At first, the novel was only going to be from Riley's point of view, but then I came across a poem by John Greenleaf Whittier. At the time, I was living in Whittier, California, which was named after him. The poem is called the "Angels of Buena Vista," and he writes about a Mexican woman named Ximena, who is nursing and tending to wounded soldiers in the battlefield. It's a short poem, but I was very intrigued by this Ximena. I started to wonder what her life was like, who she was, and what she was doing there in the battlefield, what drove her to become a nurse. So, my character Ximena was born from that poem. Then the book became a love story about these two different protagonists: my Mexican nurse and John Riley.

Maceo: You mentioned reading diaries and first-person accounts. Is that how you were able to capture the language of the Irish soldiers? I'm also curious how you balance the historical research and the fictional elements. Is there a point where you let go of the research and just enter into the characters?

Reyna: John Riley was so much easier to write than Ximena. With Ximena, I had to create her from scratch because she was based on the Whittier poem, which is short. With Riley, it was easier because of the information I had from the three books I read about the Saint Patrick's Battalion, especially from *The Rogue's March* by Peter Stevens. Nobody really knows a lot about John Riley's personal history because the parish records in Ireland were burned. After the war, he disappeared from official records, but I learned enough about him and what he did to be able to write his story. I know that he deserted on April 12, 1846. I know that he got commissioned as a first lieutenant in the Mexican Army, and I know that he was actively recruiting Irish men and other foreign soldiers for the Mexican Army. So, I know *what* he did, and my job as a novelist was to try to figure out why. Why did he desert? What was driving him? What did he dislike about the US Army, about the US in general? How did he connect to Mexico and Mexican culture? What were his motivations? Once I started to think about the why, I began to enter his mind and really tapped into his psyche.

When it came to the voice, I read nineteenth-century Irish literature. William Carleton's Irish peasant stories were helpful for me because he captures the dialect of Irish peasants and how they spoke back then. I made a list of all the vocabulary they used, and I got a feel for the syntax and diction, the rhythm of how they speak and construct sentences, so I was able to put that into my novel. Then I contacted a historian in Ireland and asked him if he would be willing to read my manuscript. He read it and corrected a few things I got wrong. He also gave me suggestions for little details that Riley would have thought about, like comparing Ireland to Mexico or thinking about the similarities or differences between Irish and Mexican culture.

MACEO: If we could go back a bit, we'd like to hear more about your creative trajectory. What have been some of the formative moments that have shaped you as a writer?

REYNA: The very first thing that shaped me as a writer was my childhood in Mexico, being poor, not having access to books; but my grandma loved listening to radionovelas like *Porfirio Cadena, el ojo de vidrio*. I would listen to these radionovelas with my grandma, and there was also story time on the radio where I would listen to fairy tales and folktales, so I developed an ear for stories. What I loved about stories is that they helped me to understand the world, to make sense of the things I was going through. In *The Distance Between Us*, I talk about how the story of the three little pigs helped me understand why my father had immigrated and why he wanted to build us a brick house. I understood the metaphor of the Big Bad Wolf and why he wanted to protect us. For him, it was the brick house that would offer that protection. I saw the power stories have to help us understand the world we live in.

Another big moment was when I immigrated to the United States, where there was more access to books than what I had in Mexico. In my neighborhood in Mexico, we didn't have a public library, and books are expensive. Even to this day, books can cost like two days' worth of wages. Who's going to spend their meager wages on a book? They're going to buy food with that. When I immigrated, we had a public library in my neighborhood in Highland Park. I went there and I checked out ten books every single week. Having access to books made me a reader, and by being a reader, I became a writer, because it nurtured my initial love of stories that I had from the radio. I went from reading stories to then wanting to write my own.

The next big moment for me was meeting my English professor, Diana Savas, at Pasadena City College, because she was the first teacher who ever told me I had writing talent. She was the first teacher to suggest I pursue a career as a professional writer. Her mentorship and encouragement helped me develop my future goal to become a published writer and to share my stories. Then, of course, a few years later, I got accepted to the Emerging Voices program offered by PEN Center USA, or PEN America, as it's called now. The Emerging Voices Fellowship was huge for me because when I was in LA, I didn't really have access to the literary community. I had lived in LA for fifteen years, and I had never even heard of the LA Times Book Festival. I had never gone to it, and I didn't know any published writers. I had no clue how to pursue a career as a professional writer. When I got into Emerging Voices, part of what the program offered was a professional writer as your mentor. I worked with María Amparo Escandón, who wrote *Esperanza's Box of Saints*. They also offered free classes at the UCLA Extension Writers' Program and brought in speakers from the literary community. They invited editors and agents and book publicists, who talked about the importance of promoting your work. That's how I met my agent. Then they would hold events for us. The first time I got to read my work at the LA Times Festival of Books was through the Emerging Voices program. This fellowship really helped me learn what I needed to do to have a career as a writer. It went beyond just learning how to write a book and focusing on the craft but thinking about the business of writing, how to get an agent, get published, and promote my books. I'm very grateful to Emerging Voices.

JAVIER: As you were developing as a writer, did you think about what literary traditions you saw yourself being part of or inheriting?

REYNA: I saw myself being part of the Chicano/Latino writing community. The writers that mostly influenced me were Chicana/Latina writers like Sandra Cisneros, Helena María Viramontes, Isabel Allende, and Julia Alvarez. My English professor at PCC introduced me to their books. Then, when I went to UC Santa Cruz, my Chicano literature professor introduced me to Alicia Gaspar de Alba, Ana Castillo, Cherríe Moraga, Gloria Anzaldúa, and Sor Juana Inés de la Cruz. In that class, I was also introduced to Juan Rulfo's *El llano en llamas* and Tomás Rivera's *. . . y no se lo tragó la tierra*. I liked their work because they wrote about poverty and I write a lot about poverty, so they really spoke to me. I found them very inspiring because I could connect with them. Their stories depicted a reality that I had experienced firsthand. That there were Latino/Chicano storytellers like me out there getting their work published . . . that was my inspiration.

JAVIER: You mention Juan Rulfo. What impact has the Mexican literary tradition had on your work? Do you feel like you are part of that tradition, or do you root yourself more in Chicana/Latina literature of the last fifty years?

REYNA: I want to feel that I belong to both. I see elements of my writing that come from both Mexican literature and Chicano literature. For example, *Across a Hundred Mountains*—I think it's a very Mexican book. *Dancing with Butterflies* is more of a Chicano book because it features three Mexican American characters, and only the fourth character is an immigrant. Through Soledad's story I write about Mexico more, but I mostly write about the Chicana experience in that book. Then, of course, there are my memoirs. I don't know where to put them. They're neither Mexican nor American, but somewhere in the hyphen.

JAVIER: Both Rulfo and Tomás Rivera write scenes of poverty that are just heartbreaking. Your books have that as well. You mentioned before that you couldn't write your memoir *The Distance Between Us* right away, so that's why you wrote *Across a Hundred Mountains*. There are connections between your memoir and the novel. I'm thinking of the scene of crossing the border; it's very similar in both books. I'm also thinking of Adriana in *Dancing with Butterflies*, her domestic abuse experiences. We see that abuse described in your nonfiction as well. What was the process of writing from that place of vulnerability? Where do you find the courage?

REYNA: When I was in my early twenties, I didn't really have the courage to write the memoir because I felt very vulnerable, and emotionally I just wasn't ready to write a memoir. Writing *Across a Hundred Mountains* helped me a lot because I was still able to write about some of my childhood experiences and some of my traumas without being the protagonist of the story. My character Juana became my avatar, and I was able to write about myself through her, but I was also able to use my imagination to change things. For example, I gave Juana a very sweet father. I could not bear giving her my father, and so I gave her a nice father who, unfortunately, later disappears. At the time I was writing the book, there were stories about unaccompanied minors, and I was able to bring that into Juana's story when she leaves her hometown and goes to the border to find her father. I also brought in stories of things that never happened to me but that happened to my family, like the little boy who died on the bus; that was my cousin Chucho, who died on a bus on his way to the doctor.

I messed around a lot with the story, and ended up writing from two perspectives, one chronological story and the other nonlinear. When I wrote *Dancing with Butterflies*, I took the same approach with multiple narrators. As I was working on these women, I gave a little bit of myself to each. Adriana got my bad, violent father as well as the instability and the child abuse that I suffered. With Elena, I was a middle school teacher at the time, so I made her a high school teacher. I also gave her bad vision, like me, and she has this trick that I have, which is when she's nervous or she wants to tune out, she takes off her glasses so that everything's blurry and she hides behind that blurriness. With Soledad, I gave her my experience as an immigrant. Her grandma dies the way my grandma died—being stung by a scorpion. Yesenia was a tough one for me to write because I was in my late twenties when I started writing the book, and Yesenia was in her early forties. I was having a hard time imagining what it's like to be a middle-aged woman! I gave her a bad knee, and now I have a bad knee in my mid-forties. I tore a knee ligament two years ago, and it still gives out on me. Now, when I reread *Dancing with Butterflies*, I connect to Yesenia in a way that I didn't when I was writing the book.

MACEO: Adriana is a good example of a troubled character that appears in your books. It seems as though you're not afraid to go to the darker places in their mind. What draws you to these kinds of characters?

REYNA: Because I'm like that. I'm totally messed up in the head! I have so much trauma, which I've been dealing with all my life. I have inner turmoil, a lot of hurt and anger, a lot of insecurities, too, and vulnerabilities. I feel like you learn to live with your trauma, but it never goes away. It always comes back in some form or another. So, I use my characters to explore my own traumas. That's why I'm not afraid to go to those dark places, because in the end, when I finish writing the books, understanding my characters helps me to understand myself a little bit more.

JAVIER: How do you perceive your role as a writer in relation to your community, to the larger society here in the United States, and then also to literature itself?

REYNA: Something I've been thinking about recently is how I've come full circle. When I was a college student, I admired all these writers like Sandra Cisneros and Ana Castillo. I admired them so much, and their work helped me to keep going with my own work. Now that I'm their age, the age they were when I was admiring them, I have college students who are admiring my work, and my work is inspiring them to tell their own stories. I feel like we're connected through this cycle of encouragement, and I'm happy to be part of that cycle. It's important for those of us who are lucky enough to have careers as professional writers to keep trying to tear down the hurdles in our path so that the young writers coming up encounter fewer obstacles along the way. That is something I really want to do—to make it easier for the next generation.

JAVIER: Your books are assigned in classrooms, and you're frequently invited to speak on campuses. What is the experience of not only having students read your work but then getting a chance to speak to them in person?

REYNA: It's a big responsibility, but it's an honor to be able to provide inspiration and encouragement to these young people. I get afraid because sometimes I think, "What do I have to say to them? I'm just this little immigrant girl from Mexico." Then it's nice to hear how they respond to my work, because a lot of them do connect with the things I write about. We were talking about how I go to those dark places with my characters, and I feel that's what these young people connect with, because it shows them that it's okay what they're feeling, we all feel that way at some point. Knowing this makes you feel less alone and less ashamed of your feelings. To me, it's important to make sure that when I meet young people, I help them understand they have nothing to be ashamed of.

MACEO: You've become a spokesperson on issues of immigration, and the undocumented experience in particular. In recent years, you've written very pointed essays, opinion pieces, about current policies and about sexual assault, and you've waded into some very complex issues. Do you perceive yourself and your work as political?

REYNA: When I first started writing, I did not see my work as political, I saw my work as being very personal, and then later I realized that the personal is political, and that you could read an article about immigration and learn about all the statistics, but when you read a memoir about immigration, you can feel it in your body, you can experience those moments in a much deeper, more impactful way. It helps you to understand what that immigration article was trying to say. I started to understand that whatever I write is political. For example, when I wrote *The Distance Between Us*, we were having a discussion as a country about the DREAM Act and what to do with our undocumented youth. There were all these articles about it, but if you read the memoir, it gives you an insight into the experience of undocumented youth, and it helps you to understand why the DREAM Act is so important. I don't have to be that explicit, I just let the story tell you what I think about immigration.

At first, I was really hesitant to write op-eds because I didn't see myself as a very political person, and I didn't see myself as someone who knew how to talk about politics. But when I wrote my op-ed about Trump's zero tolerance policy and separating children from their families, I wrote about my experience with my father and I wove in some of those statistics, some of the hard facts into my personal experience. I discovered that if I approach it from a personal angle and then widen the lens to include what's going on in the country and include some facts outside of my own experience to support what I'm trying to say, then it works. After that, I wasn't as afraid to write political pieces anymore.

As far as becoming a spokesperson, nobody told me that when you're a writer, you also have to learn how to be a public speaker. I wish I had taken some public speaking classes in college! I had to learn how to do it because I'm an introvert, and I get very shy in public spaces with strangers. I tend to find a corner and hide. I can't do that when I give presentations, so I had to learn how to be comfortable onstage. I just decided to be myself, to be open and honest and willing to answer hard questions. I got good at being able to talk about myself. I pretend that I'm in a therapy session, and I just open up. Maybe too much! Sometimes I walk off the stage, and I'm like, "Damn, I shouldn't have said that," or later, I'm like, "I hope that wasn't recorded because that's going to come back and bite me in the butt." I have to learn how not to disclose too much. It's daunting, and I get scared when I'm onstage, but I have this tic where I smile when I'm nervous, so then you can't tell that I'm nervous! It comes in handy sometimes. I still get scared because I feel I'm more eloquent when I write than when I speak. Like when I did *The Oprah Show*, I was very scared of *what* was going to come out of my mouth and *how* it was going to come out.

Maceo: In your novels you've used alternating perspectives to tell the story; sometimes it's alternating third-person, sometimes it's alternating first-person. You've returned to that style with this most recent novel. When you shift to writing nonfiction, how does the energy change when you're limited to just your voice and perspective versus the novelistic form where you've allowed yourself to move around?

Reyna: I enjoy writing fiction because of the voice—thinking about how the characters see the world, which really influences the way they speak, the things they say, and how they say it. I have a lot more fun with those fictional characters than I do when I write from my own perspective because there's really not a whole lot I can do about how I speak. What I tried to do with *The Distance Between Us* was to be aware of how old I was because the memoir covers from the time I was four years old all the way to when I was twenty. For each chapter I had to think about how old I was at the time and how I would've spoken at that age. As I get older, you can see the sentences get longer, the vocabulary gets a little bit more complex, my thoughts do as well. In fiction, when I was writing *Dancing with Butterflies*, I was very aware that Elena—who's a university graduate, a working professional, a teacher—her vocabulary is different from her sister Adriana who doesn't have much schooling. Then Soledad, an immigrant who works as a costume maker, sees the world through fabric. That's how she describes people: using the characteristics of cloth. I'm doing that with my novel right now. John Riley sees the world in a different way than Ximena. She is a folk healer. Throughout her chapters, I mentioned a lot of the flora and fauna because she's very in tune with nature. Her voice is very specific in that way, in how she sees the world.

MACEO: Do you ever feel any pressure when it comes to your subject matter, that people are expecting another book that's going to be about immigration and you feel pulled in another direction?

REYNA: I haven't felt that because even if I set out to write a story about whatever, it always becomes an immigrant story one way or another. With *Dancing with Butterflies*, I was going to write a story about folklórico dancers and the beauty of Mexican dance traditions. Then here comes Soledad, an immigrant who goes back to Mexico and has to cross the border again. Now it's the same thing with my novel *A Ballad of Love and Glory*. I thought I was writing about war and land theft, and here comes John Riley, and I end up writing about his immigrant experience and the discrimination he suffered in the US Army, his longing for his family, and his homesickness. It's an immigrant story, even though it's also very much a war story.

JAVIER: Your first novel, *Across a Hundred Mountains*, came out in 2006, and it was one of the first works by someone who had actually lived the undocumented experience. Since then, we've had many more undocumented or formerly undocumented writers come out in poetry, memoirs, and novels as well. What is it like knowing there are others writing about these experiences?

REYNA: It makes me really happy to see all these stories about immigration, and especially about the undocumented experience, because I didn't have those stories when I first started writing. That's part of the reason why I started to write my stories: because they weren't there. I was hungry for them. Now there are so many wonderful stories that have been coming out. During the Trump era especially, which was very anti-immigrant, people wanted to learn more about immigration. I saw an increase in invitations to speak at colleges, universities, and high schools because many teachers were trying to push back against his anti-immigrant agenda. In a way, one of the positive things that resulted from Trump's racist rhetoric was that people became more aware and supportive of the immigrants in our community. I'm really happy to see new undocumented literature coming out. In fact, I was just reading Karla Cornejo Villavicencio's *Undocumented Americans*. It's a great book!

MACEO: A common thread through all your books is this search for a home or family or a stability that was never there but that the character is trying to find. What do you feel are the major themes of your books?

REYNA: Home is still a major theme for me. In *A Ballad of Love and Glory*, both of my characters are longing for home. Ximena's home gets burned down by the Texas Rangers and her husband is killed. Throughout the novel, there's that longing. She feels homeless, physically but also emotionally. Riley is also longing for his home and for his family in Ireland. Their homesickness is what brings Riley and Ximena together, their longing and desire to create a home.

As I get older, I'm going to write more about aging and trying to cope with my aging trauma as my body falls apart! My bad corneas, my bad hearing, my bad knees and aching hips. I've also started to write more about parenthood. I've spent a lot of time writing from the point of view of being someone's daughter, and now I'm starting to write more from the point of view of being a mother. I just wrote an essay for an anthology I'm coediting of undocumented stories, and I write about my children. I explore how their childhood is completely different from mine, and how I feel like an outsider in my own home because there are many times when I can't relate to them. The contrast between their upper-middle-class American childhoods and my Mexican childhood of poverty creates a distance between us.

MACEO: As more and more Latinx writers get published, what is the unique perspective that they bring?

REYNA: I think they're highlighting the invisibility that seems to be present in so many sectors, so many fields. For example, in film and TV, we're not there. It's a very Black and white world, and Latinos don't seem to exist on screen. Things aren't much better in publishing, but what I like about our literature is that it says, "Here we are, we're part of American society. These are our experiences. This is our point of view, this is how we see the world." That's really beautiful. To have a truly diverse American literature, you need to include the Latino experience. I think it's crucial for us to continue to create our own content, and write our own stories, and to demand to be seen and heard and read.

JAVIER: What are the milestones of Latinx literature so far in the twenty-first century, and which directions do you see Latinx literature taking as we continue into this century?

REYNA: I'm hopeful that this year and the next few years look brighter for Latino literature in terms of being published more, having more new voices. I think things are looking a little better. I was talking to my agent a few days ago, and she told me that almost 90 percent of the books she's sold are by Latino folks. I know a lot of Latino writers who have books coming out this year or next year, including Julissa Arce, María Amparo Escandón, and Erika Sánchez. We still have a long way to go, because historically Latino writers haven't had many opportunities to publish. We're underpublished and underpaid, so we need to keep working on that. What happened last year with *American Dirt* highlighted the ways that Latino writers are kept out of the publishing industry. The Black Lives Matter movement also created more interest in diverse literature, and publishers are actively looking to publish writers of color more. Latino writers are going to benefit from that, too. We have to keep pushing, keep working hard to make sure we are being paid attention to, but I also think it's important for us to continue to work on our craft and make sure we're producing good quality work. We need to push ourselves to write the best books we can.

MACEO: You're one of the few Latinx writers who have been published by major presses. To look at your career from the outside, it looks like a huge success, but I'm sure there have been struggles along the way. Can you speak a little more about your experience in the publishing world?

Reyna: Yes, since my first novel, I've been published by a major publisher, and a lot of good things have come from that, but at the same time, regardless of whether you're published by a big press or a little press, you have to do the work. I have felt that with every single book, and it never gets better. Or easier. With *A Dream Called Home*, for example, which is my fifth book, it got worse. I got more help from my publisher to promote *Across a Hundred Mountains* than I did with *A Dream Called Home*. But I learned from the very beginning that I was going to have to do the work in making sure I have a career as a writer. I tend to see my publisher more as a printer. They're going to print my book, but it's up to me to be out there promoting it and investing in my writing career.

But it's a lot of work. It's almost like a second job. It's not enough to write the damn book. Then I have to send endless emails, create social media posts, be actively looking for ways to get my books into readers' hands. I have to pound the pavement and travel all over, get on endless airplanes—never mind the wear and tear on my body. Lugging around heavy suitcases packed with books. I have even sold books out of the trunk of my car as if they were tamales! And I'm not waiting for the grace of God to make things happen for me. I have this very vivid memory when *The Distance Between Us* came out. I had a friend who worked at the *LA Times*, and she snuck me into the building and took me to the office of the book reviewer. I said, "Here's my book. It's coming out. I hope you can write about it." I hand-delivered my memoir to one of the book reviewers, Héctor Tobar. Because they get so many books from publishers, I knew that I had very little chance for my book to stand out from the pile. That's how I got my *LA Times* book review—by sneaking into the office. We must advocate for ourselves. If we want to have a career as writers, we need to be willing to put in the work. Publishing is a business and numbers speak. You must have good sales numbers for you to get book contracts and better advances. So don't abandon your books, don't leave their success to chance.

—January 21, 2021

13

ARACELIS GIRMAY

Aracelis Girmay is the author of three poetry collections, *Teeth*, *Kingdom Animalia*, and *the black maria*, the collage-based children's book *changing, changing*, and the editor of *How to Carry Water: Selected Poems of Lucille Clifton*. The daughter of an Eritrean father and Puerto Rican mother, Girmay was born and raised in Santa Ana, California, before leaving for boarding school, an experience, she told us, that left her feeling isolated and confused. She found herself through literature, reading authors whose work made her feel less alone in the world and spurred her own writing. She would later attend college on the East Coast, graduating from Connecticut College and receiving her MFA from New York University. Girmay's poetry reflects this search for connection through uprootedness and the ways that different strands of being can be held at once—a "flickering subjectivity," as she describes it. Her work also encompasses the different routes of her family's migration and histories, viewing her own family story as a lens to understand a world defined by upheaval and survival. Her poetry is also about mixtures and juxtapositions, and often how it relates to movement and geography, spanning centuries and continents. Her poem "Fourth Estrangement, with a Petition for the Reunion of Jonathan & George Jackson" in *the black maria* begins in Venice, Italy, and explores a Jewish ghetto, tells the story of Passover, and then turns to the murder of the political prisoner George Jackson at San Quentin State Prison in San Francisco Bay and his brother Jonathan who was killed attempting to free him. Girmay asks the reader to travel with her, to forge connections where they might not otherwise be seen. "Girmay is deeply involved in the world," Martín Espada wrote in the foreword to Girmay's first collection, *Teeth*, "and her poetry articulates a passion for that world in spite of—or because of—its failings." A finalist for a National Book Critics Circle Award for *Kingdom Animalia* and a 2015 Whiting Award winner, Girmay has taught at Hampshire College and currently teaches at Pratt Institute in New York.

JAVIER: How has the pandemic impacted your writing? And can you speak more generally about your writing process?

ARACELIS: My partner, Rassan, and I have two little kids who are now four and six but were two and four at the beginning of the pandemic. We live in an apartment in a wonderful neighborhood in Flatbush-Ditmas in Brooklyn. At the start of the pandemic, once we realized what was happening and the schools shut down, both Rassan and I were able to work from home. It was instantly the four of us in this tight space with the sounds, the worries, the trying to keep up with the news. I was just trying to be there for students and for my family. I wasn't making work. I wasn't reading work except for my students' work. Then there was the horror of George Floyd's murder, and then the uprisings, and then profound family losses. I stopped reading and writing because there was so much tending to do, and I felt like I didn't want to be quiet—the quiet that my practice and process requires from me and that I love about it. I was busy and tired, but I felt that I couldn't get quiet enough. I didn't want to because I just needed to keep functioning. I was afraid that if I slowed down and really began to read, really began to follow some of the sentences or phrases or notes that were coming to me, that I might dip into my emotional terrain, and I didn't feel like I had the capacity to do that. That said, more recently I started writing again, started taking notes again, and have been deeply immersed in reading again. It took almost two years exactly to feel like I could be quiet enough to listen to what I've been feeling.

As for my practice more generally. What these last two years have taught me is that for me, writing is the closest thing I have to a spiritual practice; which is to say, I carry my questions into the writing. I try to renew my courage, my mind in writing. There's a lot of reckoning and a desire to remember that I'm small in the world and that there are bigger things that I'm a part of. That's what writing can help me to do. I knew that was true, but it was interesting to feel so devastated by these losses in the last few years and to feel like I didn't want to touch spirit. I'm often writing to learn something. I'm also often writing to try to undo a way of thinking into another way of thinking. Part of my resistance to writing, I think, had to do with a desire for a certain stillness or stability that I think my writing often tries to move away from. Of course, these feelings and ways of thinking about my writing change depending on the circumstances.

MACEO: There is a sense of play in some of the poems in your first two collections that signals a proximity to children, or at least to a sense of child's play. I'm thinking especially of the poems on letters *B* and *R*. Why was it important for you to include that sense of play?

ARACELIS: Even when I was in college, I was always doing work with young people. My major, my formal studies were in Documentary Studies and what was then called Hispanic Studies but is now called Latin American Studies and Latino Studies at Connecticut College. I was always working with children in my work-study jobs. Any chance that I had to do special projects, I found that I was often drawn to working with elementary school children. Then when I was in grad school, I studied with the Community-Word Project and had the chance to work in the public schools in New York with Community-Word and with Teachers & Writers. One of the things that I thought about a lot, and that I think about with my own kids, is just how deeply taught I was by my own art teachers. There was a ballet teacher named Sister Beth who offered free ballet classes to young people in Santa Ana. It was called Saint Joseph Ballet then, and we were in the church basement of the Episcopal Church of the Messiah, just behind Main Street, but we always called it Saint Joseph's. Sister Beth would play Anita Baker and Peter Gabriel and all kinds of music that we would dance ballet to. Then she invited a few of the Alvin Ailey dancers and the Joffrey Ballet dancers, all of them of color, to come and give us special classes, and they came and they did. In ballet classes and in this one art teacher's class in elementary school, even then I could feel how formative those experiences were for me. For somebody to say, "You don't have to say a word, but what is this gesture saying? What can you do with this one sheet of paper?" That kind of attention is profound. How amazing is it to get to pay attention to young people paying attention or to the strangeness of what they are noticing before they've had years and years of people saying, "No, it's this. Say it this way, this is the correct way to say or see."

Working with young people taught me so much about holding on to my idiosyncratic way of saying. This is what I hoped and needed for them, and it came to be what I hoped and needed for myself too. I was working on these lesson plans and thinking about pedagogy with other art teachers, really having to articulate, What are the actual objectives? Is it that I really want this person to know what a metaphor is? Actually, it's something beyond that. I would love for them to practice noticing what they delight in. I would love for them to practice naming what they notice. Scrutinizing, questioning. I would love for them to feel the powers of their imaginative capacities and the imaginative strategies of those they are in community with, family with, place with.

MACEO: What have been the formative moments in your journey as a writer?

ARACELIS: I always loved reading. I think about childhood a lot, and I have visceral memories of looking out of my eyes as a child. When I think about my roots of coming to my language, I think about how much I loved reading, how much I loved to just read anything out loud. I liked the sound, the sensation. I also really loved listening to stories. I grew up in Santa Ana, Southern California. My mom was born in Chicago and lived there until she was a teenager and her mother moved the family. My dad was born in Gondar, Ethiopia. We were around my mom's side of the family—my grandparents and my uncle and aunt were in Southern California with us. There were a lot of stories of different "back homes." I loved listening to them talk and trying to imagine the details of the places and asking them questions. That was more one-on-one, but when people got together, I just tried to listen. There were incredible stories that they would tell each other again and again, back and forth to each other; everybody knows the story but they're telling it again. That's the second thing that feels formative for me. The other thing is that I would spend so long just digging in the dirt. There was always some dirt somewhere. Even a little small patch of dirt at my grandmother's place. But that feeling of *what's down here* was important. Those three things carry through into how I see my work now.

I went to a boarding school and felt very isolated and confused by my experience there. But that's when I started reading differently and was introduced to Toni Morrison and Gabriel García Márquez by my literature teacher. That was amazing, and then I started reaching toward poets—Lucille Clifton, Kate Rushin—and I just found my way in the library. That was the first time where I was like, "This reading is helping me to feel like I'm not alone in the world." I had left my family. I had left what I understood to be how the world functioned into this very different place. Reading was the way that I could feel like I was overhearing people's stories and how they spoke. Toni Morrison, I think about *Jazz*, the orality of that work; and the imagination of García Márquez. So I felt I was losing something and was finding it again in literature. That was when I first began to write in a different way: not to show anybody, but to save something of myself. To create company on the page.

Javier: What literary traditions have you inherited or do you feel you're writing as part of?

Aracelis: I've always been drawn to what art, and especially literary art, meant or could mean to people who were engaged in political struggle. From García Lorca in Spain and June Jordan in the US to Gioconda Belli in Nicaragua. But I'm also thinking of the weather of the bomba dancer's skirt at a bombazo, the connection and collaboration between the dancer and the drummer listening to what they might make together, and the fact that these practices were named, transmitted, taught, and attended to, against erasure, over two hundred years. What are the pressures on these artists in a time of struggle? What are the ways that they relate to that pressure? How do they carry the stories? How do they fight? How do they nourish? Those were the questions that I was carrying as somebody who was reading. That's a way of saying that, eventually, those were some of the people and practices I learned from. My schools. I was drawn to that tradition of writers and artists engaged in struggle against oppressive regimes of all kinds.

When I think of how I would place my work, my way-back roots are probably in documentary poetics and folks who practice that in different ways. I'm also interested in poets who praise, whose minds are on the everyday—Martín Espada, Jack Agüeros's psalms. I am deeply informed by a range of Black diasporic poetic traditions. I think of the documentary practices of Gwendolyn Brooks, where there's world, lyricism, documentary and exquisite details of the everyday, domestic scenes. I think of Kamau Brathwaite's record and witness work as very different from Brooks's, and I am shaped by them equally. Brathwaite's ways of marking plurality, simultaneity, and the strange porousness or resonances of a single gesture.

MACEO: All three of your collections span continents—Iraq, Sudan, Palestine, Eritrea, Puerto Rico, Santa Ana, California—how did you develop this international approach to your poetics?

ARACELIS: I'm thinking about my friend, Simone White, who said something like, "Blackness is my eyeball." In Puerto Rico, Eritrea, Santa Ana, there are certain traditions of sound, of fight, of living, of relationship to empire. There are certain positions that I was just born into because of my family's routes. That is in and of itself transnational and mixed. I'm very aware of a kind of flickering subjectivity—that when I'm in this house, I'm never only in this house. A sensitivity toward the ways that ideas of nationhood and language are formed and are problematic. That's how me and my personality matched with my own heritage. That's how I exist in the world. I'm thinking about connections between these histories and also differences at every point—especially when I look at Eritrea and Puerto Rico and also African America, which is varied—but I'm looking at questions of dispossession, colonial status, second-class citizenship, relationship to land, that land being taken. Those are some of the deeply charged and ongoing violences that I grieve and wonder out of, as someone in a few diasporas, and think through on a regular basis. Of course, I don't need to have my heritage to feel those things, but I do feel them, and I'm interested in the ways that my personal histories are connected to these other histories. They feel like critical and natural connections to make.

Also, I'm interested in other people's stories, how things came to be the way they are. Over and over again our stories are each other's. Bhanu Kapil has this book, *The Vertical Interrogation of Strangers*, that starts with these twelve questions that she asks strangers. One of them is, "Who are you and where did you come from?" That question is just fascinating to me and full of sorrow and also brilliance and joy. Just a single life, all the stories, and they're all connected, and I feel the more I listened to other people singing, saying, asking, the more I couldn't help but think about the connections, and the more I wanted to read this way and that way and this way and that way. But I still know that my arms are not wide enough in my studies and my listening. I am so US-focused and need to read and listen more widely.

JAVIER: What have been your experiences in getting your works published, either negative or positive?

ARACELIS: I was living in Long Beach and I had just finished graduate school when John Murillo, who I met at Cave Canem's workshop for Black poets, sent me a message that was like, "You have to come to Arizona for this weeklong class with Martín Espada," whose work I knew and loved. I was like, "I don't know if I can afford it." And he said, "You have to figure out a way, trust me." I don't even know how I figured out the way, maybe I sold some books at the bookstore I was working at—I was working at Acres of Books in Long Beach at the time and would sometimes sell from my collection of books to the book buyer there in order to make extra cash. But I drove out to Arizona and took this workshop with Martín, who asked me, "What do you have? What are you working on now?" I said, "I've been working on something, but it doesn't feel done." By the end of the trip I agreed to send him what I had. When I returned to California, I spent some time putting some poems together and then sent them his way. A little while later, he sent me a message: "I would like to send it to somebody else to look at."

I remember the way I interpreted it was, "Maybe he doesn't have feedback and he feels like he doesn't know what to say, so he's going to send it to somebody else." I was just grateful that he wanted to see my work. I had no expectations of him sending it to a publisher, but then I get this message from Sandy Taylor, the amazing publisher of Curbstone, this beautiful soul I came to know later. Sandy said he didn't think it was ready yet but that he wanted to publish it. I remember feeling like dropping to the ground in gratitude and also embarrassment, like, "I don't know that it was ready for somebody else to look at in that way." Which is to say I don't know what ideas I had about what a manuscript should be before a publisher looked at it, but I just felt like there was some magic up there and it was far from me. Now I feel if you've got something strong and you want to share it, then you should do that. See what happens. When you get a million nos, sometimes that means change it, but sometimes that means you're doing something that other people don't understand and that's okay. Anyway, that's how it came to be published with Curbstone, which had published Luis Rodriguez, Naomi Ayala, E. Ethelbert Miller, a posthumous selected by Roque Dalton. I was just amazed and excited, and I also loved the humble hands-on, "What are we going to do? How are we going to share this work? Have you read so and so? Have you seen—?" There was just something really beautiful about Sandy's practice, and I felt very lucky to be a part of that work.

After that book with Curbstone, I was just writing poems, poems, poems, and there was a contest, the Isabella Gardner Award out of BOA. My friend Aisha asked, "Do you have something to send?" I said, "No, there's no way I'm close to anything." And she was like, "Are you sure? I know you've been working on poems. I think you have something." Then I went back and looked and was like, "You know what, I do have something. I didn't realize it." She told me to send it to BOA because Laure-Anne Bosselaar was judging a prize. Aisha knew Laure-Anne and thought she might connect to my work. So I sent it in and they said yes. One of the things I was naive about, and now I know to be true, is that books and projects and all of these things have everything to do with community. When I was in grad school, we didn't have conversations about publishing. We didn't have editors visiting. Nobody talked about it. It was a thing not to talk about. It was like, just make the most amazing poem, whatever that means, and you don't talk about this other stuff. It's not part of it. Then I came to realize that what ends up happening is that the people who are connected to publishing, to money, to these different institutions, literary and otherwise, keep getting the knowledge. It's not as if those practices aren't happening, it's just that the people who aren't connected are not in this conversation with the people who are. For better or for worse, communities that we're a part of have everything to do with our work having opportunities. It's important to be super explicit about that. In both of those cases, I feel deeply grateful to my loved ones for helping me find my way.

Maceo: You mentioned your father was born in Ethiopia, your mother's Puerto Rican from Chicago, and you grew up in California, where the Latinx community is predominantly Mexican American. There's less awareness, unfortunately, of the Afro-Latinx community. How did your mixed heritage impact your relationship to your Latinx identity? Does that have any reverberations in your work or your choice of subjects?

ARACELIS: First and foremost, I think of myself as a Black writer, and of course one can be Black Latinx, Afro-Latinx, but the Latinx identity has never felt like mine as a general identity. Puerto Ricanness, on the other hand, I feel part Puerto Rican. I feel part Eritrean. The more local or specific I am when thinking about my heritage and culture, the more comfortable I am. Who knows what it would have been like to be raised somewhere else, but growing up in Santa Ana in the '80s and '90s, and Southern California more generally, it felt like the categories were Black, Mexican, Cambodian, or Vietnamese. These were the categories. I was like, "Well, I'm clearly Black, and I'm not Mexican." Even though my great-grandfather is from León, Mexico, and he was married to my great-grandmother who was African American from Griffin, Georgia. They raised their babies in the South Side of Chicago. My grandmother was their third-youngest child. She married her first husband, my grandfather, who was from Arecibo, Puerto Rico. So there's a mix a long way back. It is sometimes a point of contention in our family. Who claims or doesn't claim what? Depending on how people look and people's commitments, for different reasons, people in my family identify differently from one another, categorically speaking. I think that my own interest in parallel possibilities and simultaneities—in reading and how one is read—is probably rooted in some of this personal history. I am also so interested in the conditions that made it so that these people even met. I am fascinated by history and the conditions out of which these unions emerge—our routes to here, which is something I continue to think about deeply across all of my work and days.

JAVIER: Urayoán Noel, in his afterword to his book on Nuyorican poetry, *In Visible Movement*, focuses on others who don't fit those categories of being from New York or those centers of Puerto Ricanness. He uses your work as a prime example of how those categories and possibilities of experiences can be opened up, where there's not just one way of being Puerto Rican or one way of being Latinx.

ARACELIS: Who would I have been had I been younger and read Urayoán's work? He's acknowledged, named, and valued a space that so many people live in. I think when I was much younger I was aware that my stories didn't fit with anybody else except for my brother. Even then they're different because of our genders and the way that we look and because of our names. I realized that I was not neatly categorized, even when I chose to be summed up quickly. There was a time when I felt almost apologetic about the confusion or bewilderment that I caused! More than that for me now, though, is a question about opportunity. I want to always be aware and thoughtful about what kinds of opportunities I am offered and when it might make sense to decline or to put forward the names of other writers better or differently suited for a program or project.

There's that on the one hand, and on the other hand, there are the truths of who I am and what my roots are and my identity is. I'm going back to that word "apologetic." I think when I was younger, I felt like I didn't fit in other people's imaginations; even the trajectories of who and where and how—they're not neat, and they are part of the story of the world. When I think about the migrations of my people, these are working people, people whose lands were taken, who were taken. My histories, as all of our histories, carry histories of the world, but for a long time I avoided that because it was too messy. Then it was like, actually, these are the stories I carry and have to share, and it's important to honor my people through them. Nobody else is going to know how to say me. I can't be spoken by somebody else. That's something that I realized in my twenties, but these are things I'm still always wondering about and wrestling with.

MACEO: Your poem "Ride," from your collection *Teeth*, imagines a little boy and the speaker robbing a bank to build houses, proper schools, and gardens for the people. Your poems express indignation at the injustices you see, but there's also a desire to do something about those injustices. How do your poems seek to be more than just witness?

ARACELIS: The poems help me to articulate something about what I want my life to be and my actions. There's something about a poem that helps you to say what you're trying to say or express or articulate to yourself, the truth about something, or to lay something bare, a revelation, a history. The poem teaches me something when I'm writing it. I'm thinking about Audre Lorde and her essay "Uses of the Erotic"—how once you've experienced something so deeply, then that can become a measure for the rest of our lives. Lorde writes: "Once we know the extent to which we are capable of feeling that sense of satisfaction and completion, we can then observe which of our various life endeavors bring us closest to that fullness." So once you've written something clearly in the poem, and then the next poem, the next one, and the next, it can start to become a measure for your hope and desire and what you want to be outside of the poem. The poem helps me to understand some of my commitments in life.

Yet during the pandemic, I'm looking at the horrors of Trump's administration from my apartment windows, and I'm like, "I'm not doing anything." I'm taking care of what's in this tiny circle—my kids and family members. Sylvia Wynter talks about when she left Jamaica to study in the UK and how she could no longer coincide with herself. And I felt like I had articulated these commitments, but what was I doing outside of imagining and trying to recover my spirit? "It isn't enough," I kept thinking. "This is who I am? I'm doing nothing even though there's this measure and this clarity?" Everybody feels in their own ways when they're engaged and in the world in the ways that feel most alive for them and fulfilling to themselves and their communities. I feel somewhat far from that, and it's a painful feeling and I must do something about that.

JAVIER: The tradition of documentary poetics is very present in your most recent book, *the black maria*. The first half of the book is the long poem "Elelegy," which is a response to an estimated twenty thousand people dying at sea making the journey from North Africa to Europe in the past few decades. One way of understanding documentary poetics is that at the center of it is this responsibility for others, being able to respond to others, but you also make us aware of your own subjectivity. Why was that important for you?

ARACELIS: That terrible number of people killed by these violences continues to grow. The organization Forensic Architecture continues to powerfully investigate these state-sanctioned crimes against humanity and the deadly patrol practices of NATO ships and European coast guards. Since 2020 they've been investigating the illegal "drift-backs" within "Greek waters." Their work is exquisitely vital and necessarily exact. Fierce.

As for my own writing and thinking about my own subjectivity: when I was in college I did a couple of long-form narrative pieces, documentary pieces, and was really lucky to get to work with folks at the Salt Institute for Documentary Studies. This was in 1998. At the time, one of the things I really struggled with was how you're supposed to write so-called objectively. How you're not supposed to think of your own subjectivity in the work or name your subjectivity. These are the lessons of then, the teachings of then, which have been problematized. When I was thinking about my last book of poems, there were some stories and histories I wanted to tell and think about. There was research I wanted to do, and I did not want it to seem like I was anything more than myself. I wanted to really point to the limits of my own subjectivity or the specifics of my own subjectivity as a thing to read, as in, "Don't think I'm speaking for anyone. This is exactly who I am with my specific histories and this is what I'm writing and noticing and trying to write toward." I wanted to try to write toward as opposed to about. There's a way that, in that book, I'm trying to show my hand and my shiftful self and my imagination and limitations and vulnerability, especially when writing as somebody in the diaspora who's connected and removed by distance and experience to these more recent migrations.

MACEO: You edited a volume of Lucille Clifton's poetry, and you remarked that one thing that drew you to her work was that she wrote poems out of the truth of her life, "insisting that a poem is and can be made with the truth of one's experience and in the languages that are your own." How does that resonate with your own poetry, your work that's personal but also when writing about experiences that you haven't lived?

ARACELIS: There's something so tiny and capacious in Clifton's work. People are doing things. Her aunt is ironing, the lights are blooming. Things are happening. Not just people but things are doing things. Those feel like anchors and teachers for me. I'm reminded of Bhanu Kapil, who writes about her family's experience of Partition, and there are these tiny details. One of them that I remember is about the print on the back of a leg, a print from sitting somewhere. It's just like, "Oh, my God, we're made of bones and flesh and breath and so were our ancestors many years ago." The details of each specific body have been really important for me to remember, and I feel this as I get older, having children. I remember just thinking, "Now I know a little more what a child is." Suddenly my relationship to certain stories in my family but also other historical stories is different having this new relationship to this tiny body and knowing the sounds of certain cries. I think we live, I live, in those tiny details.

When I'm writing toward histories I was not there for, one way for me to ground myself is to think about the details of the earth or light or to remember the way someone stood, or the words they used to tell the story, or where they were looking as they spoke. What are the peripheral details that can help to anchor me, to remember the flesh and bone and breath of it? What are the ways to ground myself in the physical and tangible? That feels like a way to ground a poem in a larger history that I was not there for. I also think it's important to name the wondering and to wonder toward what is outside of the poem—unsayable, even, by the poem. Lucille Clifton models this too. I'm thinking of her poem "Study the Masters" and the part that goes: "it was her iron, / or one like hers." That "or one like hers" is so stunning, how it points to relationship and makes room for what is unknown.

JAVIER: Your poem "Elelegy" speaks to a combination of traditions, two different cultural ways of dealing with grief: the Western literary tradition of elegy, grief in reflection, and the ululatory expression, which is more immediate, more bodily grief, and in some ways, non-Western. How did you envision combining those?

ARACELIS: I love the distinction that you're making, which I hadn't made before, thinking about embodiment versus something that feels removed or reflective. For sure, there's something to the "elelele" part. Immediately in my mind, it's plural—there are many voices. It's always a rise of many voices doing it. It feels like a flock of birds just taking off. With the elegy, there's a way that, in the tradition of poems that I've read mostly in English that are European or US American, there's something that feels a little more solitary to me about the word. I don't know if that's true. I'm just saying this for the first time. I love Brathwaite's work. There's a deep, deep beauty and practice in being alive to one's associations and the experiment of the way things touch inside of us. There's a point where Brathwaite is talking about the word "widow," and he's thinking about his wife who has just passed and he writes "window" instead of "widow." What are the ways in my English that I carry other sounds that are alive in me? What does that do to my English? That's what I was also trying to think about. What else can I find here digging in the dirt? English is fairly new in my family, and it's the only language that I'm fluent in, but what else can I find in there before English just because of the associations I carry?

MACEO: In editing Lucille Clifton's selected poetry, you organized her work, listening, in your words, "to the repeated resonances and reckonings across her life," and I'm curious as you think about the arc of your own work, your three collections so far and the poetry you're writing and hope to write, if you can identify those repeated resonances and reckonings in your own work?

ARACELIS: One thing that's true is I've been trying to honor my beloveds and notice the details of certain lives and gestures. I feel like life—the word, the idea—is so big, and I've come to realize we have these memories with people and ways that we shape each other's lives, even between strangers, these things that stay with us, that feel so molecular. The poems are trying to pay attention to what moves me, the things that positively move me, and to honor and remember them. I'm thinking I'm offering small petals of flowers to this, to this memory, to this person who will never remember me who was on the bus with me once. I think that across the books. I'm so amazed by how we shape each other and how that lasts, and also how we hurt each other and how that lasts. Again, how did we get here, and how do we live now knowing what we know? I think that's the heart of the reckoning and the resonances.

I realize, especially having my kids and sending them off to school, the extent to which people harm each other. It takes no time for somebody's cruelty to just change everything for thousands of people in a second. What are the ways that people have imagined something that could resuscitate themselves or imagine something different? Even things that don't feel explicitly profoundly political, like a Bustelo can lunch box or cardboard inside a shoe to cover the hole or earring backings made from erasers, whatever the thing, I just want to carry for myself what people do with their imaginations, the beautiful things people do with their imaginations, and that's part of what's at the heart of my work.

—April 22, 2022

14

CARMEN GIMÉNEZ

Through her work as an editor, publisher, and poet, Carmen Giménez has become one of the most influential figures in contemporary Latinx letters. Awarded a Guggenheim Fellowship in 2020, she is the author of six poetry collections, including *Milk and Filth*, a finalist for the 2013 National Book Critics Circle Award, and *Be Recorder*, a finalist for both the PEN Open Book Award and the National Book Award. Her searingly honest memoir about balancing motherhood and creativity, *Bring Down the Little Birds*, won the American Book Award in 2011. Throughout our conversation, Giménez frequently mentioned the impact of her working-class Peruvian mother, whose love of art and beauty she imparted to her children. Giménez attended San Jose State University, where she worked with the poet Alan Soldofsky, an experience that not only "unlocked the key" to poetry but also gave her a template for what it meant to be a literary citizen and surrounding oneself with a community of writers and artists. She would later receive her MFA in poetry from the Iowa Writers' Workshop. In 2002, Giménez founded Noemi Press, which started publishing chapbooks and evolved to publish some of the most innovative writing by writers of color in the last decade. Shortly after our conversation, we learned that Giménez had left Noemi Press to become the publisher and executive director of Graywolf Press. After years at New Mexico State University, Giménez joined the faculty in the English Department at Virginia Tech. She spoke to us from Blacksburg, Virginia, where she lives with her partner and her two children, Jackson and Sofia. Her son, introduced to readers as a baby in her memoir about motherhood, is now about to graduate high school. Giménez was bleak about the future in our conversation, half joking that all of her hard work on behalf of her children would pay off when they had to pay forty dollars for a bottle of water. Her most recent collection, *Be Recorder*, has the feel of a manifesto with righteous anger calling out the evils of consumer capitalism and the ravaging of our environment, a theme that she believes now supersedes all others, and one she has carried into a novel in progress.

JAVIER: How has the pandemic impacted your writing? And can you speak to your writing process more generally?

CARMEN: I felt like I was in a nightmare—so isolating and strange. My last book came out in August 2019, then the pandemic happened and I shut down. The pandemic changed the way that I was connected to the world: traveling to be with other writers, for example. I was stuck in my house with myself, saying, "Damn, you're lonely, you don't have much going on. That was your whole world. You don't even have a book in you right now. What are you going to do except lose your mind?"

As an artist, I want every book that I write to be different from the last one, and that book took a lot out of me, but maybe I need to let go of not wanting to be the person who you're like, "Is that the fourth book or the fifth book? I can't tell the difference." Most recently, I do have a new series of poems that I'm working on that have given me a little momentum, and I've been working on a novel as well, which has been a real charge—to do something radically different that might reconnect me with a new aspect of poetry. I definitely have to be looking outward. Translating also keeps me alive as an artist, as does being an editor. Even when I'm not producing, I have a relationship with art sustained by communal art making.

MACEO: Your memoir, *Bring Down the Little Birds*, speaks to the anxiety of being both a writer and a mother. One of those anxieties, of course, is the loss of time. Yet you've been profoundly productive in the years since. How have you balanced motherhood and your creative practice?

CARMEN: Frankly, I made a lot of sacrifices. There were a lot of things that I wasn't available for, things I didn't do. Sometimes the family pays a price. I am contending with that now that my kids are older, but I don't know that I'd have done it differently, despite everything that has happened.

JAVIER: What have been the formative moments in your journey as a writer?

CARMEN: I always loved reading so much—escape and fantasy. If I wasn't reading, I was making stories up in my head: elaborate, complex, multilayered, multiverse worlds. I read the dictionary when I was young because I so loved the material life of language and the idea of rhetoric, of trying to convince someone to do what I want or to get something that I wanted. That's the mezcla of being a writer, and particularly of being a poet, although when I was young I wanted to be a novelist. My father was a voracious reader, an indiscriminate reader, and indiscriminate in handing me books. I was reading *How To Be a Good Manager*, Dale Carnegie, Wayne Dyer. I read Marx when I was twelve. It didn't matter. I read textbooks. I would go to a flea market and wipe people out.

But I didn't read a ton of poetry until high school. I had a teacher who had grown up in North Beach during the Beat era, so in 1985, '86, I'm reading Ginsberg and Yeats, and something clicked in me about the puzzle part of poetry, that if you solve this or if you figure out how this image works. I remember in my body what it was like to read "The Second Coming," that moment of seeing the image system unfold, the music that rose up from it—literally, the dark violins playing while I was reading it.

When I went to college, I studied with Alan Soldofsky. He introduced me to Juan Felipe and he just knew everything about poetry—was a true zealot. He unlocked the key: "If you do this," and "This is what meter is," and "This is what a turn is," and "This is what a line break does." My head was blown. I look at a poem and I see an engine. I see how it works, and this is what cools stuff, and this is the liquid, and if you don't have this, then it's not going to run.

He also brought so many readers through the Center for Literary Arts at San Jose State, and I was his assistant the whole time I was there. I got to pick people up from the airport and chat with them. I was like, "Yo, Joyce Carol Oates." So it wasn't just that I wanted to be a writer, but also an organizer and an editor. All of that connection was formative, shaped my path.

JAVIER: When you started Noemi Press in 2002, what was your vision?

CARMEN: I had friends who had just bought a Vandercook that I wanted to play with, so I said, "I'm going to do a chapbook for my friend." At the time, I had a boyfriend who was a graphic designer, and I told him, "Come help me. Let's all do this together." That's how it started. I just wanted to play around, and then it became a desire to do something different in how people of color were represented in a catalog, to say we publish cool shit and we publish a bunch of people of color because people of color write a bunch of cool shit but we're not super worried about it because that's not the only lens we use.

Noemi started as a chapbook press, but at a certain point, I realized that with two kids, hand-bolting, hand-printing, and hand-sewing two hundred books was not going to work. Digital printing made publishing books affordable and accessible and made it possible for a person to have a solid full-length book, and we did not struggle looking for writers of color and centering their work. When J. Michael Martinez hopped on board, we saw that there were books out there not getting picked up by other presses in part because they were raw, because they didn't have the pedigreed mentorship. We all know folks of color, including ourselves, who went through MFA programs not getting acknowledged, not getting named, being marginalized, being microaggressed, and they were coming with books that weren't ready. We developed the idea, which has been a big ethos of Noemi, to do collaborative revision and long-term revision with writers. Sometimes we worked with writers for up to two or three years revising their books.

We tried to recognize talent, give people room to play and room to question, and when writers know they're getting published and they're being told they can do whatever they want, they develop a sense of freedom. Additionally all the players picked books. Suzi Garcia and Anthony Cody, Noemi's new publishers, were key in acquiring important books, as were Sarah Gzemski and Diana Arterian. We created this laboratory of collaboration, learned how to edit together and learn from each other, and that's how Noemi became what it is now.

MACEO: You've talked about being a literary citizen. Can you speak more about what that means? And to what extent does being a literary citizen make you a different kind of writer? Can one be separated from the other?

CARMEN: Art doesn't happen in a vacuum. It happens in movements, whether intentional or not, centered around groups of people, shared affinities, connections with other art forms, or around community organizing. Take the art collective Asco—they emerged from social justice community organizing, which informed their art and their aesthetic. The Dadaists were processing World War I trauma. The idea of a literary citizen is part of that, but it's also being suffused by connection and energy, being surrounded by people who are hungry and excited by art and sharing affinities. One of my favorite things to do is sit in a room writing with other people.

I often think about being that girl, nineteen, twenty years old, in that class, opening up Lorna Dee's *Emplumada* for the first time, in San Jose reading about Cervantes's San Jose. That was so formative and important to me—life-changing. Literary citizenship is based on creating love for art in someone else who doesn't have access to it. My mom took us to every museum, and she would be like, "Bye, go look at art." We didn't have any context, but for her, it was, "This is yours. You can do this." I learn from every book I edit or every reading that I set up. Living beyond your own work connects you to other communities and to other aesthetics. I don't know that I would be the writer that I am or the thinker that I am if I hadn't reached beyond my own page.

JAVIER: In "Remembrance of Their Labors," in your most recent book, *Be Recorder*, there's a line that says, "In homage to different models of discourse, particularly the work of my pantheon." Then there's a list, including Gloria Anzaldúa, bell hooks, Ana Mendieta, and Patssi Valdes. How would you describe this pantheon? And what are some of the literary traditions that you feel you have inherited?

CARMEN: What all those artists have in common is that they transcended genre. They're not *a* poet, *a* visual artist. They play. They also activate a rigorous politicized aesthetic through their work, like bell hook's radical pedagogy of engagement or Gloria Anzaldúa's work of self-definition and inscription. The artists I love work against conventional notions of the canonical, the historical. These are all artists of obsession, of recurrence. They're also very powerful women of color who didn't give a fuck. That was important for me to see.

So often you're shaped by who your teachers are. My first teacher in college was Aldon Nielsen, a scholar of Black experimental traditions. I was nineteen years old, and this guy's like, "We're going to read William Carlos Williams and Ishmael Reed." The books he introduced me to were wild, like, "Okay, a poem can be this weird space where you do weird stuff and it's super metaphorical and it's super philosophical. Okay. Check. You can do that."

Translation was also formative for me, in part because of James Wright. I read who he translated, and then I read who was proximal to them. I discovered César Vallejo, a Peruvian, and I was like, "Okay, represent," especially having grown up in a country where they talked about "down south" as primitive. As a consequence of reading Latin American surrealism, then reading Eastern European surrealism, I became a fan of the uncanny valley quality of surrealism as well as the political charge.

Over my career as an editor, I have read thousands of manuscripts. The more I read, the better I get as a writer. It's like my superpower. I'm just sucking the juice out of everything, still that little voracious girl. My influence is being influenced widely, by anyone who draws me in.

MACEO: Having inherited these different traditions or having been influenced by them is a little different from where you see yourself. Is there a tradition that you situate yourself within?

CARMEN: It's aspirational, but at the end of the day, I situate myself in proximity to poets and friends who are very dear: Rosa Alcalá, Farid Matuk, Susan Briante, Roberto Tejada, Douglas Kearney, Sara Borjas, Anthony Cody, J. Michael, and of course all the Noemi authors. I like people who ask the same kind of questions, which is what's great about surrounding yourself with artists. I feel remote from category, especially since poetry has evolved so much to resist it, but the backdrop, the influence is vast because I've drawn a range of tools from so many poets, which is probably a quality I share with the poets I mentioned.

JAVIER: A lot of the influences that you mentioned are radical and experimental, which often is trying to get away from the lyric. Can you speak to this idea of a more radical, experimental lyric?

CARMEN: I like the excessive. It's the rococo Lucie Brock-Broido, but if Lucie Brock-Broido was a brown waitress's daughter. I like the combination of the high and the low. In the '90s, the lyric was all boring white women. They were great and wonderful writers, but their world was so defined by their class. What I wanted was the high excessive lyric. Like Nicanor Parra, the high excessive lyric with the bass. I wanted that ample, sexy, complex lexicon, but that wasn't moving in this rarefied class. I consider myself on a continuum with J. Michael Martinez. I told him when we were much younger that he was "Little Keats," because he loves the sublime as much as I did. I wanted to dirty the sublime, the heavy, clangy bass of the sublime. I wanted the dirty South of the sublime. That's what I was thinking about for the lyric. I'm always acting as an instrument for what my mother never could say or what my mother never could do. I'm vengeance. I'm vengeance wrought from my mom but in the most constructed and sonic way I can.

JAVIER: Your poems "Be Recorder" and "American Mythos" take a turn into the speculative. How did you imagine the role of the "future" in this latest work?

CARMEN: It's writing from the Anthropocene. This is the end. We're not coming back from this. It's hard to ignore the excesses and abuses of capitalism. Miami is going to be underwater in our lifetime. New York City probably will be decimated within the next hundred years. There are island countries that are going to be destroyed within our lifetime. There are climate refugees. All of that is fueled by excess, wanting things, spending money on bullshit like fast fashion, me drinking this fucking thing out of a plastic bottle. Social media, television, films—all of it is propaganda, it's all complicit, and when we're watching TV all the time, we're not doing anything. That just felt like something I had to address as a writer.

I've always been a fan of sci-fi, and I love seeing writers of color engage with the speculative. I didn't think you could love sci-fi movies and do something with it. I've only seen that in the last few years, and it's because writers of color are doing that in their work. We can be telling our stories, and that's important, but when all is said and done, we're watching the world burn. There's no coming back from it. Poetry feels almost elegiac at this point, when writing about climate and speculative writing is the most aligned both traditionally and rhetorically for those investigations.

JAVIER: What are the milestones of Latinx literature so far in the twenty-first century, and which directions do you see Latinx literature taking as we continue into this century?

CARMEN: Visual poetry comes to mind, the culture and lineage of visual art—Juan Felipe being an OG, and other folks like him making art in tandem with poetry. Now the visual can live inside of a poetry book and draw from traditions which on the surface have been super white avant-garde traditions. Noemi had the honor of publishing Joshua Escobar's book *Bareback Nightfall*, which exemplifies what's exciting about vispo and also reifies that there's a new generation of writers who paint and collage.

Even though it's not an entirely Latinx modality, I'm excited to see the traditions of spoken word being integrated into the poetry conversation. If we identify spoken word as a movement or as an aesthetic that has lots of off-ramps, you have someone like Elizabeth Acevedo and, at the same time, someone like Edwin Torres, which underscores the flexibility and ampleness of spoken word. There's this core of a tradition, and you see all of these ways that these writers are being celebrated as performers as well as writers on the page.

MACEO: Your mother has appeared in most of your poetry collections, from *Odalisque in Pieces* and *Goodbye, Flicker* to *Be Recorder*. In a way she's this mystery, an inaccessible figure who nevertheless is a yardstick by which to measure yourself. Her inaccessibility becomes literal in *Be Recorder*, when we learn she's suffering from dementia. Seeing the passage of time in your different views of your mother made me think about the arc of the poet's creative journey, and I'm wondering how you've come to see the different stages of that journey.

CARMEN: I'm obsessed with my mother. I'm always going to be writing about her, thinking about her, because she was an enchanting mystery. She's still living, but she's not what she was. She was so full of life. She had the most beautiful singing voice and sang all the time and had these fantasies about being an artist, which probably is a foundation for the path I chose.

—January 23, 2022

15

JENNINE CAPÓ CRUCET

Born to Cuban exile parents in Miami, Jennine Capó Crucet's first story collection, *How to Leave Hialeah*, focuses largely on second-generation Cuban Americans' attempt to define themselves and create a new sense of identity and community separate from their parents' preoccupation with the past. She continued this exploration in her critically acclaimed 2015 novel *Make Your Home among Strangers*, which tells the story of Lizet, a first-generation college student trying to balance her new life at a prestigious college in the Northeast and the pressure of family and home back in Miami. Crucet's novel is one of the few coming-of-age Latinx stories that addresses the complexities and intricacies of leaving one's community and navigating white spaces and institutions without preexisting knowledge. Adopted as an all-campus read at over forty universities, in 2019 the novel was drawn into the heightened culture wars and polarization of the Trump era when her book was burned following a presentation at Georgia Southern University. Video of the book burning went viral and Crucet became the subject of intense harassment, an experience she was reluctant to talk about. We respected Crucet's wishes, but we did talk about her work's willingness to wade into controversial issues, exemplified in her book of essays, *My Time among the Whites*, which shifts the anthropological gaze away from brown and Black bodies and trains its eye on white America. Crucet also spoke to us about her forthcoming novel *Say Hello to My Little Friend*, which centers on a Pitbull impersonator named Ismael who turns himself into a *Scarface* Tony Montana impersonator and also features a whale at the Miami Seaquarium. Having become disillusioned with her life in academia, Crucet recently resigned from her tenured position at the University of Nebraska, a decision spurred by the pandemic, and spoke to us from her new home in Greensboro, North Carolina.

JAVIER: How did the pandemic impact your writing? And can you speak more generally about your writing process?

JENNINE: In my new novel, one of the perspectives that it inhabits is Lolita, the orca who's been held in captivity for over fifty years at the Miami Seaquarium. During shelter-in-place, I was hunkered down in my house, far from my family in Miami, and I started thinking, "How does that whale keep from going nuts?" The idea that she's just in this one tank and there's very little coming in or out. One way that she might keep herself entertained is watching videos of herself on her tank's screen. What must that be like? I'd already been writing to explore these questions in the book, but the pandemic made me realize that the question I should be asking wasn't, How do you keep from going insane? but, How do you manage your insanity? How do you manage that sense of feeling trapped and bring yourself back from the edge of terror or panic over and over again? That was something that the experience of being in isolation early in the pandemic helped me understand in a new way, and it also helped me realize that what Lolita is living through—having lost her family and not being near another whale for so many decades—could absolutely make you nuts. I remember when the pandemic first started and we were all being told, "Well, you're not going to be able to come close to or hug anybody for six weeks." I was like, "I'm going to die." But by month three, I was like, "No one can ever touch me again! Ha!" Being in that deep physical isolation and it feeling completely beyond my control gave me a way into imagining, as best as I could approximate, the psyche of that whale. I firmly believe that orca are much smarter than we are. Lolita has somehow invented tools and coping mechanisms that have allowed her to survive in that space—tools that we weren't able to access, that we still haven't accessed. We failed as a species in a lot of ways during that time.

My least favorite thing about writing novels is how lonely it is and how much you're in that world by yourself for so many months and years. A lot of my process is mitigating that loneliness. I'm married to a novelist now—another pandemic miracle—which is a gift from the universe. We'll write near each other, have a long writing day, and then come together at the end, knowing we'll both be in a daze and that's okay. We'll order takeout because nobody can be responsible for food and talk about the day's work and read to each other from it. I do a lot of writing by hand and write a lot very late at night. I'm in edits now for this weird novel, and during this process, I'll wake up in the morning, and the notepad I keep on my side of the bed will have writing all over it. It's a strange sensation: I'll know I wrote those words on the notepad; I'll know I woke up sometime in the night and wrote all those ideas, but I won't really have a solid memory of doing it. Then I read it and it's as if Dream Me gave Waking Me the instructions for the day's work. A lot of my process feels mystical like that. That's something I resisted in the past because it sounded a little bananas, but the pandemic taught me to accept that life is bananas. Now I'm like, "The only way the work is going to get done is if the ancestors are intervening." If it's going to be worthwhile as a project for me, it has to have that inexplicable element to it.

MACEO: Your first story collection, *How to Leave Hialeah*, details the lives of residents of Hialeah, most of them second-generation Cuban Americans. I've heard you describe your characters as neighbors and Hialeah as the ten blocks of your imagination. Can you speak more to the experience of writing about place and how Hialeah became a framework for your collection?

JENNINE: Because of climate change, most of South Florida is going to be under water in my lifetime, so there's a sense of needing to capture or preserve my idea of it in order to give the future a blueprint for what was there before and how we could've let this happen, this erasure. My first impulse back in 2006, 2007, when I was writing my first book, was homesickness. I missed being there so much, so I was writing from a place of longing, wanting to write the kinds of stories that I would read for comfort. Now there's this sense of almost anger at the city for being such a part of its own demise when it comes to climate change. Like the fact that every time I go back to Miami there are new skyscrapers being built. I'm like, "What the fuck are you doing? This can't be here." There isn't a sense that what's coming is really coming. With this next book, I'm trying to write an archive of what I've come to think of almost as an Atlantis. Bizarrely, this has allowed me to identify with the sense of the exile my parents' generation experienced for a place that they can't—or won't—return to, a place that just doesn't exist anymore. Their version of Cuba now exists only in their imaginations. The aim of honoring place is something my earlier work tried to speak to in a way that now feels somewhat disingenuous to me, because maybe the real way of honoring it would've been not preserving it through literature but literally preserving it. Literally combating the things we need to keep the city above sea level, and we didn't do those things. I don't think everyone really believes it's going to happen. I remember at Florida International University they were putting pieces of painters tape on all the walls and saying, "This is where the water is going to be in twenty-five years." How did that not change people's behaviors drastically? I don't know, maybe it did. I'm not on the ground there as much as I used to be, and I'm sure there is a crop of young builders and thinkers and artists who are trying to reimagine the city, but it's all about how we adapt it to the water. It saddens me to think that my niece, who's five right now, isn't going to be able to grow old in Miami because it won't be there. I'm not saying anything new here. If you think about our ancestors, even just our parents and grandparents, those of us who are part of an immigrant or an exile experience, they've had a version of this same feeling: home is gone and it's not something we can return to, or it'll never be the same even if we do return to it. In some ways, in retrospect, I can see the immense privilege it was to have had the sense of South Florida that I did as I wrote the first book.

JAVIER: What have been the formative moments in your journey as a writer?

JENNINE: When I was a kid I would have dreams and I would write them down, and then I would start editing them, and then I would read them out loud to my family. I remember very specifically writing down this dream—I was maybe eight or nine—about being a dolphin who was growing tomatoes under water and then starting to change the "facts" of the dream to be a better story and being really thrilled about that. I felt this excitement for something I knew that nobody else knew yet, and I couldn't wait to tell people. That's when I thought, "I wonder if I'm going to do this the rest of my life." I just felt that possibility really distinctly in that moment. Then, when I was in college, I was lucky enough to take a workshop with the writer Helena María Viramontes. Her work, her mentorship, and her teaching inspired an entire generation of Latinx writers. She was the only Latinx professor I had the entire time I was at Cornell. Working with her, she told me some hard truths about the ways that I was whitewashing my fiction. Not that I was doing it intentionally, but she could sense I was afraid to be in an all-white workshop space. I was very protective of the characters, and so they'd have sort of ambiguous names that could be read either way, but I couldn't really hide who they were because the family dynamics in the story would play out a certain way, and then my workshop colleagues would say, "Why are they all yelling at each other?" or, "Why does this get so dramatic so fast?" There was this sensibility that was different, and Helena protected me from those criticisms and pointed out that this sensibility was in fact connected to my work's strengths. She said, "You're not going to listen to this, we're going to work together, I see something in your work." It was what I really needed at that juncture in my career: someone telling me that what I had to say could be valuable.

Helena once gave the whole class a writing exercise, and it's an exercise I use as an instructor now, which was to write about a family event for which you were not present but which has risen to the level of family lore. Most people in the class went back very far, great-grandparents meeting or something like that, and I wrote about this funeral, which ended up in my first book as "El Destino Hauling." It was a funeral that everyone in my family went to, but my mother somehow intuited that there was going to be un show Cubano, and she was like, "You and your sister are not going." We were pissed because everybody was going; all our cousins were going to be there. My family's funerals back then were a twenty-four-hour affair, and there's crying and there's laughing and there's food and it just turns into a big reunion, and we didn't get to go. Every time the family would get together after that, they'd start telling the story of what happened at the funeral, laughing and all telling the story together, and I always felt so left out. So for this exercise Helena assigned us, I wrote this two-page scene, and I did it very sincerely, putting myself there in fiction as I hadn't been able to in real life. I thought it was hilarious, the way it all played out on the page. I turned it in, and the next class, Helena said, "I want Jennine to read hers." I had never even talked in the class, and I remember reading it and the class sat there stone-cold silent, just in shock with their mouths open and their eyes humongous. But Helena was cracking up, falling over her chair laughing, the only laughter in the room, and she's clapping in all the right spots. Clearly it was a highly comedic scene, and because Helena was the authority in the room, everybody thought, "Oh, I got it wrong, the professor's right and this is funny." It made me think about audience and who it is you're writing toward, and should you even think about that question because you cannot control the answer. That was a really formative moment for me as a writer because I realized, here I am, reading this scene, and *this* person is laughing hysterically, which is what I would do because in writing that scene I'd centered my own sense of the world—of grief and mourning and family, *that* experience, that gaze—and these other people, who weren't the intended audience because I'd never imagined myself reading this piece aloud in class, were horrified by the exact same scene.

MACEO: Your novel *Make Your Home among Strangers* is about the experience of being a first-generation college student. What drew you to tell this story, and what were some of the challenges in writing this novel?

JENNINE: When I went to college, the identity category of first-generation college student hadn't really gained the traction and popularity that it has now. I was very secretive about it, and when I would find out somebody else was the first in their family to go to college, I'd be like, "Are you having the same feelings I'm feeling?" It felt very underground almost. I moved to Los Angeles after finishing my graduate degree and was working at this nonprofit organization called One Voice. Part of its focus was preparing and placing first-generation college students into small liberal arts colleges around the country. Working there, I saw so many things come up again and again that I had experienced. A decade after I had finished college, people were still going through the same shit. College had taught me that a certain amount of progress was going to happen, and now I was realizing that was a lie—or at the very least, a mirage. I wanted these students to know that they weren't alone. The book is dedicated to three people—Jose, Angelica, and Amara—and they were students who I worked with at One Voice who were constantly asking me for reading recommendations. I was like, "I'm going to finish this book, I'm going to print it out, and I'm going to mail it to them as a graduation present from college." I'm thrilled that the book has found a much wider audience, but honestly, it was those three people who I cared about the most, that they would have a sense of seeing themselves reflected on the page, of being seen, of having that camaraderie.

Part of what I wanted to get at with the novel is that the feeling of being a first-generation college student never really dissipates; it never really goes away. You just start to feel comfortable moving between worlds, or you grate against it. And another big impetus for writing the book was to create a blueprint or a roadmap, though I didn't want Lizet's story to be read as *the* story of the first-generation college student experience. The danger, especially when you think about the whiteness of publishing, is that this becomes *the* story that fills that void, and that there isn't room for other writers to add to that conversation to make it a robust one. Some of the challenges in writing the book came through the publishing process, where I had editors who ultimately turned down the manuscript saying this book could be hurtful to the white women who read books because they would see themselves in the character of Jillian: they had the Latinx roommate when they were in college and didn't realize how much they'd hurt her, so some editors wanted me to tone it down. I actually got told by one white woman editor, "Look, I find the story really compelling, I want to publish it, but how do we make the New York literati care about a girl like this?" *New York literati*? Who did she mean by that? Who was she leaving out? What a euphemism.

So the process of selling that book was eye-opening, to put it mildly. The wonderful editor I eventually went with was the one person who was willing to start our conversation by saying, "Okay, so basically I'm Jillian." She wasn't afraid of the book's refusal to pander to the white gaze—she understood that that's what made it powerful, what would make it resonate so deeply with readers. One of the biggest discussions I had with that editor was that she admitted she was hoping a romantic relationship would occur between Lizet and Ethan, who's the redheaded white RA character. But it just didn't feel possible given the rest of the story, given Lizet's relationship with her boyfriend, Omar, back home. Plus, Lizet's just way too hot for him. Marketing folks had envisioned this whole hashtag "Team Omar," hashtag "Team Ethan" angle to promote the book. It's very hard to keep your book from becoming a product, and if you don't play along, then the book doesn't always get the support in-house that it needs.

What's remarkable to me about *Make Your Home among Strangers* is that my publisher did not at all anticipate the need the book was meeting. By the end of 2018, something like forty-five thousand copies of it had sold, which is huge for a debut novel, and a good percentage of that was through adoptions of common reads. Over forty different colleges and universities in the United States have adopted it for their first-year classes to read. My publisher had no idea, even as I was trying to tell them about the need I'd seen through my nonprofit work. They were like, "Oh, it's a little book." They didn't pay very much money for it, so it wasn't a priority to promote. I've heard from so many readers directly saying, "This book made me stay in college," or, "This book made me drop out of college." The book gave them what they needed to hear—validated them in some way. That's priceless to me.

MACEO: One thing your novel does is point the finger. Lizet doesn't passively accept the way things are. She's able to describe the ways that white people and white institutions are constantly corralling and patronizing and belittling marginalized communities. Do you think this is partly why it made white people feel uncomfortable?

JENNINE: Oh, I don't know. I'm not going to try to inhabit the white gaze here. It wasn't something I anticipated and it wasn't something I was writing toward. It was something I was surprised by. I really can't say why it makes white people uncomfortable other than it's pointing to some truth that they don't want to face. We have two choices when confronted with something like that: either we can learn from it and become a more compassionate person or we can fight it and dig our heels into the sense of injustice that we're perpetuating. You can sit in that discomfort and learn from it, or you can reject that discomfort and project it into rage against an object or a group of people. I've had hundreds of white readers come up to me at events and say, "I needed this book. I didn't realize I was doing this stuff to my roommate. It was so uncomfortable to read and I really needed it and I'm grateful for the experience." That's great, but I'm also so happy for your roommate. Their college experience is going to hopefully be better because you're now aware of the ways you were potentially harming them, and now you've made the choice to stop that. The novel was not marketed as an easy read or a beach read. It was accurately packaged as a serious book because it takes on serious issues. If a reader doesn't like it, they can put it down and come back to it. Maybe they aren't ready for it, and that's not the book's fault. The book is just doing its job, showing you the truth of one character's experience.

JAVIER: What literary traditions have you inherited or do you feel you're writing after?

JENNINE: Lately I'm aspiring to be on a shelf next to writers like Percival Everett. His book *Erasure* is a work of genius, and I've been thinking about his novel *The Trees* almost every day these days—the way he plays with genre and humor in order to talk about the history of lynching in the United States. That book is brilliant. I feel the same way about Zadie Smith and the way she works across different literary genres and takes such big risks on the page. Toni Morrison is also a huge influence. One of the reasons I went to Cornell was because she studied writing there. *Beloved* is such an important text to me. Zora Neale Hurston's *Their Eyes Were Watching God* is another. When I read these authors I think, "How do I write something that this writer would appreciate?" Octavia Butler's work, too. She's a prophet. My new book has more fantastical elements, and I think I'm moving in the direction of the "marvelous real" in my work, which is something I resisted for a long time because I didn't want to feel pigeonholed as a Latinx writer, so I decided I was going to be hyperrealist. I wasn't going to move into magical realism because I saw it as an excuse for writing bad plot that white editors let you get away with, but I've hopefully gotten a little more sophisticated in my thinking and no longer feel that way.

I recognize when I look at this pantheon of writers I've mentioned that there are no Latin American or Latinx writers. You asked about literary traditions, and sometimes I don't know how I became a writer because I didn't grow up reading a lot. We had some books in the house, but my mom was not a reader. We were a TV family. I started reading more seriously at the end of high school, mostly Black and African American writers like Hurston and Morrison, and then in college I was like, "Oh damn, I haven't read enough to be here. I need to read all the things." I didn't read any Cuban or Latinx writers until college, when Helena Viramontes introduced me to their work, but then in grad school those names and backgrounds disappeared again.

If there are any traditions I've inherited, I'd say it's not being afraid of or struggling with plot. I've never shied away from action, and I've never understood why plot seemed like a dirty word to many of the "literary" writers I've known and worked with. But probably I got that fearlessness from television more than anything else. Television, and my abuela's natural storytelling abilities.

JAVIER: Do you sense any affinity with other Cuban American writers? Maybe it wasn't what you read as you were becoming a writer, but now do you keep up with other Cuban American writers?

JENNINE: I'm in this weird in-between place where a lot of those stories, a lot of those books felt like a way for me to understand my parents and what they had been through, except that when I would try to share these books with my parents, they were like "¿Qué es esta mierda?" They just didn't see themselves reflected in it, even though they *are* reflected in it. Their approach was like, "Why does anybody want to read about this stuff?"

Achy Obejas's work has always been very important to me. The bizarre structure of her book *Memory Mambo* showed me, "You know what? I can do whatever I want because Achy is doing whatever she wants." It's funny, my husband is Cuban American and he's super well read and a Reinaldo Arenas fanboy. When we first got together, he was shocked at how little of Arenas's work I'd read, and my excuse, or my defense, was: "Oh, I'm a Miami-born Cuban. Arenas is a Cuban-Cuban." Which is no excuse at all, of course, but it ties into part of what I appreciate about Achy's work: she writes about Cubans in Chicago, Cubans back on the island, queer Cubans, Cubans conflicted in their sense of Cubanness—she makes so much room in her work for all sorts of connections to Cubanidad. And by doing that, her work helped me understand the limits built in to my idea of Cubanidad, of how those concepts were being hemmed in by Miami-Dade County.

MACEO: Your work seems to resist the expectation that your stories should delve into your parents' homeland and entertain the Cuban imaginary. Can you speak to this decision to focus on the present as opposed to reaching back in time to tell other people's stories?

JENNINE: I just find the ramifications of exile on more recent generations more fascinating to me, and it's something I know more intimately. I can write fiction from that space much more convincingly than if I were trying to reach back or reach over into that other experience. I have access to it. I feel I'm allowed to do that. What I feel that I can do well is my particular sensibilities as they pertain to Hialeah and Miami-Dade County, but also moving outside of that space, too. I started to do that with *Make Your Home among Strangers*. Half that book is set in Upstate New York and is trying to render that landscape just as much. I don't think you have to live through something to be able to write about it, but it's almost as though I've heard those stories you're talking about, those stories about Cuba, so many times that they felt well told already. I'm talking about within my own family. What nobody seemed interested in was the impact of being told about things that have happened that you didn't get to experience or see. I felt like my job was not to put those stories down but to say, "Well, here's the next chapter." Here's how a story like that finds its way generationally into what comes next. I was really interested in the *legacy* of those stories more so than the stories themselves. It's admittedly a very American project. It's an accident of history that my family came here and not Spain, or Canada, or Mexico. That's the accident that I find worth exploring. What does this very particular brand of American experience look like in a place like Miami? Trafficking in nostalgia doesn't appeal to me as subject matter because I would just be rehashing what I've already read and heard rather than trying to push past the cultural imagination of what exile literature is allowed to look like. An agent once told me, "I can sell things if they look like this," meaning, the recognizable tropes of Cuban exile literature, "but I don't know if I can sell this stuff," meaning, what I was actually writing. Well, that's the stuff I need to be writing. I know the ways in which I'm expected to perform, but it's just not real—it's incomplete. I've gone into interviews in the past being like, "I wanted to honor my grandparents and the sacrifices they've made, and that's why I wrote these stories." I look back at that now and I'm like, "Yeah, it was great being twenty-six. That's no longer the whole answer."

JAVIER: You and your work were very much drawn into the political polarization of the Trump era. How is your collection of essays, *My Time among the Whites*, a result of this period?

JENNINE: I never intended to write a book of essays, but a publisher came to me based on my work in the *New York Times*. It was initially supposed to be a book about higher education and the first-generation college student experience, pitched almost as a nonfiction companion book to my first novel. It very quickly turned into a book about whiteness, and race, and ethnicity as it's tied into race. I wanted to provide a tool for people to have difficult discussions around these topics. I believe that things change for the better with individual conversations, but this was a way I could spread the conversation more widely. There's an essay in the book about encountering a bigoted rancher in Nebraska and the things he starts talking about. Most of my friends are in California, New York, and Miami. A lot of these essays were put together before Trump was elected, and I would hear those friend say to me, "Oh, he's never going to get elected, it's never going to happen." I was like, "You are in a bubble. It's a big bubble, but it's still not a complete reality. You're not hearing people who are different from you. You're not in volatile enough spaces." I was living in Nebraska at the time, and I felt it was almost my duty to report what was happening, to share the kind of crazy-ass conversations I was hearing in these spaces.

MACEO: There's this expectation of writers of color that the gaze is going to be on themselves and their community, but your essays largely focus on your observations about whiteness. Why was it important for you to shift the anthropological gaze, and what were the risks inherent in that?

JENNINE: I was really intrigued by a lot of the pushback to the title that I got from my publisher. If you go to Amazon and type in "my time among," it starts filling up with, "my time among the African peoples of Zimbabwe." "The Sioux tribes." There's this long literary history of white folks parachuting into a community, observing it, and then reporting back to their people what they observed. I wanted to turn that on its head. What if we heard from people embedded in these communities, these predominantly white spaces, making observations and bringing them back? I think I initially did that with a sense of humor. A sense of pointing out how ridiculous that looks. It's like, yes, if you can admit that it's ridiculous, then it's ridiculous for all these other books that have come before. Hearing white people say, "It's racist to have a title like this. It's racist to have this approach in these essays," but that's impossible, because the lens is being put on the dominant culture. It's examining the power, it's not exploiting someone with less power. The distinction is in which community you're looking at, and how much power that community yields in relation to other communities. The risk is that white people don't trust you. I often get talked about like, "Oh, she's so fierce in her work." I don't know that I agree with that assessment. I think I approach a lot of these things with humor—not that humor can't be fierce. But the idea of "Oh, she tells the truth. Oh, she's fierce"—or the word "sass" has been used—those are all really loaded terms when you are describing a Latinx woman. If I were a white writer doing these things, critics would talk about my work in a very different way.

JAVIER: What are the milestones of Latinx literature so far in the twenty-first century, and which directions do you see Latinx literature taking as we continue into this century?

JENNINE: I sense there's a difference now. There's an energy, there's a momentum in Latinx literature in this century so far that feels like we're right on the precipice of really breaking something open in a permanently transformative way. I don't know what it is. All I know is that I'm here for it, that I want to continue being part of it, of whatever's coming. There's this feeling of needing to be prepared, even in a physical way—like lifting weights, drinking water, getting stronger in every way.

I might be sticking my foot in my mouth for Future Me, but what I would like to see is more divestment from institutions, industries, and structures that were designed with our exclusion at their core. I would like to be able to say, "I'm just not going to participate, I'm going to be over here doing something else entirely." I don't know what that "something else" is, though resigning from my tenured position at University of Nebraska felt like the first step of that. But it's easy for me to say "divestment" when I have an MFA from a well-regarded program and I held on to that professor job for long enough to write my way out of it. It's easy for me to say "divest" after I've already used and consumed all those systems—and still do, with my latest book contract—to get me to a place where now I can divest in some more significant ways. It's now my responsibility to use that privilege to create opportunities for other people to divest sooner.

I would like to see our work creating more opportunities. I'd like to see the "Highlander" mentality continue to fall away—this idea that there can only be one—and not just lip service of it falling away but it really falling away, and that's not going to happen if we keep trying to work within these structures because they're designed for that. What's fucked up is that, especially through graduate writing programs, we are taught to value systems that were built to exclude us. The dominant publishing industry is designed to take as little risk as possible, but we can't afford to do that in our work. If you just have books that are rehashing a white idea of what our lived experience is and not representing it in its vastness and complexity, we're going to be having the same conversation in twenty years. They have their box, they check it off, they move on—and there's decent money to be made if you're okay being in that box, if you can trick yourself into being okay with that, if you can trick yourself into thinking you aren't even doing that rehashing in the first place. But I want to see us do more than just step into the shoes of the systems that have been oppressing us, because in its place we've invented something new. I don't know what these alternative structures look like, but I want to imagine them really ambitiously. I talk with my husband about this all the time. Do we found our own press and do work in translation, publish Cuban writers in the United States, and hope it's financially viable? Is *that* what it looks like? Is that ambitious and inventive enough? Is it big enough? I would like to see the need for the idea of Latinx literature to almost evaporate, if that makes sense, because *all* of it becomes ours. Is world domination really my answer? I think I mean creating justice, or maybe I mean continuing to create community—*that* being the goal.

And at the same time I hope that any Latinx writer working today is doing whatever the fuck they want on the page—whatever they want, and that we do no harm in that fuckery. That nobody feels some subconscious pressure to purport to be writing to represent anything, or to speak for anyone, because we no longer have to. In the future of Latinx literature, anybody who wants to speak for themselves can, and they find readers and an audience. That's what I would want. That would be beautiful.

—June 13, 2022

16

EDUARDO C. CORRAL

Born in 1973 in Casa Grande, Arizona, Eduardo C. Corral is the son of Mexican immigrant parents. He received his undergraduate degree from Arizona State University, where he first encountered poetry in a Chicano Studies course. He went on to receive his MFA from the Iowa Writers' Workshop, an experience, he once described, that nearly broke him. He returned home, working at a Head Start and Home Depot, and slowly rediscovered his love of poetry and found a supportive community, much of it online through his influential literary blog, *Lorcaloca*. He went on to become the first Latinx recipient of the Yale Younger Poets Prize for his 2012 collection, *Slow Lightning*. Corral embraces a plurality of modes, as he describes it: lyrical fragments, narrative, sonnet sequences, and persona poems and influences from corridos, visual art, and popular music. This plurality is most evident in his use of multiple languages, employing both Spanish and English as well as code-switching. In his work, he acknowledges the influence of early Chicano poets such as José Montoya and Lorna Dee Cervantes but also poets such as Bei Dao, C. D. Wright, and Robert Hayden. As Corral shares in our conversation, his first obligation is to language and process: "dwelling with language," as he calls it, and patience with his process, which is often painstaking and slow. But Corral's poems are far from abstract, as they're rooted in the Sonoran Desert and the US-Mexico border, in grief and survival of migrant and working-class lives, and in deep explorations of masculinity and sexuality. A recipient of a Whiting Award, a fellowship from the National Endowment for the Arts, and most recently a Guggenheim Fellowship, Corral's second collection, *Guillotine*, published in 2020, was also critically acclaimed, longlisted for the 2020 National Book Award for Poetry and a finalist for the 2021 Lambda Literary Award for Gay Poetry. Corral spoke to us from Raleigh, North Carolina, where he teaches in the MFA program at North Carolina State University. Several of the poets we interviewed and many of the younger poets writing today cite Corral, both his poetry and mentorship, as being influential to their work.

JAVIER: How has the pandemic impacted your writing?

EDUARDO: The first few months of the pandemic, I was in shock. I would sit in front of my TV and just take in the news. I rarely walked. I lost the ability to enjoy reading poetry. For the first time since I discovered poetry as an undergrad at Arizona State University, I couldn't go to poetry as an escape or as entertainment or as something to enrich my daily existence. I couldn't go to it because what I encounter in poetry is interiority and others' thinking or experiences. Somebody's soul and mind. Somebody's interiority luminescent on the page. I had enough of my own damn interiority, sitting on the couch, going through the scenarios, dwelling inside of myself. It makes sense looking back that I could not go to poetry, especially the lyric, because it's a space of interiority, of indwelling.

What I did instead, because I'm a reader and I had to read something, I latched on to fiction. I loved falling into that world-building, which took me out of my own world, out of my own mind for an hour or a weekend or a few days. Just the propulsive nature of the sentence, "this happens, that happens," was very helpful in pulling me out of myself. That's one of the big differences between prose and poetry, especially the lyric. You play with time in the lyric. There can be momentum, lyrical momentum. There's often a slowing down of time, of experience. I love that. But during the pandemic, I didn't want to be there. I wanted movement. I wanted world-building.

JAVIER: Can you tell us about your writing process?

Eduardo: My writing practice is rooted in attentiveness. I move through the world with my five senses attuned, ready to pick up anything. No matter what catches any of the senses, if I mishear something, if I touch something, if it reminds me of X, Y, and Z. No matter what comes into my mind. No matter what in the world has paused and stilled me, it goes into the notebook. This hyperattentiveness is at the heart of my creative practice because I'm building up pages and pages of interesting language and sensory-rich details. That's how I build a first draft. Plucking something from the notebooks and putting it into what I call "dwelling with language." Putting pressure on it. Letting it stay with me. What else does it give me? The first part is the attention, moving through the world hyperattentive to everything.

It's also very important to be attentive to my attentiveness. I pay attention to what I'm paying attention to. For example, years ago I walked through a park and noticed the yellow throat of a bird, and immediately I thought of my abuela's stained apron. For the Eduardo working on his first book, that first leap, that first gift sufficed—the yellow throat of a bird and my abuela's stained apron. There's an image there, maybe a metaphor or a simile. I've made a connection. Something from the interior world and something from the exterior aligned and sparked. Louise Glück calls it the first circle of discovery. After a while, though, I actively started refusing the first gift. The first circle. The surface. I started interrogating the leap, the gift. What else is in the gift? What else is in the box? What's in orbit of that? Why did you go there? That was a very important step for me as a poet. Be attentive, and be attentive to my attentiveness—put pressure on what I observe, what's given to me, and where my mind goes. My best images, the best kind of phrasing comes to me when I put pressure on the first gift, when I unravel and unpack it.

Another thing that's very important to my practice is patience. I'm a very slow writer. The language will come. I will be bewildered by it at first. I will not understand what it's trying to lead me to. But eventually, by dwelling with it, I'll figure it out. My second book is titled *Guillotine.* I carried the word "guillotine" for months before I finally realized what it was suggesting. I didn't force it. I just carried it. I wrote it out on a piece of paper, again and again. I just coexisted with it knowing that it was going to give me something eventually. A spark. Another gift. Centering language itself as a material is also important. Painters have a canvas, oils, or acrylics; sculptors have their materials—stone, wood, etcetera. Writers have language. And with the hand of the imagination, we can shape it. We can mold it. Centering, not subject matter, not emotion, but the language itself. The very building blocks. Words. This is why I obsess over a phrase or a linguistic snippet or a word itself. I'm patient with that. I just live with the words. See how many shadows it can cast. More than one. What else is there besides the obvious shadow of this word?

MACEO: What have been the formative moments in your journey as a writer?

EDUARDO: I went to a very underfunded school system in Southern Arizona. I have a learning disability that has never been diagnosed. We didn't have the resources. When I read words, the letters leap out. I transpose letters and numbers continuously. Vowels disappear. It's just the way my mind handles language. Growing up, I would stutter continuously. Giving a presentation or talks filled me with fright. This learning disability forced me to develop strategies to navigate language, to navigate sentences. Easy things, like taking a bookmark and then using it to isolate the sentence on a page. Divorcing the sentence from the rest of the page of text was very helpful because I was overwhelmed with the rest of the words. I had to slow down the reading process and take in the words at the syllable level. Then I had to be patient with myself, because my mind would scramble the syllables, especially a very long word. I had to read it a couple of times to figure it out. My dyslexia forced me to develop reading comprehension strategies.

I became a poet by accident at Arizona State University in the late '90s. I signed up for this Chicano Lit course taught by Dr. Arturo Aldama. The first day of class, Dr. Aldama handed out the syllabus, and I saw that there was going to be a poetry workshop in the middle of the semester. I thought about dropping the course because I didn't see myself completing that poetry assignment, but when I wrote that first poem, I realized that my dyslexia had been preparing me for this moment. Dr. Aldama explained that poets play with language. They look at the words as building blocks. In a sense, I'd been doing that just for comprehension because of my dyslexia. The difference was that this time instead of gleaning meaning, I was the one who was going to create meaning as a "poet." So this thing that had been hampering and haunting me I could now use to my benefit to create something, to generate something. There was immense joy in that moment, immense joy realizing I could do this, that I'd been doing it in a different way all my life. This is why I took to poetry so easily. I couldn't stop revising and thinking through those first prompts. Dr. Aldama read my first poem and encouraged me to write more. He's the one who changed my life.

Near the end of the semester he said, "Now that you're writing poetry, you should actually be reading poetry." He gave me a list of poets: Gary Soto, Lorna Dee Cervantes, Derek Walcott, Phillip Levine, David St. John, Rita Dove. Like a good undergrad who wants to get a good grade, I checked out those books, and another moment of joy happened. I remember a line from Derek Walcott, "The wind stretches its blanket over our heads." I had a visceral reaction to that image, that line. I remember my body trembling with delight and pleasure. Then immediately after joy—the same kind of joy that came to me when I realized that all along my dyslexia had been preparing me to manipulate and work with language—audacity set in. Ambition. I said, "Well, what can I do?" I instinctively knew it was going to take me time to get to the place where I would feel comfortable calling myself a poet. I knew years and years of work were ahead of me, but again, I had patience.

MACEO: Several of your poems in *Slow Lightning* are based on visual art by Latinx artists. In your citations you include the medium of the pieces—oil on wood, mixed media, a Cibachrome print. Can you speak to this focus on materials, on the process of constructing an image, and the importance of visual art in your work?

EDUARDO: The visual appeals to me because it's not word-based, text-based. It's outside of the linguistic. When I look at a painting, I'm not stressed out as I am when I look at a paragraph or a page of text, because I don't have to navigate my learning disability to enjoy or to interact with a painting, a performance piece, or a piece of music. The anxiety isn't there. I just take it in.

Also, I was raised as a Mexican Catholic. If you've been to Mexican churches, you know how visual they are. They're sensory-rich with aromas and textures. The vestments of the priest, the splinters of the pews or the sandalwood, the holy water. The visual was all around me. I had no interest in that faith because once I realized I was queer, I was like, "What am I doing here? They're not going to like me." So I would just dwell on the visuals and sensory details around me—the colors of the walls, the textures, the aromas. In a sense, I was preparing myself for being a poet.

When I write about visual art, I make visible the materials in part to honor the process of the visual artist. They used all these materials in the process of arriving at this painting, or this collage, or this photograph, or this installation, and for me process is important. To make visible another artist's process and materials was a way to encourage myself to be comfortable with my own process and materials. Visual artists, even people who are not visual artists, know that a painting doesn't just happen. There are sketches, studies, multiple models of a sculpture before it's made into a cast. Painting a masterpiece doesn't just happen, a still life doesn't just happen. A poem doesn't just happen. No matter what Allen Ginsberg said: "First thought, best thought"—that was bullshit. His own archives show that he was revisionist. It's not about the poem as the end product, it's about the process, and it's very important to me to center that.

JAVIER: You've spoken elsewhere about how your MFA experience at the Iowa Writers' Workshop wasn't a productive environment for you. Where did you find a positive, productive, and supportive community of writers?

EDUARDO: After graduate school, I went back to Southern Arizona, Casa Grande, and lived with my parents. I started working as a Head Start teacher for a year and a half. I didn't know many writers and was isolated from any literary community. But I noticed, doing internet searches for poets and writers, that there was this thing called blogging. This is the late '90s, early 2000s, and poetry blogs were starting to take off. I decided to start one myself called *Lorcaloca*. It was a wonderful way to find community. There were all these writers scattered around the country and around the world, too. We just came together on these virtual platforms, these daily diaries. We communicated with each other, told each other about opportunities, or shared great essays. We'd have little controversies, too. Being a poetry blogger gave me access and entry to a literary community. It wasn't always wonderful—people would fight, there were jealousies—but for the most part, it felt very communal to me, and I realized I could be a participant in a literary landscape. The blog took off and a lot of writers discovered me. Even now I'll get invited to read at a university or a college and someone will say, "I first started reading you years ago on your blog." In a way, I was also helping Future Me as a published poet, because there was a lot of goodwill engendered by being a member of that community. There's a nostalgia for those days because Twitter or Facebook are different kinds of platforms. They don't allow for a deeper conversation, and there's less of a communal feel.

I also found community through the mentorship I received. My mentor is Rigoberto González. He's a mentor to many folks. That mentorship has become a friendship. That happened pretty quickly after we met at Arizona State. When I went to graduate school, he moved to New York, and we would have conversations daily. Here was somebody who was already publishing and entering spaces where very few Latinx/ Chicano writers have ever been, and also as a queer person, he was a role model for me. He was showing what might be possible if I put the work in because I saw that he continuously put the work in, not only as a writer but as a scholar, literary activist, and citizen. I was very lucky to have him as a role model, teaching me how to work as a writer, work on your craft, work on your language, but also be there for other writers. One of the best things he taught me is that when the door is open for you, it's so easy to rush into that space that's been given to you and say, "Look at me, look at me, look at me." "Do that a bit," he says, "but also go back to the door and prop it open for somebody else to enter." Not only did he tell me that, he showed me; he modeled it. I have internalized that. Whatever success and visibility I have, it is important for me to make spaces for other writers, to ensure I'm not the only one there.

JAVIER: In 2012, you were the first Latinx, the first Mexican American/Chicano to win the Yale Series of Younger Poets for *Slow Lightning*. What was the importance of that milestone to you, personally, but also for other Latinx poets?

EDUARDO: Simultaneously I was proud and then wounded by the very fact. It's the blade of being a visible writer of color. When you are the first to enter a space or one of a few in a space or a table of contents or a list of award recipients of an organization, your pride is tempered by your singular presence there. For me, it has never been, "I must be really good, better than everybody else in my field and my community." No, I start questioning, "Is my work so accessible and easy even the gringos are going to throw roses at my feet?" It really starts messing with your mind. The trick for me is to not internalize the good or the bad or the in-between when it comes to things outside the page. I have a ritual that I do every time something good or bad or not-so-good happens to me career-wise so that I don't internalize it. I allow myself to celebrate the good stuff. I allow myself to mope, to be sad about things not happening for me. The nos. Whatever it is, I feel it, I navigate those feelings, and I tape a blank piece of paper to my front door, because a blank page signifies what's important for me: the next poem, better music, more interesting imagery, a new approach. New possibilities for me as a writer. That's what matters to me at the end of the day.

That said, year after year, I sense and see the influence of *Slow Lightning* among Latinx poets and writers of color. They were given permission to center their experience, to make their experiences universal, just as whiteness has been centered by default. They were given permission to use their native languages, their home languages and grammars and music, and make the reader lean closer to their language, their memories, their histories, instead of explaining things with a footnote or a bit of italicized language or a glossary. I do sense that the book has a legacy, but these kinds of legacies are very cyclical. There will soon be another poet, another book that does something that surpasses and complicates what I put out there, and that next book will be for the next generation, something to emulate and to push against. I wrote *Slow Lightning* as a young Chicano poet—we now say Latinx, but I still think of myself as a Chicano poet, and I think of *Slow Lightning* as a Chicano text—and I did one thing very consciously when I was working on my first book. I absorbed every book I could get by a Mexican American, Cuban American, Boricua, Central American—all that branch of American poetry: the Latinx branch. I took it all in, but I was not passively taking in. I was doing two things as I was reading and taking in all that Latinx poetry. I was simultaneously absorbing and jettisoning, taking in what was important to me, what resonated with me as a poet in the twenty-first century—I love that approach, I love that use of language—and jettisoning what was not going to work for me in the twenty-first century. Italicizing Spanish, goodbye. Made sense in the '60s or '70s, even in the early '80s, but we don't need that nowadays. Jettisoning internalized homophobia, misogyny, racism, sometimes the national-centric tone and fever of some of these earlier books. I want to be influenced by Octavio Paz, Lorna Dee Cervantes, Bei Dao, and C. D. Wright—all of it is up for play as a poet from the borderlands. I'm going to treat the whole world as a borderland, where things are mixing, veering off—a gorgeous nexus. It's important to absorb the literature that's meaningful to you, but you can't just take in; you have to actively jettison what's not going to work for you now. Otherwise, you're doomed to repeat what people did before. Lorna Dee Cervantes wrote *Emplumada* in the early '80s. I can be informed and shaped by it, but why do I have to rewrite it?

I remember people would say, "Oh, I don't want to be a Chicano poet, a Latino poet, African American poet, Asian American poet. I'm just a poet." That's fine, you call yourself whatever you want to call yourself. More power to you. But your work is legible to others often through those different kinds of lenses that you're trying to ignore. Personally I thought, "I *want* to be a Chicano poet." I respect those books and a lot of those writers. Maybe they weren't equating Chicanx poetry to the best of us, but for me Chicano poetry meant early Gary Soto, Sandra Cisneros, Lorna Dee Cervantes, Luis Omar Salinas. I was seeing myself at the table where the good writers were. I'm proud to be a Chicano poet, to pull from this branch of American literature, because I see what's possible.

MACEO: You've emphasized the importance of language and process, but I also read in your work the thrill and enjoyment of storytelling. What was it about inventing and imagining other characters, other personas and voices that opened up your poetry?

EDUARDO: It was an easy shift for me to move from the lyric "I" to persona, to imagine and to voice experiences outside my own. I'm obsessed with language, but I'm also a poet who distrusts language. I think it's very important to have this very human, intimate bond with language. Some days you're enthralled, it's full of pleasure, and some days you're mistrustful of it, even wounded and hurt by it. I am the son of Mexican immigrants, and growing up in my little hometown in Southern Arizona, I would hear horrible things about Mexican immigrants said in the grocery store, in the park, at school, even by my teachers. I would go home and look at my parents and say, "My parents aren't that." When I realized I was queer, all the things internalized by queer people, my orientation, I said to myself, "I'm not those things." Because of the way language *othered* people, my parents, the way language othered myself to myself, I was always suspicious of it. I knew it had its own agendas and could be used for people's agendas. Language is malleable and I, as a poet, can shape it with my imagination, but language also *others.* When I apply that mistrust and love of language with the notion that I could see other shadows of myself, I could see other people having other kinds of lives, it was easy for me to work with persona, to slip into other voices. If language others, especially for POC people, queer individuals, why can't I, as a writer, occupy that otherness in the shape of persona or character?

A lot of the poems in the first book and even the second book feel like autobiography. They're often very fictive. Like "In Colorado My Father Scoured and Stacked Dishes"—my father has never been to Colorado. He's never worked as a dishwasher in Colorado. In the poem "Watermark" in *Slow Lightning*, the speaker's mother gives him a pack of cigarettes on his thirteenth birthday. A lot of people say, "Wow, that must have been very rough for you," but that never happened. What's true about those poems is the emotional resonance. That's what matters to me, not the details. When I was working on *Slow Lightning*, I would ask myself, "What makes you excited about your own work?" I was code-switching, putting English and Spanish side by side on an equal footing, no glossary, no italicizing. My modes would shift. Sometimes a lyrical fragment poem, something more narrative like a sonnet sequence, a persona poem, a long riff on "El Louie" for the Monchi poems, poems about AIDS, poems about the border, the father, the mother. A plural of approaches, a plural of modes, a plural of linguistic choices, a plural of aesthetics. The word "plural" stuck with me, like "the self." The self is plural. I am many things at once, simultaneously. That's what my poems are enacting. In the first poem, "Our Completion," the ekphrastic poem, I bring in Emily Dickinson, Prince's song "Little Red Corvette," Mesoamerican rain gods, and code-switching. These plural approaches gave me a charge. Why can't my lyrics or aesthetics have this plurality of choices, of possibilities? I wasn't centering "a self," I was centering "selves," a plurality of a self, who I was, and who I am.

JAVIER: Do you view yourself and your work as political?

EDUARDO: The very fact of my body, my queerness, my brownness, my fatness, my dyslexia, my working-class background, son of Mexican immigrants, the mere fact of my existence, of my body, is political. I inhabit a political body. I have to acknowledge, of course, economic stability and safety nets; also, whiteness. I'm a very pale Mexican American compared to some of my brothers and sisters, so there's colorism privilege, too. But I occupy and navigate the world in a politicized body. My very name makes my work political. Our names attached to our work, our author photo and biographies, immediately conjure up certain genre content expectations. There's no way around it. People have these expectations. The question then is to make visible what people expect from you, and how to upend those expectations. I'm from Southern Arizona. I'm Mexican American, son of immigrants. "He's probably writing about the border." Yeah, because I have to. It's something very important. I can't not write about it, but I'm going to include Spanish in a way that might throw you off, might piss you off. Yes, I leaned into that expectation because I had to, but I also upended it by my linguistic choices.

The aesthetic, the mode, the subject matter all have an agenda or specific narrative, and that's just a fact of who I am, what I look like, what my last name is, and where I come from and who my parents are. It doesn't bother me. I don't care because once the poem is out of my hands, the way it's read or misread, I have no shape over that, no control. I wouldn't want to. It's never been a point of stress or anxiety. The poet Jericho Brown has this wonderful way of thinking about it. "Queer, Black poet are often before my name," he says. "People see those as constrictions, ways of limiting what I can see or write. But I see those as ways to enlarge what's possible for me." Different ways of seeing. Whatever kind of modifier you put in front of my name, Eduardo C. Corral, they're not limitations or constrictions; they're ways for me to magnify, to enlarge, to complicate the way I see the world. I do that in my lyrics, the plurality of influences, of modes, of approaches, typographical play. I give myself permission to navigate and experiment and pull in whatever I need at the moment as a writer.

MACEO: Is there ever a tension between your focus on language and the politicized subject?

EDUARDO: Yes. This is where my practice of centering language, privileging the material itself, often hits a barricade or obstacle, but I need to say it or I have to write about it, so I allow myself. You have to write about your abuela. Write it, submit a draft of it, and keep it in your files on your desktop. Return to it eventually and figure out what bit of this draft, which is full of intentionality, what you can salvage, what bit of language or an image you can plug into the next draft. I don't refrain from the intention or the need or desire to want to write about X, Y, and Z. I realized early on that if I didn't get it on a page somehow, it was going to ghost and misshape everything else that I was trying to write. If I have to write about something, I do it. Then I go back to it. I try to pluck something or isolate something that imagistically, linguistically, or on the level of syntax is interesting to me, then I isolate that and work on it.

That was one of the huge problems for *Guillotine*. Outside of the "Testament" sequence, *Guillotine* is a book about unrequited love, what happens to the lyric "I," a speaker, when they desire to fall in love with somebody who cannot return those feelings. How can they navigate that? It's an experience that happened to me. For two, three years, it was almost impossible for me to write one of those unrequited love poems because I kept going to the factual, the actual, and I usually don't do that—my language veers off and does its own thing. But here, because I was so broken emotionally, I kept forcing the language into this container of experience, of brokenness. Later on, I realized, okay, there are a few things you can do as a writer to help you navigate this. One, make him a composite figure; not who you remember or who you had this experience with, but make him something else. Yes, he had a beard, but maybe in your poems, he will have a beard and other traits that were not who he was. That allowed me to handle the poems in a different way. Stop making experience a constriction. Don't pour all your language into a specific memory experience because there's no space in this memory/constriction for the language to veer off, to blossom. I had to relearn the things I learned for the first book. I had to relearn those things because the experience of this unrequited love was so intense that I had to write about it. I knew that the poems I first generated were not interesting to me as a poet. There was no linguistic charge. The imagery didn't surprise me or do anything for me. But I was patient with the process. I had to rephrase the familiar to make a breakthrough.

Javier: How has Arizona, as a place and a landscape, impacted or influenced your imagination and how you write about the place?

Eduardo: Outside of my plurality, there's duality. Binaries are more than one possibility. That has been a constant presence in my life, growing up Mexican Catholic, as a young boy believing and being enthralled by the tenets of that faith and then realizing your difference is going to make you illegible or an outsider to that faith system, so you only go there because you have to. So it's not a religious experience anymore but an aesthetic experience for me. That duality for me. Realizing as a young gay man, coming of age at the height of the AIDS epidemic in the late '80s and early '90s in Southern Arizona, that sex for other people, or desire or lust, was just pleasure or procreation. But for me, it could mean death. Again, a duality. The desert itself, all the beautiful postcards of the saguaros, all the beautiful wildflowers around Acacia Peak outside of Tucson; I saw that too, but I saw what's also behind those postcards—the stories of people moving from Central America, Mexico, into the United States; the death, the violence, the sexual assaults, happening in those wildflowers, deeper in those groves of saguaro. I've always had what Ilan Stavans calls "double vision." I think most writers of color, people of color have this double vision. I could see the beauty of the desert, but I could see the chaos and the violence and the human utterances in the distance.

That said, I feel no obligation as a writer to my queer communities, to my Mexican American communities, to my family, to my generation. I feel no obligation to any of those communities, no matter if I was born into them or if I forged them on my own. My only obligation as a poet is to language—to my language. If my language veers off into this politicized landscape or the subject matter, it goes there, but I never see it as an obligation because obligation means audience. And audience for me is toxic for my writing process because when you are writing toward an audience, you're writing to be legible, understood by a certain subset of society, and that limits what's possible for the work.

You could argue that a lot of my work is very legible to people who dwell in the borderlands, Mexican Americans, Latinx people. There's more resonance, I think, for those readers. They see what I think the poem is trying to do on various levels, but I've never worked that way as a writer. I never think of audience. I find it very limiting. The paradox was that when I released those anxieties about audience or that I was too queer, not queer enough, too Latinx, not Latinx enough, was when the work became queer and Latinx, more richly and deeply, but in ways that startled and surprised me. One of the things I noticed when I was working on *Slow Lightning* and taking all these Latinx/Chicanx poems and texts was how straight the borderlands were, how heteronormative—but that's not true. Any time a window rolls down and Juanga pours out, it becomes queer, just that little detail. One of the major tasks for me as a writer—and here is where I contradict myself—is to queer border narratives, to queer the borderlands. You could say I'm working with intention, but writing processes are full of contradictions. There's an inherent tension between what I'm saying, between my ideal practice and what I want the work to do eventually. But again, I'm from the borderlands. I'm happy with the contradictions. They make sense to me. They don't stress me out.

MACEO: What are the milestones of Latinx literature so far in the twenty-first century, and which directions do you see Latinx literature taking as we continue into this century?

EDUARDO: I see the new generation questioning the older frameworks. For example, the notion of Aztlán, being mestizos, la frontera—theories beautifully articulated by Gloria Anzaldúa. Those were default thinking in my generation. We bought into them. They seemed important and necessary—our way to articulate what we've been through as a gente and where we are now. But the critique of it makes sense, the idea that mestizo and notions of Aztlán are Indigenous erasure, and I'm curious that nobody thought about it before the newer generation. There's a willingness to upend the theory or critical aesthetic, linguistic frameworks, and ways of thinking of previous generations. The new generation is doing this continuously. They view themselves as writers who've taken art, literature, movies, music from all around the globe to shape what their voices can be, yet there is still something of who they are, who their parents are, and where they come from. At the same time, there's more willingness to shed rose-colored lenses and be confrontational about the familial. This is the task of the next generation of writers, of thinkers, of artists—to ask questions that nobody asked before, to reframe things, specifically in a queer community. Why didn't we have this conversation about gender norms or the constriction of gender? Why weren't those conversations happening earlier? That's why I find it very enthralling, just being somebody who takes in the thinking and the writing of the next generation of writers and thinkers, how they reframe and pushback and veer away from what I thought was sacred and central.

—March 11, 2022

17

GABBY RIVERA

In Gabby Rivera's 2016 semi-autobiographical YA novel, *Juliet Takes a Breath*, the central character, Juliet Palante, travels from the Bronx to Portland, Oregon, for the summer to intern with Harlowe Brisbane, a white feminist writer and activist. The complex relationship that ensues reveals for Juliet, and by extension the reader, the complex divisions within feminism—specifically, the disconnect between white feminists and women of color. As disillusioning as the experience may be, it forces Juliet to discover her own definition of feminism and the kinds of supportive communities she wants to cultivate. The novel is also about the discovery of Juliet's lineages, including stories about powerful women from Puerto Rican and LGBTQ+ history that she had never learned about in school or from her family. While frustrated by all that she doesn't know and felt had been denied her, her new discoveries also push her forward to learn more and give her a greater sense of her own agency. The intertwining of knowledge and empowerment are central to Rivera's groundbreaking work on the comic series *America*, Marvel Comics' first solo series about a Latina LGBTQ+ character. The project expands Rivera's goal to increase visibility of positive and powerful queer Latinx characters. In a 2017 article, Rivera says of her role as the first Latina to write for Marvel Comics, "I've always dreamt up wild, powerful and carefree superheroes that look like me and my family: thick, brown, goofy, beautiful. And now I get to see them come to life." Rivera has worked for many years for LGBTQ+ organizations and publications and knows the important role that visibility and support can play in keeping queer youth alive and thriving. We see Rivera's guiding hand in the affirmations sprinkled throughout *America*, such as, "Scrape knees for love. Tell hard truths for love. And definitely run heart-first into the unknown for love." All of her projects, including her most recent original comic *b.b. free*, are about young people and queer people of color being empowered to transform the world in their own image. Originally from the Bronx, Rivera recently moved to California, first to Oakland and now to Sacramento, where, she told us, she hears birds chirping and which is the calmest place she's ever lived.

JAVIER: How has the pandemic impacted your writing?

GABBY: Before the pandemic, I was working with BOOM! Studios and Royal Dunlap, an incredible Black trans illustrator, on an original comic called *b.b. free* about a fifteen-year-old Boricua teenager living in the Florida swamps a hundred years in the future after a plague that ate greed and killed off 80 percent of the powers that be. By the third issue, COVID hit the States, and it knocked us out. That one comic distributor got shut down, and because of that they had to cancel the *b.b.* series as well as so many other new, original, independent comics. They just got canceled. That was one of the first ways that COVID really impacted my work. It took away this really beautiful love letter that I was working on.

b.b. wasn't Puerto Rican just because I'm Puerto Rican. It was also because of the big protests in Puerto Rico to get rid of the governor at the time, Ricardo Rosselló. He and his cronies had gotten busted with this group chat. In the middle of all the corrupt things that happened in that group chat, they were caught joking about how beautiful it would be to have a Puerto Rico without Puerto Ricans. They also made jokes about feeding the unburied dead from Hurricane Maria to the crows. They said some nasty vile stuff in that group chat. When I was thinking about an original comic for BOOM!, I was like, "Well, if I put Puerto Rican teenagers—even if they're Diasporicans from the States—in the future, then no one can ever take us from the future." I wanted to honor my grandmothers. I wanted to honor all the queer kids on the island,

and have this bouncy comic where all the people who thought like that man and his friends are gone, and we can tap into our power as healers and as vibrant people connected to the earth. This will be the offering. When *b.b.* got taken out, it really hurt. I get it. It didn't have anything to do with *b.b.* itself, it was this whole other machine, and this whole pandemic that took out so many industries and so many authors who had their first book or people doing their first movie.

Then I was just numb from the pandemic itself. In the beginning I don't even think I left my house. We were doing nothing. We were washing our groceries, not talking to people, letting the mail get delivered and then waiting a couple of hours because maybe the disease would wear off the mail. Afraid to even take a walk around the neighborhood because you're like, "Where is it? How do we spread it?" Then in California we had all these wildfires, and Oakland and San Francisco were doused in smoke and ash. We woke up one morning to no sunrise, just a red sky. It was apocalyptic. I wasn't writing anything. I was frozen. Then we're protesting George Floyd and police brutality. I'm from New York, so none of that is new. I remember Abner Louima and Amadou Diallo from back in the day. Our whole lives have been impacted by these incidents of brutality. So now we're experiencing this on a global scale with all these other environmental disasters, I'm in the emergency room with my asthma because I can't fucking breathe, the neighborhood is popping off, and people are getting shot in front of my apartment every night. I had nothing in the pandemic. The saving grace was that I was falling in love. That was the one nugget, like, "I don't know how this is all working out, but in the middle of this, I met a person right before the pandemic and we are falling in love." I couldn't write anything. I could only viscerally experience what was happening to me.

JAVIER: Your novel *Juliet Takes a Breath* is meant for young adult readers, and in important ways so are your comic series. Why have you been drawn to write for a younger audience, and why is it important to reach them?

GABBY: I'm going to be forty years old, but inside of me is all this bubbly, excitable, joyful energy. I have so much respect for grown-up fiction, but sometimes it's so serious that I find myself stuck in it. There seems to be more room for playfulness, for joy, in books for younger readers. There's also this idea of what is professional and what isn't. So when you write the way that you talk, and you talk like you're from the Bronx, or you talk like you're from Oakland, automatically people shift into, "Oh, that's for younger people." Adult writing is more like this, or adults speak this way. I was writing Juliet when I was twenty-three, twenty-four, twenty-five. I'm writing the way me and my friends talk. I'm writing the language of my neighborhood. I didn't imagine it would necessarily be for teenagers, but because Juliet is nineteen—she's almost an adult, she's just getting there, but she's not a little kid either—people are like, "Okay, young adult fiction."

At the same time, there is a vulnerability in young adult fiction where characters are allowed to not know what is right or wrong. There's still this area of, "I'm figuring this out. I'm figuring out myself." For Juliet, it's her queerness and her feminism. It's also, How does she love? How does she love herself? What does she want to do with her life? Does she have to be a good girl? These quintessential things that you're figuring out in childhood and teenagehood. Whereas in adult fiction, if somebody is too naive or makes too many wrong decisions, then they're a disaster. I'm also very close to my queer kid self. My queer teenage self. I think about her all the time and how little there was for her to see herself in, and how damaging that was. To speak personally, I'm currently seven months pregnant. I'm a masculine-presenting Latina butch. I can tell you in my teenage years, I never saw anybody like that. I didn't even know we were allowed to have families. We couldn't get married yet. I was literally the worst thing you could become if you were a Latina woman. So to be here now and have this gorgeous experience of crafting and building my own family, that's something that I want to put into everything I do, so that it can be seen by the people who need to see it. We think that because kids have access to the internet that they're fine, but these images and this representation and these true-life stories still need to be crafted and brought to them.

In *America*, issue number seven, her origin issue, one of my favorite scenes is her birth narrative, and it's her two queer moms spiritually manifesting America Chavez between them in this orb of golden light, because why not? Out of the million-and-one hetero birth narratives, here is one queer one where two women could make life just because of the powers of the universe and their love for each other. At a very core level, little kids get that stuff. Teenagers get it. They see it, and they're just like, "Okay, of course," and if you can just have that acceptance, it makes it easier for you to imagine yourself having that experience.

MACEO: I saw *Juliet Takes a Breath* as a conversation or an argument about divisions within feminism, and specifically white feminists and their disregard or obtuseness when it comes to communities of color. That's a layered, complicated discussion. When did you decide that was the ground you wanted to cover?

GABBY: Originally, *Juliet Takes a Breath* was Juliet ends up going on a party summer and just hangs out and makes out and has a blast. Then I started thinking about offerings. If this was the only book I ever got to write, was this the offering I wanted to give? I just had to sit with it, and folks like Ariel Gore, a prolific feminist writer, and Vanessa Mártir, a poet and writing teacher out of Brooklyn, they were reading my work and they were like, "If this is what you want to do, we support it, but where is your growth in this book? What are the things that you have learned about navigating this life that you want to offer to other people and that you want to let Juliet experience?" That's when you get into the grappling with white feminism and being harmed by white women who think they're doing the Lord's work as far as their feminism goes and what their white saviorism complex dictates. How do you want to let Juliet experience not just being LGBTQ but being LGBTQ with other Latinos, with Black folks, with kids of color? What are the questions that you had to figure out? That was a whole other layer and a completely new way to rewrite the book.

Even thinking about Juliet's relationship with her mom—originally her mom just stays mad at her, and they figure it out, but it's unclear, and then I had to think about my mom and her growth and how much work she did to meet me where I was at. To give that to Latina moms, to say, "Okay, you can have your feelings about this, but there's also work you get to do, and you can keep your love on the table for your kid." It was about modeling other possibilities. So many of our kids are taught by predominantly white institutions and white educators, and there's a lot of good things that you learn and then there's also ways where you have to say this isn't enough, I need to learn about my culture and I need to protect myself from your good intentions. Juliet's relationship with Harlowe was one way of exploring that.

JAVIER: In a TED Talk, you describe Puerto Rican women in the Bronx as superheroes. In your novel, Juliet is learning this well-articulated feminism that doesn't necessarily account for the strong women in her life already. Can you speak to the feminism present in that family and community?

GABBY: In *Juliet,* the book opens with a letter to Harlowe, and in that letter she goes on about her mom. She's like, "My mom has a master's degree, and she takes care of me and my brother, and she runs the whole house, but she also irons my dad's socks, so is that woman a feminist?" By the end of the book, it's like, "Hell yes, that woman is a feminist." She may not claim that particular title, but in every way that she hustles and shows up and takes care of herself and the whole freaking neighborhood, she is going above and beyond, and she is showing what women are capable of, what mothers and grandmothers and folks that aren't often at the head of power, what we are doing to care for our families and for our livelihoods. It was also important that her mom have a whole career outside of the home to show how much women in our neighborhoods are doing.

When you talk about allyship in LGBTQ communities, there's this whole language and performance of what being an ally should look like. Respecting pronouns, and not asking too many questions when people tell you all the different identities they hold, to just accept and to listen. There's that genteel language of allyship. Then I think about my cousins when I go use the bathroom, and they're like, "Yo, do you need me to go to the bathroom with you? I'll fuck up anybody that looks at you funny." That's allyship too, but it isn't in that same acceptable, respectable politics way. I think that's what feminism in our neighborhoods looks like. It's just showing up because it's the right fucking thing to do. You have no choice. You have to be the one that makes the breakfast, and makes sure that the bills are paid, and make sure that each of the seven kids living in the house is home at night and takes a shower, while you're also working your three jobs. Maybe you don't have time to declare yourself an official professional feminist. Sometimes, that type of energy is more trustworthy than any performative feminism or academic feminism.

JAVIER: How do you perceive your role as a writer in relation to your community, to US society, and to literature itself?

GABBY: I once took a writing class with Willie Perdomo. He did a workshop, and his big thing was writing as a conversation. When you're reading a poem, one way to honor that is to write a response to it and be in communication with it. When I think of myself as a writer, I imagine myself as part of this greater communication. I am lucky enough to have my work exist at the same time as Roxane Gay. It exists at the same time as Claribel Ortega and her *Ghost Squad*. Yesika Salgado. Even Junot Díaz. We are all offering our pieces of this story. I think of myself as somebody who is offering my little bit of magic, my curiosities, and my rage to whoever wants to take it in and listen. We are all writing and creating in communication with each other. I don't even think I would be a writer if it wasn't for Cristy Road, who wrote *Bad Habits*, or Erika Lopez's *Flaming Iguanas*. That book gave me permission to write how I speak, that I didn't have to be the next Isabel Allende, that I could just be goofy Gabby Rivera and tell my stories. There's this old cartoon from Dr. Seuss called *Horton Hears a Who*. It's about these people who live on the back of a speck of dust and nobody believes they exist. They just keep shouting, "We are here, we are here, we are here." That's what I feel like I'm doing. I'm just reminding myself and all the other queer kids, butch kids, gender-nonconforming kids and adults, elderly folks. We are here. We are here. We are here.

MACEO: In your introduction to the collected volume of *America Chavez* you write an inspiring letter to the "Dandelions of the Revolution" and you speak of the project as a chosen family. Is it accurate to say that your work seems to know that there's a reader out there who is struggling and that this comic or this book will be a lifeline?

GABBY: Yes, 100 percent. I've worked directly with LGBTQ youth. At one point, I was running a national student council for queer kids. We would come together virtually, even before the pandemic, and figure out what they needed in their schools, what supports they needed to advocate for. We did programs together. We went to DC and met with the great John Lewis, the Black congressman. In all that work, I still lost kids, kids that took their own lives because it was just too much, because no matter how much day-to-day support someone like me could give, I'm still far away in New York. They have to go to school every day. They have to be in a house where they're being abused and harassed and silenced by people who are supposed to love and care for them. Stories where twelve-year-old kids are fighting fifteen united pastors in their small community. Pastors who want to tell them, "God doesn't love you and you're not trans. We want to stomp you out. We—grown-ass men, positions of power in the community—are going to rally together to destroy you." So I know firsthand how precarious the line is between having a teenager that stays alive and a teenager that takes their life.

"Dandelions of the Revolution" comes from when I would talk to the young people, and it was a way for me to include all of their genders. It was a greeting with a lot of love and care and also purpose. They would respond so well to that language. Even in work emails, I made sure to use soft language but language with a purpose. If it's too soft, you're patronizing them, and you're not really doing anything. If it's too hard, then you're pushing them in a way that isn't making room for all their needs. Seeing how well they responded to that language and then seeing them use it in school, in their papers, with each other, and having them tell me, "This makes me feel calm. It also makes me feel respected. I can find the energy to advocate for a GSA at my school. I can find the energy to feed myself, take that nap, start fresh, dye my hair pink," whatever it is. It's a lifeline. Statistically with LGBTQ youth, it's one supportive adult in their direct life—literally, mom, dad, teacher, somebody like that, but specifically someone in the home—one supportive adult increases the life expectancy of an LGBTQ youth by 80 fucking percent. When I write that way, it is so intentional. I may not be the adult in your house, but when you're reading my stories, you're going to feel like you're part of my family, that we are part of one big chosen family.

JAVIER: You have spoken before about how we don't always have to tell only the stories of trauma, that you also have to tell the stories of joy. Could you speak more directly to how joy takes a central place in your work?

GABBY: Listen, I'm from New York, so it's not like I grew up joyfully skipping around, you know what I mean? I grew up ready for anything, keeping an eye on my belongings, ready to fight if I needed to, ready to run, stressed out. Joy is something that I experienced as I started to grapple with the world around me and all my identities, and that when we came together, there was this revolutionary joy. With all the ancestral trauma that we have experienced, there's also ancestral triumph. When we allow that to become center stage, then it's always there to protect us. That's when joy really started taking a core place in my life and my work. When I was writing *Juliet*, I don't know if I could articulate it that way, but I knew that I wanted a story where the queer Latina lives to the end, and where she's not depressed and sad and hating herself the whole time, because that's all I had. If you watch old lesbian movies like *High Art* with Ally Sheedy, Lord, man, the drug addiction, the death, the angst, the wishing you were something else. I didn't want to be mired in that anymore. Now there are so many queer stories where the kids live and they're having fun. Joy is being woven into the fabric of LGBTQ narratives, and that is just so necessary and vital. You have to know that the joy is there for you, and if you don't have it, we're going to offer you ours.

Maceo: You mentioned that you started early drafts of *Juliet Takes a Breath* in the 2000s, but it wasn't published until 2016. Can you talk about just your experience in publishing and how you ended up writing for Marvel?

Gabby: I was writing forever. I was in the writers' club in high school, and then I was an unemployed lesbian writing in my mom's basement. I was doing open mic poetry like Mike Geffner's spoken word in New York City. I was doing open mics at the Nuyorican Poets Café. I was part of the Latina Writers Group, which was early 2000s, just a bunch of Dominican, Puerto Rican, Colombian women and queer folks doing writers' workshops together in Harlem led by Alicia Anabel Santos and Vanessa Mártir. I was immersing myself in writer community, doing workshops with Ariel Gore and Inga Muscio, white queer feminist writers from the Pacific Northwest. I was also writing back when people were still blogging, when people still read what people wrote on the internet that's longer than a tweet. I was writing for this website called Autostraddle.com, an independent lesbian queer folk website—entertainment, pop culture, news, and personal essays. I was really working the "writing industry" in my communities. There was no mainstream anything. A handful of folks were published, but mostly we were self-publishing each other on our blogs and our websites. Vanessa Mártir would feature me on her open mic night along with all sorts of other folks in the community. So I always start there. The community had my back.

Ariel Gore was gathering stories for an anthology called *Portland Queer*. The year that it came out, it won a Lambda Award, and the original iteration of *Juliet* is a short story in that anthology. I was reading the story at different events, and an editor came up to me and said, "If you turn this into a book, I'll publish you." I never thought I could write a book. I just thought I would be a scrappy New York City poet the rest of my life. I think I'm undiagnosed ADHD. I have no attention span, but I was like, "Here we go. I'm going to write this book." I started working on the draft, and again, my community took me in. All the women that I have mentioned so far are reading my work, I'm watching their kids, I'm washing dishes, I'm caretaking while they're editing. We are exchanging all this mutual energy, so that I can have a published work.

A couple years later, I have a full draft, and it gets published. Indie published. I can't say too much, but basically, you should always have an agent before you sign a contract. Even after signing it, my girlfriend at the time and I did most of the editing for the book. I was purchasing my own books. There was no distribution. There was no publicity. There was no assistance. I was buying my own books and giving them to people. I was fundraising in my community so that people could buy books, get books, and help me ship them to other places. My apartment looked like a postal service. That was the hustle. I was only making a couple of cents on the dollar for every sale of *Juliet*. So it was super indie, and then it just started getting picked up.

All those people that I was in community with were writing about *Juliet*. I met Roxanne Gay a year before *Juliet* was officially published at a reading that she did in New York City. I went up to her and I was like, "I'm Gabby. I'm going to publish a book. I love your work." She said, "When you publish that book, let me know," and she gave me her email. When I published, I let her know. A couple months later she tweeted about it, five tweets, and then it was like a rocket ship. Around that time, Joanna Volpe from New Leaf Literary & Media reached out to me. When *Juliet* was just on the indie blogs and the indie list, I had a couple of agents reach out to me, but they made it seem like I had to razzle-dazzle them, and I don't do that. Don't make me feel like I have to tap dance for you. Jo Volpe was like, "How can I tap dance for you? What do you need? How can I protect you? How can I give you all the resources I have? You don't even have to sign with me," and so of course I was like, "Done." A couple years later, Nancy Mercado from Penguin Random House came around and said, "We love this book. We want to uplift it to even more folks." That's when I got republished. I got my film rights, my TV rights, I got a better deal.

After all of that, here comes Marvel. Marvel read *Juliet Takes a*

Breath while they were doing research for the *America* solo series. Again, I didn't have to tap dance for anybody. They found my work, and they came to me with offerings. I have an interesting little road to publishing. It is very nontraditional, but it has been the right road for me.

JAVIER: What literary traditions have you inherited?

GABBY: With *America Chavez* especially, I was running with that *Love and Rockets* energy from the Hernandez brothers. That madcap, zany, always on an adventure, emotional, dramatic, gritty, fun, punk kind of energy. That's what I brought with me to *America*. It doesn't follow the Marvel formula. I went bonkers. If you read the *Love and Rockets* series, you get everything from Maggie and Hopey—two punk Chicanas from the '80s falling in and out of love, being reckless—to Penny Century who's a gorgeous viejita that fights crime in outer space. You get all these luchador abuelas fighting crime in the future in retro outfits. You have comics within *Love and Rockets* that are just vignettes and don't really lead anywhere. They're just goofy, wacky moments that the Hernandez brothers threw in there.

I've mentioned Cristy Road, I mentioned Erika Lopez, I'm also thinking of the book, *Gabi, a Girl in Pieces* by Isabel Quintero. Writers that don't speak the old-school romantic language of Gabriel García Márquez and Isabel Allende. We are bringing in this rush of Spanglish and Nuyorican speak, and I'm a punk-type language. Together we are busting open what it means to write from Puerto Rican, Dominican, Cuban perspectives—the diaspora Latinos.

I also want to acknowledge how much Audre Lorde impacted my work, and her storytelling in *Sister Outsider* and in *Zami: A New Spelling of My Name*, where she's detailing her life as a lesbian in the '50s and '60s, reflecting what America looked like at that time. I want to name James Baldwin. He also has a romantic element to his writing, but he's also very much critical of the world around him and speaks with a lot of love and expectation for young Black folks. I took everything I could from those writers as far as finding myself and trusting my voice.

MACEO: What about the Nuyorican poets who emerged in the '60s and '70s? Were you aware of them as you were coming into your own as a writer?

Gabby: If you had asked me when I was like seventeen, eighteen, nineteen, twenty, I could've told you all the names of the poets who founded the Nuyorican Café. I was obsessed. I went to a predominantly white high school. In our poetry classes we were reading Sylvia Plath and Robert Frost. My teacher was writing poems about the maple tree. I'm writing poems about the subway. Then I went to the Nuyorican for the first time, and it was like my spirit just burst out of my body. That first slam, I had never heard people use language like that. This is before YouTube. This is before you could really follow an artist on a platform and see videos of their work. The only way you could experience the Nuyorican was going there. I didn't even know people could do this.

Then I looked into the legacy of it, Afro-Latinos in New York and Chicago starting this spoken word style of poetry. Much like hip-hop, it's an expression of language, and an expression of what you're experiencing in the world around you—inequality, racism, sexism, homophobia—coming out of you in this certain style. I felt inspired by all of it. I thought maybe I could have a little space here, maybe I could express myself. I'll never forget this one line. I don't even remember the poet. I've never heard anything so brilliant in my life. He was like, "I don't smoke weed, I smoke the dust of ancient pyramids rolled up in pages of the Bible." Almost twentysomething years later, I have never forgotten that, me and my little notebook writing that down. I used to know all those names, all the founders and the poets back in the day. It has been a long time since I've been part of the Nuyorican family, but the impact that it left on me is forever.

Javier: *Juliet* ends with a quote from Gloria Anzaldúa, who has been an inspiration for a whole generation of artists, scholars, queer folk, and communities of color. In recent years, there has been criticism of some of her ideas, mainly the concept of mestizaje erasing both Indigenous and Black identities and communities. Much of *Juliet* focuses on white feminist inability to handle critique. Black and brown feminists are mostly viewed in solidarity. How have you come to understand critiques within communities, even when those trailblazers helped to create the very spaces that have allowed us to thrive?

Gabby: When I grew up they called us Spanish kids. You could be Puerto Rican, you could be Dominican, but as a group it was Spanish kids. Then it was Latinos. Then it's like, "You're a Latino, but you're also a person of color." Now "a person of color" is considered racist, too, because it decenters Black folks and erases Indigenous folks. Personally, I'm always trying to keep up and understand and learn new things and just listen. Alán Pelaez López is an Afro-Mexican scholar who has written about getting rid of "Latino" or that "Latinidad is dead." I've learned a lot from reading folks like Alán or listening to Zahira "Bad Dominicana."

With Anzaldúa, here's this beloved figure who has done so much good and has offered a pathway for so many folks coming to find themselves and identify in their ethnicity, and they're hitting up against these grander critiques of folks saying, "What about anti-Blackness, and what about transphobia, and what about your people erasing this whole Indigenous culture?" When you fight against that, you're doing yourself a disservice. When you try to say that your way is still the right way and you're not listening because you also feel like you're part of an oppressed minority group, that is when we have big problems. That is when you can lose your status as a beloved person, which is a small price to pay compared to the erasure of all these other groups. There's a lot to be said about just being quiet. Not as in silent and not supportive, but just being able to say, "Yo, I don't know the answer to this. Since this is your lane and your world, you take center stage. I'll be right here supporting you."

MACEO: Does Latinx literature offer a unique perspective on the society and culture of the US in the twenty-first century?

GABBY: Latinx feels like this big generic term that has lumped us from so many different places together. I think this era of literature gets to tear away at that term and remind folks, "Hey, I'm from Colombia, I'm from Venezuela, I'm from this tribe in Mexico, I'm Puerto Rican by way of the Bronx"—whatever the grouping is, the reality is that we all come from different places. Our cultures are different, our experiences, our historical ties to the US are all so nuanced. "Here's what I've experienced. Here's my joy, here are my heroes, here are my triumphs"—that's what our work is. Maybe our predecessors had to hold on to this identity of Latino or Hispanic just to gain some ground, to gain some protection politically, to gain some power, to gain resources. We get to bust that up and force people to dig deeper.

When you write about queerness and when you write about disability, when you write about those particular identities, you're also educating your own people, and offering ways to be more accepting. You're offering reflections of what people and their families are experiencing, and so it's multilayered work. That is what contemporary Latinx writers are doing. We're bringing ourselves, our politics, the things we want to dismantle, the things that we want to love on, and we're saying, "Here, here." Because I'm not going to accept your version of me. I am showing you what this life is really like.

JAVIER: What are the milestones of Latinx literature so far in the twenty-first century, and which directions do you see Latinx literature taking as we continue into this century?

GABBY: There are a bunch of these different moments where you feel the tide changing and you're not just going to be "maid number one" on the TV show. You're not just going to have this book that nobody reads. It can be impactful. It can stand out in the mainstream. Claribel Ortega's *Ghost Squad* just hit The New York Times Best-Seller List, and that is a middle grade ghost story by an around-the-way Latina. I couldn't have even imagined that five years ago. Look at *The Poet X* by Elizabeth Acevedo, and not just one book but *Clap When You Land* was also a New York Times Best Seller. She's just killing it. There's so much forward movement, and I think it's just going to continue to get better, and more raw, too. I'm still in community with LGBTQ youth, and when I read works that folks have shared with me, their manuscripts about being queer and punk and coming up as Peruvian kids in Detroit or wherever it is, it's gritty and it's anti-capitalist. It wants to tear down the system, and it doesn't give a damn about presenting this squeaky-clean image of this *George Lopez*–style American family. It's gritty, punk, pro-immigrant, defund the police. They are creating a whole new society, and I am here for it. I'm here to be the butch tía helping when I can—usher in all the babies and let them dismantle everything in their path and make it new.

—March 22, 2022

18

ERIKA L. SÁNCHEZ

Erika L. Sánchez is the author of the best-selling novel *I Am Not Your Perfect Mexican Daughter*, a finalist for the 2017 National Book Award for Young People's Literature and now a staple in high schools across the country. Set in Chicago, the story is told by Julia, whose distinctive voice is by turns raw, honest, humorous, sarcastic, even caustic, capturing with precision a smart teenager constantly questioning and challenging the truths that everyone around her seems to have accepted. An aspiring writer, Julia pushes against her parents' confining cultural and gendered expectations all the while struggling with depression. Formerly a sex and love columnist for *Cosmopolitan for Latinas*, Sánchez's novel doesn't shy away from themes often considered taboo in Latinx households, including mental health and suicide. Born in 1984 and raised in Chicago, Sánchez is also the author of the poetry collection *Lessons on Expulsion*, which was published by Graywolf Press the same year as her novel. The collection alternates between poems about love and sensuality and poems about violence, including narco violence and violence against women on the border, weaving the intimate and personal with societal critique. Sánchez strikes this balance again in her 2022 memoir, *Crying in the Bathroom*, composed of personal essays reflecting on many of the same themes that appear in her previous work, including growing up the daughter of Mexican immigrants, dealing with depression, sex, love, and relationships, and feminism, humor, and spirituality. In the introduction to *Crying in the Bathroom*, Sánchez writes about growing up not having access to literature that spoke to her experience—but a whole new generation of Latinx students are coming of age having been exposed to *I Am Not Your Perfect Mexican Daughter* in junior high and high school. It is now being made into a film directed by America Ferrera. The pandemic brought many changes in her life. She got married and had a baby daughter, and she spoke to us from her writing space, the attic in her new home in Chicago, where she is the Sor Juana Inés de la Cruz chair at DePaul University in Chicago.

JAVIER: How has the pandemic impacted your writing? And could you speak about your writing process more generally.

ERIKA: It's given me more time. Unfortunately, it took those circumstances to be able to work on my writing for longer periods because we weren't distracted by life. Life was inside. I was able to get a lot done, but I was worried all the time and still am. Having a child really changed the way that I work, and I was trying to do everything señora style, taking care of my kid all the time and then writing, running the house, of course with my husband's help as well. But I realized I couldn't do it like that. I started putting my child in daycare and she's been thriving, having a great time. I need my writing time or else I'm going to go crazy.

My writing process is quite erratic, and I don't think it makes sense to people who are more rational minded. I make a lot of art a lot of the time. That helps me in my process. I take walks. I play music. There are days that I don't write at all. There are days that I just read. And it comes when it comes. I harness it when it does. It's nonsensical. I really just want to live a creative life and feel nurtured by art and literature. Then the writing reveals itself, and I'm up here in the attic writing like a crazy person. It's all instinctual. It is very emotional. Also intellectual, because once I have a draft, I'm meticulous about how I edit.

MACEO: Your poetry collection, *Lessons on Expulsion*, was published in 2017, the same year as your YA novel, *I Am Not Your Perfect Mexican Daughter*, and there are some thematic similarities. You now have a forthcoming memoir, *Crying in the Bathroom*. How do you draw a distinction between your different voices as a writer?

ERIKA: The truth is that I'm never going to get over a lot of things. I am the daughter of Mexican immigrants and that is my identity. That's how I grew up and that's how I see the world. I will probably always write about that fact. It manifests itself differently in the different genres. Poetry is a more spiritual experience, a catharsis. I write about trauma because I'm not over it, and I don't know that I ever will be. These are themes that people resonate with and have not often been in the mainstream. The novel was based on a lot of my own experiences, but I got to imagine different scenarios, different worlds. I wasn't subject to the literal truth. The memoir is all true and was emotionally intense to write. Similar themes again, but every writing experience is different. I assume it is for the reader as well, because the delivery is very distinct. It was somewhat liberating for me to write the truth without any of the embellishments found in poetry and with fiction. I had to be much more literal. I couldn't just be, "And then there was a beautiful flower," which I probably did, but I had to harness or pull back on that. I had to get the story across to the reader. I was trying to be as honest as I could about my life. It was the hardest book so far that I've written, but it was also probably the most cathartic. I hope that happens throughout my life, where it just keeps getting harder and better. I always think about how my voice manifests itself in the different genres and what kinds of images I use. Things are repeated but with a purpose, and it's all part of a larger work that I continue to expand upon. I try to challenge myself with every single book, to make it different from what I've done before.

JAVIER: In your memoir, you write that you've wanted to be a writer since you were twelve years old. How did you know at such an early age, and what have been formative moments in your journey as a writer?

ERIKA: My childhood was quite lonely. My parents were often working and exhausted. We lived in a pretty tough neighborhood. There wasn't a lot for me to do. I began to read, and I loved it so much because I could escape to different places. Unfortunately, the stories were mostly about white people because that's what was available to me. In the sixth grade, when I started to read poetry, in particular Edgar Allan Poe, I thought, "This is so beautiful. I want to say those types of things." I felt very connected to it because I was very lonely and he wrote about despair and solitude. At twelve years old, it's sad that was relatable to me, but it's true. Something awakened in me and I had to write. One of my teachers thought a poem that I did for the class was really good. She said, "I'm going to get this published." She didn't, but it sparked something for me, and I realized that I was good at this, because there wasn't a lot that I had going on in my life in terms of feeling valid as a person. When I started writing, I felt I could say things. I could be free. I could feel everything that I wanted to feel and no one was going to judge me. That's essentially how I came to love poetry, and ever since I've insisted upon being a poet. For a working-class Mexican girl, it doesn't make a lot of sense. I was just very tenacious. In high school I was known as a poet. I introduced myself to people as a poet. I was that girl. I wore very poetic clothing, I thought. Like thrift store clothes and black. And I was very brooding. I made it known. My teachers were great and encouraged me. One of them would let me borrow books and give me packets of poetry.

I had a featured poetry reading at fourteen. It was really cute. I was so excited. I felt so proud of myself. It is so rare for a brown girl to feel that way because we're often so invisible. We don't matter to the world. I got excited about what that life could look like. I would read books about writers and poets, and I wanted that romantic bohemian life. I just kept doing it and doing it. Then I went to college and started publishing here and there. I went to Spain and took a poetry class and wrote all sorts of poems. It was just something that I felt I had to do. I don't think most people choose to become poets, and I don't know who I'd be without it. It had to be this way. A lot of that has to do with being the first woman in my family to have a voice. I can educate myself. I can write things. This is a new experience for my family. One of my grandmothers can't read, and my mom only had a sixth-grade education. She always felt disenfranchised by not being able to express herself. I was the first girl to have that opportunity, and I just exploded. It's intense a lot of the time, because I write so much about my own life and it's scary. I feel vulnerable, but I also know that it has the power to heal a lot of people. That's what gets me through.

JAVIER: What have been your experiences in getting your works published, either negative or positive?

ERIKA: The hardest part was getting my foot in the door, having people take me seriously. That was frustrating for a while. I felt that no one understood what I was trying to do, and I had to be patient and wait for the right people to find the work or for me to find the right person to show my work to. With poetry, my editor Jeff Shotts at Graywolf was good at allowing my voice to remain the same and not pulling back from the hard subject matter or making me feel like I needed to change something about myself in order to get published. I'm grateful for that. It did take a long time to find that person, but once I did, it was a beautiful experience because he respected my voice and my vision.

The experience of publishing *I Am Not Your Perfect Mexican Daughter* was frustrating because I knew that the story was good. I knew that a lot of women, young brown women in particular, would relate to it. I knew that the voice was strong, but agents weren't interested because they felt that the voice was too vulgar and aggressive. I'm like, "Well, I guess you've never met a Julia because we exist all over the place." I got comments such as, "We love your writing, but we don't love the voice," as if the voice wasn't part of the writing. Or they'd ask, "Do you have another book to show us?" I'm like, "No, I don't. I've been working on this for five years." Eventually, after many rejections, I was put in touch with my agent. I met her at AWP and she loved what I had to say. I sent her my work and the rest is history. Still, a lot of people didn't vibe with the book. They would say, "This is too much." I've been told my whole life that I'm too much, so that was annoying. But we sold it. There was no auction, no one was clamoring for the book. One editor wanted it and she got it. She was incredible and made the book better.

By the third book, the first two books had done so well that it wasn't hard to sell. People were hungry for it, and there was an auction and it was intense and exciting, but it was because the previous book had been a bestseller and won all these awards. So it was much easier for them to accept and be excited for the memoir even though it's edgy and I write about tough things. My editor was Georgia Bodnar, a Black woman, which was such a gift. She pushed me in my thinking and made me so much better in the process. I've had an unusual experience because a lot of people complain about their editors, and I love all of mine. I want them to be my friends.

MACEO: In the introduction to your memoir, *Crying in the Bathroom*, you write about not having access to literature that spoke to who you were, a daughter of Mexican working-class immigrants. I have students in my Chicanx literature classes talk about how happy they are for their younger siblings, that they get to grow up having read your novel.

As a writer, this is rarefied air. How has the success and reach of *I Am Not Your Perfect Mexican Daughter* made you think about your future works? Does it change your approach to the page?

ERIKA: It makes me a lot more audacious to be honest, because I'm like, "Well, if they like that, then I can get away with so much more." The memoir is intense and the subject matter is not easy, but I felt emboldened by the success of *I Am Not Your Perfect Mexican Daughter*. I saw how much it meant to young women, and especially young brown women. The reach has been unbelievable. I never really conceived of it in that way, but I'm grateful for it. I think about how much influence I can have on young people, and I take it seriously. As a professor, too, I know that I can make a difference in my students' lives, good or bad, and I'm very conscious of that fact. I want to help empower young people of color to be themselves and go after what they really want to do in life regardless of what others may think, to be who they are without any apologies. The more I write, and the more success that I have, the more committed I am to my community. I always write for us. I don't ever pander to the white gaze. I'm not interested in doing that. I want to uplift other writers that are emerging and give them more of a platform. I'm always thinking about the community. It's not just me writing, and the older I get, the more that is true, because it's very healing for me. It's good for the community to expand the riches. I don't want to be in my ivory tower by myself. That's not what success looks like for me. I started a podcast with my brothers and my husband called *No Chingues*, and I want to put people on. I want other young Latinx folks, Black and brown folks to have opportunities to express themselves. The plan is to build, not necessarily an empire but, a community of people and spread the opportunities. Sometimes we live with this scarcity mentality where it's like, "I have to be the only one." I don't feel like that at all. I want a bunch of other people to join me on this journey because it has been amazing.

JAVIER: How do you perceive your role as a writer in relation to your community or communities or in relation to our society?

ERIKA: I write for brown women, and everyone else who enjoys and engages with the work is extra. My point of view is as a Mexican American daughter of immigrants, and that doesn't change because I don't change in that way. I want to write stories that feel familiar to people like me, who have never really been seen or recognized. We have such a strong tradition of literature in Latin America and we have a strong tradition here in the United States, but we haven't been given the opportunity to be as visible as we should be, especially based on our population and how long we've been here. It's incredible that there's not more in circulation. I didn't have many books to draw from. I had a few glimpses here and there. Sandra Cisneros, of course, blew my mind, and there were other authors that I read, but it was really scarce. Now that I have this opportunity, I want to create stories that make our communities feel seen and that can encourage healing as well. I think about what my work can mean to young women because I didn't have many models. I didn't know what I was doing half the time. When I was a young budding writer, I felt very alone. I want to change that. I want to create a community of people telling their own stories. I want it to be a giant tapestry.

I think about this experience I had in Texas. I was a keynote speaker at an event, and at the end I saw this señora weeping. She was wearing a cleaning uniform. She was the janitor at the school, and she had a broom or a mop, and she was crying. She came up to me and said, "Thank you so much for doing this for us." I was honored that she felt connected. She told me she was proud of me. I couldn't even comprehend the gravity of it all. She reminded me of my mom. She reminded me of my tías. I remember people who talk to me after readings and share that emotion with me. Sometimes it takes me by surprise, but it's something that I'm conscious of and that I care about a lot.

MACEO: You were a sex and love columnist for *Cosmopolitan for Latinas*, and your novel deals very directly with those themes; specifically, how they're taboo in our society and especially in Latinx households. Your novel also deals with suicide, shows the positive impact of medication and therapy, and concludes with resources for young people who are thinking about suicide. When you first started the novel, did you see it as an educational tool?

ERIKA: I didn't want to compromise the craft of the novel in any way, but I was aware of what reach I could have. I really wanted to talk about mental illness and suicide and medication and therapy, all of that, because we don't really do that much in our community. It's still very much taboo to say, "I'm depressed. I have this illness." It's not really accepted. It's like, "Well, you should just work harder and be quiet." In writing these books, in which I grapple with all of these issues, I want young people, and older people too, to understand that it's a part of being alive. Some people suffer from it because of trauma, and some people have a biological reason. There are many reasons why one can be depressed, but it shouldn't be something that should be judged. I write about it so openly because I don't feel ashamed of it in any way. I write a great deal about it in the memoir. I also write about sex very openly. We've never been given that permission as a culture for women to talk openly about sex and to be independent and have agency. A lot of women are craving that, and they don't know how to go about it, and that was me. I was so confused. I was like, "I'm a feminist. I want to be free, but I feel bad because my mom made me feel like I shouldn't have sex because it's dirty." All these layers of trauma, and I just want to peel that back and say, "It's okay to be a sexual person. It's okay to have a mental illness. It's okay to struggle. You're not a bad person. There are ways to cope with these things." I almost lost my life to my mental illness, and I don't want that to be pointless. I don't want that to just have happened. I want it to mean something.

MACEO: What literary traditions have you inherited?

ERIKA: I am very indebted to the Chicanx literature that came before me. I teach it. I celebrate it. I'm also very much influenced by African American literature. One of my greatest influences is Toni Morrison. I've learned so much from Black writers in the United States. James Baldwin is someone I think about all the time that I teach and refer to. Most recently, Jesmyn Ward. She is one of the most incredible writers of all time, and I'm inspired by her work. I love the book *Americanah* by Chimamanda Ngozi Adichie. I have so many books and artworks that have impacted me that it's really hard to encapsulate. It's pretty vast, and I love that I can draw from so many different communities and be in conversation with them, and that I can read about people who are so different all over the world and feel a deep connection. So it's hard to say. I'm all over the place. I love it all.

JAVIER: The city of Chicago is very present in your work. We get place names and streets. We travel through the city on the trains and buses. Can you speak to your own relationship to the city and the way that it figures into your work?

Erika: I love Chicago. There are times that I hate it, and I'm appalled by the leadership and all of the corruption. That aside, I love the people. I love the community, or communities, plural. I love the art available here. For Julia and for me as a young girl, going to the Art Institute was pivotal. I was so starved for art all the time that to be able to enter this place filled with gorgeous art pieces from everywhere, from different time periods, really affected my thinking. The Art Institute is important in the novel, and it's going to be in the movie as well. I am hoping that I can show a lot of brown kids that it's cool to go to the museum, because I know the kids that I grew up with were like, "What? Why would you do that?" Chicago is a city that has shaped me. I've gone through terrible times here. I've gone through amazing times here. I have all of these mixed emotions for the place.

There's a lot of stuff that I don't care for. The segregation and the violence. There's a lot of disenfranchisement. Some communities are just completely ignored, and I see that when I drive to my parents' house. I don't forget where I come from. Even if I feel comfortable and successful, I know what it can be for a lot of people. I'm often angered by the decisions that are made. There are these speed cameras, for instance, that have given out more tickets than there are people in Chicago. That sort of thing gets me worked up because I know that for working-class people, paying off such a huge sum can be devastating. There are so many different ways that we are disenfranchised in this city, but I try to think of all the good parts, too. I feel very embraced by this city, so I try to show it love through my writing. I want to make the city proud.

Javier: Do you perceive yourself and your work as political?

Erika: I think everything's political. Even when someone chooses not to write about things that affect other members of society, I think that's political, because they're making the choice to be myopic in their worldview. I don't love the label "political" because I don't know that it says much of anything. Of course, I write about things that affect people. I'd like to see something that's not political to understand what that means. White writers have the luxury of just writing whatever they want and no one really asks them to categorize it in that way. I think their writing, if not addressing real societal problems, is political because they've chosen not to do it. They've chosen not to see people outside of themselves.

MACEO: Your memoir is composed of essays that jump across time, focusing on a wide range of subjects such as humor, depression, and spirituality, traveling in Spain, and ideas about colorism and beauty. How did you go about conceiving your memoir, and what appealed to you about this essayistic form?

ERIKA: I started writing essays because someone asked me to write one about ambition, and it turned into "Crying in the Bathroom." When I wrote the essay, something shifted for me, and I realized, "Oh, this is what I have to do." I'm the kind of person who likes to weave in many different facets of life and art, and so writing a book of essays felt very natural and exciting—that I could focus on certain topics and also write about my own experiences but bring in all these other influences. It was fun to put it together. It ended up being called a memoir because it does have a narrative arc. It's not like a traditional memoir necessarily, but it does tell a story. I feel very comfortable with it now because it's a story about my life told in essays. It's something that just came to be because someone suggested it, and that was it, and I just couldn't stop writing essays after that.

MACEO: Your poetry collection alternates between poems about love and sensuality, poems that feel intimate and personal, and then poems about violence—narco violence, violence against women on the border. There's intimacy in these poems as well, but they're also, in some cases, prefaced by headlines. How were you thinking about this juxtaposition?

ERIKA: Eduardo Corral has been a big influence. I've known him for a long time now, and speaking with him over the years, I learned how exciting it could be to juxtapose poems that are very different from one another, that speak to each other but also almost repel each other. I like that notion of organizing my poems in that way because I thought it added an element of surprise and intention; even though they're different, they're related in many ways. I wanted readers to make those connections and to allow their minds to conclude whatever it is that they want to conclude about why they're together. To me, life is that way. It's a lot of beautiful moments and a lot of pleasure, a lot of trauma and violence. I wrote a lot about the violence against women because I think about it a lot, and I think about it as a brown woman and how lucky I am to not have to endure that sort of thing. I have this voice, this platform that could ultimately show the world what is happening. That's part of my responsibility as a writer. I care about the way that women are being exploited and hurt, and that shows up in the work. I'm very much a feminist, and I think that's clear throughout my work.

MACEO: In your memoir, you push back on Virginia Woolf's view that a writer needs to have distance in order to write, and that in fact, you feel rage and you want to write from that position. Can you speak to that place of rage as a source of your creativity?

ERIKA: When I was younger, I was just so angry, but I didn't really understand why. I didn't have the language. I didn't have the concepts. I didn't truly know how to put it all together because I was just so blinded by it. As I've gotten older, I've started to realize what it is that enrages me, and I feel a need to harness that energy in my work because there are so many women in the world that are suffering greatly in many different ways and that makes me mad. I just don't understand how in a supposedly civilized society, we still have these horrible acts of violence against women and against people of color. I'm still mad now, perhaps I'm even more angry, but now I know how to channel that anger. I know that I can use that to write. I can make a podcast. There's a movie now. There's a possible TV series based on the memoir. I can use all of this. I can give it meaning, and I can feel somewhat healed by it because I'm not letting it consume me. When I was younger, I just didn't have the capacity or the agency to really do something productive with it. I was just extremely pissed about how women were treated, especially brown women. I was extremely pissed about racism and inequality. That hasn't changed, but now I have more knowledge and more resources.

JAVIER: In your memoir, in the essay "Down to Clown," you mention comedians like George Carlin and others who are examples of how to turn rage into comedy, how comedy isn't just about making people laugh. There's speaking truth to power in comedy. You say that one of the uses of comedy for you is to make white people uncomfortable in their privilege. George Carlin has also said that comedy should never punch down. That it should always critique those who are above us, those who are in power. How do you use comedy or humor in that way? And how do we make sure to not punch down?

ERIKA: My anger is usually directed toward white supremacy and patriarchy, so I feel that because of that lens, I probably won't punch down, and if I do, hopefully someone tells me and I'm not canceled. I try my best to always break down what I think is oppressive, and for me, that is racism. I'm going to make fun of racists because they're absurd. I'm going to make fun of white supremacists because they're irrational. Race is stupid because it's made up. It's very frustrating to break it down. What is racism? I am better than you because your skin is darker. It's insane to me. I will make fun of people who believe in these things. I will make fun of men who are patriarchal and who hurt women. I feel that it's my right. It's the very least that I can get away with in this oppressive society. I hope to never hurt people who are more disenfranchised than me. I think it's fair game when it comes to white supremacy, oppression in any form. I'm going to tackle it because it's stupid, and I'm tired of it, and I'm going to laugh about it as well because it's that irrational.

JAVIER: That same essay opens up with a description of your laugh as a cackle. I like the description of a Mexican grito. Humor is intellectual, but then laughter is very bodily, and that's what you're describing. You say that you upset white people with your laughter. Not even with the jokes. It's just the laughing itself that takes up space. Can this be a form of resistance?

ERIKA: I've often noticed that I make white people uncomfortable just with my way of being. My laughter is something that I cannot suppress. It's just who I am. That's how I sound. I've been in so many spaces where they're upset that I'm laughing so loudly. I find it sad for them that they are essentially criticizing me for joy or that they don't have the same capacity for joy that I do. I wonder why they're so out of touch with their own bodies that expression frightens them. I find that a sad way of living. My work is going to be upsetting to them because I don't shy away from things that are uncomfortable. I'm going to call out what I see as nonsensical. It makes me laugh even more that they don't like my laugh. I'm okay with that. I will take up space. I refuse to make myself small in order to appease them. I know a lot of people of color feel similarly. It's like, "What can I do? Either I'm myself or I'm not." I can't shut myself down just because they feel a certain way. I want to show women, especially young brown women, that it's okay to be who you are, to be boisterous, to take up space, to love yourself, to be bold, etcetera. It's all right. We're allowed.

JAVIER: What are the milestones of Latinx literature so far in the twenty-first century, and which directions do you see Latinx literature taking as we continue into this century?

ERIKA: We have so many important books that have changed literature and have become part of the canon. A lot is also forgotten, which is frustrating, or not taught in schools. I just taught *The Rain God* by Arturo Islas, and it's a great book, but when do people teach it? Why is it so obscure? I hope that as we progress that Latinx literature will be given more of a place in the canon, at the table, whatever metaphor you would like. I don't think that we need to beg white people to let us in. We just need to do our work and do it really well, and the audience will find us.

We've had some really important figures in our community, such as Juan Felipe Herrera. He has been so incredible in spreading this love of literature. Rigoberto González has been a mentor to me for many years and has provided so many different opportunities for other people of color. He's a beacon in our community. Sandra Cisneros similarly has paved many roads for us. I hope to bring other people on board and try to help writers who are emerging because I know how difficult it can be. I'm very hopeful. They teach my novel a lot in Chicago, which is nice, but it's not enough. We need to read more than that, and young people deserve it because they need to see themselves, and other kids need to see others who are different from them.

MACEO: *I Am Not Your Perfect Mexican Daughter* is being turned into a movie. It's going to depict a young Latina in Chicago. Can you speak to your own sensitivities or reservations when it comes to how you imagine the project and what you want it to be?

ERIKA: It's important to me that the portrayals are very authentic, that they feel real, that they feel recognizable to everyone who lives here. I've worked with America Ferrera and Linda Chavez on the script. I didn't do any of the writing. I just gave commentary. I didn't need to do much because they were so good at their job. I think Chicago and our community is portrayed accurately and beautifully. They did their research. They came and visited me, and I showed them around town. We've had many conversations. I had a lot of reservations at first when I was approached to option the book. I said to the producers, "I don't want white people to ruin this." I said it just like that, and they were in total agreement. They're like, "Don't worry. We're going to work on getting you the best Latinx people." They did. They followed through. As a coproducer, I do have input, so that's great. It's not something I ever conceived as a child, so it's still blowing my mind that it will become a movie. The care that has been given so far has really shown me that the integrity of the book is intact. Of course, it's going to be different because it's a movie, but it's still going to remain true to the novel. That's something that I feel good about, so I'm no longer afraid. I'm just nervous and excited.

—May 25, 2022

19

CARMEN MARIA MACHADO

Carmen Maria Machado's debut story collection, *Her Body and Other Parties*, a finalist for the 2017 National Book Award, is steeped in genre, a mix of gothic, horror, and dystopian traditions that Machado acknowledges, plays with, and often subverts, transforming them into powerful meditations centering women's bodies and sexual violence. In her novella-length story "Especially Heinous," the endless episodes of a police procedural reveal the mind-numbing consumption of that violence. Many of Machado's stories can be read as societal critiques—the harmful body shaming of the fashion and diet industry, the ridiculous self-absorption of artists' retreats—but to focus on the sociopolitical issues of her work is to miss its strangeness, dark humor, and unpredictable turns. Perhaps Machado's work can be best described the way she describes the writers she's drawn to: "I just want to read women writing about fucked up shit in a weird fucked up way." In her experimental memoir, *In the Dream House*, which won the Lambda Literary Award for LGBTQ Nonfiction, Machado continues her focus on women's bodies, desire, and sexual violence, this time through her own experience of an abusive relationship with a woman she met in graduate school. But Machado's personal story, as painfully as it is rendered, is simply a vehicle into a larger discussion about women story traditions and tropes, the ways that abuse in lesbian relationships is silenced, and the inequitable justice for brown and Black queer bodies. In addition to her two books, Machado has also written a graphic novel, *The Low, Low Woods*, and is a contributor to multiple publications, including the *New Yorker*, *Granta*, *Vogue*, and *Harper's Bazaar*. She is a recipient of countless awards and fellowships, including a Guggenheim Fellowship and a MacArthur "Genius Grant." Machado spoke to us from the house she shares with her wife in Philadelphia, which is about an hour and fifteen minutes from where she grew up in Allentown, Pennsylvania. "I've lived all over," she told us, "but I'm kind of back to where I started."

JAVIER: How has the pandemic impacted your writing? And can you speak more generally about your writing process?

CARMEN: On one hand, I feel extremely lucky. I was able to work from home, my spouse was able to work from home, nobody in my family got sick in a serious way. But my work was very much interrupted. I teach at Penn, and I took off 2020 with the intention of finishing a new book that I had sold a partial of—then COVID just barreled through. Even this year when I had time and I was home, I was way too stressed out to even begin thinking about writing and I got nothing done. I'm only just beginning to slowly get back into it now. I also go to residencies to work and usually have a pretty rigorous residency schedule. There have just been a lot of moving parts that make getting my work done much more difficult in the last couple of years, like everybody else.

COVID and all the interruptions aside, I'm usually working on multiple projects at once. I was working on the memoir while I was working on the short story collection. I work best if I can switch between things quickly. If I get bored or if I get stuck, I just go to something else. Then I tend to do these big pushes. Basically, I spend all my nonresidency time gathering ideas and writing things down and keeping notes and doing a little bit of research and poking away, and then when I have a moment, I'm like, "Cool, now I can hammer out a really intense draft." Whenever I get ideas, I just put them somewhere, so when I sit down to actually work, I have this very robust document or series of documents or readings to get me going.

MACEO: Several of your stories involve cataloging, writing lists, creating inventories. In your memoir, in the chapter "Dream House as Half

Credit," you describe how your father encouraged you to write down everything you know about a topic to find understanding. How did that become a storytelling device for you as well as a way to explore specific themes?

Carmen: My father is a chemical engineer and I am his wayward artist daughter, and when I said I wanted to be a writer he almost had a heart attack. He's a second-generation immigrant, and he was just like, "What? Where is your health insurance coming from? How will you be able to retire?" He was very agitated and stressed out, and I was like, "I'll be fine." When I was in high school and basically struggling in all the subjects that weren't English, I remember him saying to me that "even if you're stuck on a test and you can't think of what to do, you can just write down the things that you do know." This act of list making as a way of demonstrating knowledge or accruing meaning is really interesting to me. Umberto Eco wrote a critical text about the list, the practical and poetic list, and it's its own form that has existed for a long time. When it's hard to pull things together, sometimes you just have to write one thing and then another thing. When I was going through the worst events in the memoir, I could simply write one thing down and then another. I think a lot of artists do that already. They do it as a way of getting into something when they're feeling stuck or so that they can make connections, but for me the list as a form also has its own energy.

Javier: What have been the formative moments in your journey as a writer?

Carmen: I was a kid who was read to a lot. Neither of my parents are huge readers themselves, but they were big believers in reading to their kids, and so I was read to constantly as a child and it became a part of my life. As soon as I could hold a pen, I was writing stories and poems, and as soon as I was reading, I was imitating writers that I knew. I wrote my own Shel Silverstein poems, my own Roald Dahl stories, my own *Sideways Stories from Wayside School.* They weren't even my own versions, they were just rewritten versions. But I got the flow of language. I read a ton and was lucky that I was always encouraged. I had really good English teachers and librarians looking out for me. One of my English teachers, Mrs. Stinebaugh, gave me a bunch of novels outside of our assignments, a random assortment of books like *One Hundred*

Years of Solitude, which was my first exposure to Márquez, and she gave me Gloria Naylor and Henry James. So I feel like I have been oriented toward writing in this very specific way since I was a small child.

In college, I went in wanting to be a journalism major. I hated it. I switched majors eight times and then eventually made my own major that was basically photography. While I was in college, I had this incredible writing instructor, Harvey Grossinger. I took a bunch of workshops with him. I wrote an essay about him in the *New Yorker* many years ago. Harvey was wonderful and was very encouraging. He told me, "I think you're really good. I think you should keep writing." He was an important presence in my life. Then after college, I moved to California, and I was miserable, and it was the recession—I graduated in 2008, so it was a fucking nightmare—and I was like, "I just want to go to grad school." I never had a job in my field. I ended up applying and going to grad school, and in my first semester, I was writing and handing stuff into workshop, and I remember a classmate saying to me, "You write good sentences, but you seem bored by what you're doing. You seem bored by your own story," which is a profound and interesting note to give somebody. There was a scene in my story where death appears to this woman and speaks to her, and he was like, "That is the moment when it comes alive, the whole thing comes alive, and so you should investigate that."

I was already primed to think about nonrealism in this interesting way, but it took that bump in grad school. I remember just sitting down and reading a bunch of authors all at once, like Kelly Link and Karen Russell and Helen Oyeyemi, and getting into mostly women writing nonrealism or women writing horror. Something just switched in my brain, and the next semester I wrote "Difficult at Parties," the final story in my first collection. It was the first time I wrote a story that felt like it was in my voice, in the voice you would recognize as mine now. It was the first moment where I felt form and genre and voice and theme just all came together. It was such an interesting feeling, too, because as I was writing, it felt different from anything I had written before. When I look back at the stories from my first semester, they're just boring, not interesting. This story, I loved it and felt like I had just done something new and special, at least for me.

MACEO: You're steeped in different genres—gothic, dystopian, the endless episodes of a police procedural—you borrow from these genres, only to subvert them, make them your own. Can you talk about the literary traditions that you've inherited, and when did you start to make the realization that you could subvert them? That you could turn them on their head and make them into something that's uniquely your voice?

CARMEN: People call me a magical realist sometimes, and I don't think I'm a magical realist. I feel that's a very specific genre that has a very specific history, and it's an influence, but it's not the tradition that I'm operating in. Most people are just like, "But you're Latina and you write fantastical—" and I'm like, "That's not what that is." But anyway, I think for me, a lot of the genre play was influenced by writers like Kelly Link. Every story she writes is so actively engaging with its own source material. There's this sense of play, and it's funny and it's dark and it's so aware of itself at every moment. There's a great deal of control, and you can see it in the story. It's work that is consciously metafictional. Then you have someone like Helen Oyeyemi who is deeply engaged in folktales and fairy tales and those sorts of traditions—the traditional gothic ghost story. It's very high register, very deeply literary, and every sentence is crackling with this very specific voice. Karen Russell is the same way. They're engaging on a continuum of seriousness in relation to the genre, and sometimes it's like Shirley Jackson's *The Haunting of Hill House*, which is my favorite novel in the world and it's a haunted house novel, and then you have writers like Kelly Link being a little more winky, but not in a bad way, a little more aware of itself. I'm interested in that continuum.

As I began to write stories that felt special to me like "Difficult at Parties" or "Especially Heinous," I was asking myself, "Can I do this? Is this too self-aware or winky-winky?" I was trying to figure out my exact relationship with the genres themselves. What I discovered was that I feel invigorated by genre, and by exercises in genre. I love disaster movies, and I love haunted house movies, and I love demonic possession movies, and I'm interested in these super specific genres and subgenres and the mechanics of them, the tropes of them, the way you can subvert those tropes and mechanics and use them to your own end. "Inventory" is a pandemic story, which is also another genre that I find interesting. Maybe less so now, but back in 20-whatever—I think I wrote it in 2012—I was very interested in pandemic narratives, but what does that mean? There are pandemic narratives where lots of scientists are saying, "My God, we're all going to die," and there's a sense of silliness and a scope and scale that feels very global. But I'm way more interested in the question, which, as it turns out was very prescient, and that is: What does it mean when you can't touch people or when you can't be near people because of illness? This thing that makes us so human, the desire for human contact and touch, whether sexual or not—what happens when that's taken away? What does that look like? That's an example of a genre being utilized and also subverted or deepened in a way that feels very specific to the story. That's what makes my brain click. Every time I think of an idea for a story, it always begins as a genre. I'll say, "I want to write a demonic possession story, or I really want to write a historical story set in this time period with this speculative element," and then it always ends up becoming this other thing.

JAVIER: You talked about working on your story collection in grad school. How did you move on to publishing with Graywolf, which has brought out both of your books?

CARMEN: I graduated in 2012, and I got an agent the next year. My thesis at Iowa was also called "Her Body and Other Parties." It only shares three of the stories with the final version, and one of them, "Real Women Have Bodies," is very different. I looked at this thing that I had made, and I stripped back every single story that I didn't love, and I thought, "What do we have?" We have "Especially Heinous," which is this weird long novella, "Difficult at Parties," and "Real Women Have Bodies." These felt like the seed of something. They're all about women's bodies and the politics around them and sexual violence. For me, the most interesting thing about a short story collection is when it has a shared sensibility, when there is a sense of meditation because we're chewing on something, there's something being turned over and over in the stories, and you can see the author's brain at work. I knew what I was interested in, and I decided to add the stories that fit this theme, and I would see how long it took to get a book's worth of stories. And that's what I did. Selling a story collection on its own without a novel is very hard to do, and the odds of it are low. We went out to forty publishers and we got one bite, which was Graywolf. It's weird to say that now because the book has done so well, but if Graywolf hadn't picked it up, I don't know if I would've ever sold it. I had an incredible experience with Graywolf. I loved my editor there. I had no complaints. They were truly wonderful and did a beautiful job with my book and took really good care of me. I'm very grateful. The book getting picked up changed my whole life.

MACEO: All of the stories in *Her Body and Other Parties* except for "Especially Heinous" are told in the first person. What was behind this choice?

CARMEN: I always start from a place of concept or premise or idea. I want to write a demonic possession story, or what if I wrote a story where this thing were true? Some writers are like, "This character spoke to me," or, "There was a character I wanted to create." That's not my way. When I start writing something that's an idea, and I'm trying to write into it and figure out what's going on, I write in the "I" voice, because I don't know who the character is. If we say I, you can just be like, "*I* this, and *I* that," and eventually the character begins to take shape on the page. It's my scratch work. You can see me doing something around it and I'm trying to figure out what the story is. That didn't happen with "Especially Heinous" because I was beginning with two very strong characters, Benson and Stabler. I remember writing that story and being Benson this, Stabler this, Benson, Stabler, and that incantatory quality is suited to the story. It didn't need a first-person narrator because I just needed these two protagonists who already existed, even though I was reshaping them to my own ends.

MACEO: Your memoir, *In the Dream House*, is also a catalog—an archive, more specifically, as you discuss in the prologue. You include footnotes connecting your story to an index of folk literature. You also include digressions on subjects related to your story, such as the origins of "gaslighting," derived in part from the 1944 film *Gaslight*, or the director George Cukor's manipulating actresses in order to pull performances out of them. How did you arrive at the structure of the book, and when did you realize the story you were trying to tell required an unconventional, expansive form?

CARMEN: I was trying to write the material that became that book for a while, and every time I sat down to create something, it was dreadful. It was boring. I would write it, and then I'd read it and I'd be like, "Ugh, this is terrible." Which is not something I normally feel. When I'm on fire, I feel it. But I was reading every word and was like, "This is awful. It's really fucking unforgivable." Then I remember having this series of insights. I had gone back to Iowa City where I went to grad school to do this summer camp for students. I was teaching these intensive workshop classes—two students, every single day, for two weeks. I always talk about writing through genre, and that's the way I organize my classes. So one day we're talking about fantasy, then about horror, then science fiction, then realism, then mystery, then suspense. The thing about teaching is you have a lot of out loud thoughts because you're explaining how things work to somebody. I've found that teaching is super helpful because it forces you to articulate things that you would not normally have to articulate. I was talking every day to these students, and then one day I was just walking around, getting eaten alive by mosquitoes, and I was like, "What if the way into that book is through some kind of genre fuckery, some sort of thinking about the gothic or haunted houses?" Then the idea just kept growing. By the time I left town, I had written a bunch of these premises or ideas. Something opened up or unlocked. And this is a thing that happens to me all the time as a writer, which is that sometimes I feel blocked until the form is correct.

JAVIER: Do you perceive yourself and your work as political?

CARMEN: I'm one of those insufferable people who would argue that everything is political. The decision of what to write or not to write or what gets elevated or does not get elevated—all of those have political implications. Yes, I would say my work is political. I think people would maybe argue the definition with me, but whatever. Yes, I think it's political to be fat, queer, Latina, and write weird shit about stuff people don't want to talk about with a lot of sex in it.

JAVIER: In your memoir, *In The Dream House*, you talk about the "battered woman" defense, and how the ones who benefit from that defense are cishet white women, and that Black queer women or queer women of color do not. Why was it important to you to talk about who has access to justice?

CARMEN: When I pitched the book to Graywolf, what I sold them was very personal, but I told them I wanted to research the history, do more of a cultural criticism. When I started doing the research, it was difficult because we don't value queer archives, so I was hunting down a lot of weird shit in a lot of strange places and just running into a lot of natural barriers of "that doesn't exist anymore" or "we don't know where that document is" or "no one is really saving this material." There was also the fact that a lot of the documentation I was finding were legal papers, papers that heterosexual lawyers had written, saying, "The weirdest thing happened to me the other day. I had a battering case with two women. I'm going to write a paper about it." So even the documents that did exist weren't contemporaneous in the voice of the people who were involved. I talk a lot about Deborah Reed and this group of women, all of whom were in prison for killing their abusive lovers, but she was the only one who was gay, and even the material at the time, which was groundbreaking in terms of thinking about this idea, did not benefit this Black woman who was also a lesbian. Again, this was something that I was learning. I'm not a historian. I'm not an academic by trade. That is not what I studied in school. I kept having this feeling of just pulling these pieces together, and then I would have these moments of clarity where I'd realize, "Oh, when women are queer, it decouples them from their gender, and we don't know how to talk about things like violence or sex," or, "Battered woman syndrome is like a tool that only heterosexual women and white women will be able to take advantage of." I was having these revelations every day, which was interesting but also really sad. The project of the book is trying to give myself context, which is, "Where do I fit in the middle of all this?" This is obviously a very intimate and specific question, and I can only answer it from my own perspective—I can only be me. I can only answer it from this very specific place, but I hope that if I can do this, other people will also feel like this is a thing that they can do, which is think about this question or similar questions on their own terms.

MACEO: You write that "fantasy is the defining cliché of female queerness." Much of your memoir dismantles this utopian idea that somehow queer women are different than straight folks, that they're above "the muck," as you say. How difficult was it to write against this cliché, even though you had experienced the abusive relationship? Did you face outside pushback, say from friends or readers, or was the struggle more of an internal dilemma?

CARMEN: I would say it was 85 percent internal, but that's not an accident, and it doesn't just apply to queer people. I think that any person who exists in any kind of minority group understands the pressure of not airing dirty laundry that is intracommunity, keeping it on the DL and not sharing. After the book came out, I remember one of the first interviews I gave was with this journalist, a Black woman, and she said, "There's this thing that we talk about in the Black community, but we never talk about it in a public way because we're worried—" It's this problem of not wanting to present ourselves in a certain way, this need to present a good face, which comes from homophobia, racism, sexism, etcetera. But at some point, it becomes less about that and more about the need to be honest about the problems our community, my community, one's community, is facing. I am really losing patience with people who don't understand that.

I once did an event, before COVID when I was still doing events, and this older lesbian stood up, she had a cane, and she thanked me for what I was writing about. Then she said, "I feel like every ten years we try to have this conversation and break the silence and we do. Then ten years later we have to break the silence again." I appreciated that, because this is the problem. It's this thing that is constantly recurring, and it's obviously something we have not excised from our community. It's not like it's just over. It's never over. Did I address it right? I don't know. All I can do is write my book. All I can do is write the book and have half of the conversation, and then other people get to have their half of the conversation. Which does not necessarily involve me directly, just the book that I wrote.

JAVIER: How do you perceive your role as a writer in relation to your community, your society, and then literature itself?

CARMEN: Literature itself? I write for myself primarily. I'm not super interested in what people say about my work. I guess with the memoir it was a little more complicated because there was a community element to it, but I did not feel that way about the first book. I don't think I'm going to feel that way about my next book. I'm doing what I'm doing. I'm confident in my work. Again, if people want to talk about it or with it, it's not about me. Then, on the other hand, I also feel like there's no way for a writer to understand her role in literature in her own lifetime. There's no way to understand in one hundred years—well, also in one hundred years, are we going to be here? Who the fuck knows? Assuming we are here, that we're not under the fucking sea. Assuming that humanity still exists—I don't know if people will be reading my book in one hundred years, which I know is not exactly what you asked, but literature as an idea, literature as an enduring art form, I don't know if people will read my book in one hundred years. I hope so. I don't know. I will never know. That's why all I can do is write the best books I can write and be the artist that I am. I'm lucky to be successful in my lifetime, which is not a thing that every writer gets to experience. I understand that's a deep piece of luck for me. I don't fully understand my role relative to my community and literature. Not really. Because I'm just me, nothing has changed. All I can do is what I do.

Maceo: But a lot of your stories speak to specific societal critiques, whether it's the harmful effects of the fashion and diet industry or the fetishization of violence in the media.

Carmen: I would hope it's not quite so didactic. I'm interested in what it means to consume violence, I'm interested in what it means to be a body in the world, to be a fat body, to be a woman, be queer, to have desire. All those are things that interest me specifically, not because they're a relevant political issue. I don't think of it as being a certain political angle or a role that I have to play. It's not my job to wag my finger. My job is to make art and expand human consciousness, which is a very vague and unhelpful way to describe what you do, but it's also my job.

Maceo: A lot of Latinx writing centralizes place, but the places where your stories are set, though vaguely reminiscent of the East Coast, could really be anywhere. Was it a conscious decision on your part not to name a place?

Carmen: Conscious is a strong word. How much of what I do is conscious? Not that much. I do feel there is something, which I feel is reflected in this question of geography. It's also reflected in this question about my racial-ethnic identity, which is that I feel unfixed in a lot of ways. I feel like I exist in a space of not being quite one thing or quite another. This is a thing that dominates a lot of my own thinking—this state of liminality. I just feel unfixed in this very specific way, and you can see it. Even in "The Resident" I do that literary redaction of location, which is funny because it's supposed to be the Poconos, which is where I grew up. There's just something about that sense of unfixedness or liminality that really speaks to me and speaks to my process, and which speaks to my identity, for better or for worse. It's not good or bad, it just is. It just is the way that I am, and I think that's a piece of it. If

I were to make an educated guess, if I were a literary scholar studying me, that's what I would guess. I am not a scholar. I'm not an academic, as I've said, but if I were, that would be my thesis. It would be, "She's unmoored. The location is unmoored."

JAVIER: You've mentioned a couple of times that you're not a literary scholar. Reading through both of your books, you seem very conversant with theory, with literary studies.

CARMEN: Basically, what happens is I will say a thing to somebody who knows way more than me, and they'll be like, "You know who you should read? So and So." I'll be like, "Great, thanks for the recommendation." I'll write it down and I'll try my best to read it. Occasionally, it's too weird, and I'm just like, "I don't know what the hell is happening in here." It's just stuff that I've read that I think is interesting, but it's not my area of education at all, not even slightly.

JAVIER: As a reader, what do you think the milestones have been in Latinx literature in the twenty-first century?

CARMEN: I think for me, Mariana Enriquez's *Things We Lost in the Fire*, Samanta Schweblin, Valeria Luiselli. Those are the women whose work is the most interesting to me, the stuff that has really spoken to me in the last decade of my life. Also again, I'm not a scholar, this is just as a personal reader. I just want to read women writing about fucked up shit in a weird fucked up way.

MACEO: You write about sexuality with great frankness, and sexuality and desire are essential to many of your female characters' lives. Sexual violence is always there as well. You're also very critical of how we consume the fetishization of violence against women and how it's turned into entertainment. How do you walk that line in your own writing?

CARMEN: It's a question I think about a lot. There's a kind of writer right now who would say, "I would never consume media with sexual violence. I reject that as a thing." I've always found it odd to be like, "You know what would be helpful? If we never talked about rape again. That would be super helpful." Obviously not; that'd be fucked up. I remember years ago reading this extremely interesting essay about rape jokes and the nature of the rape joke as a genre of comedy. The author ends the essay with the fact that she was raped and how she was going through the process of trying to figure out who the rapist was. At some point, they figure out it was a man named Jesus, and she was like, "I am an atheist, and Jesus raped me." That's funny. I mean, it's fucked up. It's very fucked up, but it's also funny. One of my favorite Wanda Sykes bits is about a detachable pussy, where she's like, "Wouldn't it be great if you could just put it in a box unless you wanted it." Then she's running and someone jumps out of the bushes, and she says, "Sorry, I don't have it on me. Bye," and she keeps running. That's really fucking funny. I don't think that rape or sexual violence is a topic that is off-limits. There are people who disagree with me and don't feel that we should put it in the media at all. I think that they're very wrong. For me, I think it's something you have to talk about. I think that the reality of sexual violence, like the reality of so many other things, is that if it exists, for a certain kind of writer, how do you avoid that? You can't avoid it.

On the other hand, it is also possible, of course, to fetishize things. It's possible for something to become talked about in the way that—for example, *Law & Order: SVU*, a show that I watch a lot of, which I've also been critical about in all kinds of ways, is just propaganda for the police. Once you see it, you can't unsee it. When you see it, you're like, "Oh, this is a really fucked up show." Whether you like it or you don't like it, the existence of the show is a symptom of a way of thinking that has influenced society and killed people. That's a very serious situation, and you can't untie the show from its politics. Both of those things can be true at the same time, where things mean other things. Something existing in a piece of media is meaningful, and it matters that it's there and it's important, but also it is possible for it to define something in a way that actually does affect culture in a negative way. We are always doing this dance. When we are watching something or reading something, we are engaging these simultaneous realities of what it means that this book exists. Who wrote the book? In what spirit was the book written? What did it mean to you when you first read it? What did it mean to you when you reread it? What role did it play? There are all these ways in which it's moving simultaneously, and that's just the nature of art—that it exists in all these spheres at once.

—December 17, 2021

20

IVELISSE RODRIGUEZ

Ivelisse Rodriguez is the author of *Love War Stories*, which was published by Feminist Press in 2018 and was a finalist for the prestigious PEN/Faulkner Award for Fiction. As the title story suggests, the collection largely focuses on the turmoil of young women dreaming about and suffering as a result of love. Almost anti-love stories, they also speak to generational trauma and the ways that gender expectations warp our understanding of relationships and sense of selves. Born in Puerto Rico, Rodriguez grew up in Holyoke, Massachusetts, the setting for many of her stories and an overlooked Puerto Rican enclave that her work seeks to highlight. Her story "Holyoke, Mass.: An Ethnography" is both a history lesson, taking a broad view of the different waves of migration in Holyoke, and then a very specific ethnography focused on the story of a young Puerto Rican girl coming of age. This juxtaposition between the individual and history, or the individual and community, highlights Rodriguez's attention to identity formation within a very specific neighborhood as well as within a broader historical context. Bringing this kind of nuanced portrayal to settings such as Holyoke is part of Rodriguez's larger project to expand Puerto Rican literature beyond what has historically been written about migration, language, and place. In addition to a BA from Columbia University and an MFA in creative writing from Emerson College, Rodriguez received a PhD in creative writing from the University of Illinois Chicago, where she immersed herself in Puerto Rican literature, understanding that she needed to know what came before in order to push her stories in new directions. As an extension of this work, Rodriguez founded an interview series at the Center for Puerto Rican Studies at Hunter College dedicated to contemporary Puerto Rican authors. She has also served as a fiction editor at *Kweli Journal* and the *Boston Review*. After teaching English composition at a community college in New York that left her little time to write, she decided to leave her position and follow her mother to Whitsett, North Carolina, where she's currently working on a novel about identity formation in Puerto Rico in the late nineteenth century.

Javier: How has the pandemic impacted your writing? And can you speak more generally about your writing process?

Ivelisse: Other than COVID being the scary pandemic that's going to kill us all, it's sort of like the introvert's revenge. We finally get to stay home and live like introverts. Even though people are trying to get me on Zoom calls, I'm like, "I'm still antisocial, nothing's changed. I'm not getting on your Zoom calls." So I think COVID has helped my writing because I have more time to write without the same expectations to socialize, so that's good. For example, I no longer have to go to the mall with my mom on Saturdays. I hate the mall.

My writing process has shifted now that I'm working on a novel. I started the first story of *Love War Stories* in 1996. I got an MFA right after college and then I got my PhD in English and creative writing in 2006. All that time, I was basically learning how to write. MFA programs teach you how to write, but they don't teach you how to be a writer. I had to learn how to be a writer, which meant dealing with a lot of emotional factors that nobody shows you how to deal with. I had serious fear and anxiety when I sat down to write. When you're an emerging writer, you're so focused on the future, this idea that "I have to finish my book so I can get published, so I can be famous and get accolades, and then I don't have to work." But this isn't really the way things work at all. You're so focused on the future that it creates all this anxiety, and then you sit down to write and you write terrible things and you berate yourself for that and feel hopeless. But the reality is that when you see somebody else's work, unless you're in an MFA program, you're seeing the finished product. You're not seeing those hundred drafts that somebody like Sandra Cisneros had to do. When you are looking at your own work, all you see is the crap that's in front of you. Then you have to deal with the insecurity and the questions of "am I good enough?"

Now that I'm working on the novel, there's still pressure to get the book done. I was just talking to another writer this morning, and she was telling me about her book deal, and she was like, "Hurry up and finish your book." I'm like, "I'm working on it, but I can't hurry." I'm much more patient now. Before, I used to send things out when they weren't ready, but I don't do that anymore. I've worked as an editor, either as a guest editor or as an editor for the *Boston Review*, and when you're reading from the editorial side, you realize, "No, I don't have time to edit the submissions that much." So when you submit your work to journals, it needs to be at least 90 percent done. It has been helpful to see things from the writer's side and from the editor's side. I also don't have the same anxiety or fear that I used to. One thing I did to combat my fear was to tell myself, "You're not going to write for five hours. You're just going to write for thirty minutes and that's it." Writing for thirty minutes isn't as scary. You set a timer, you turn off your phone, and you just do it. Do it continuously and the fear starts to abate.

I had to learn what my writing process was. When I was writing the short stories for *Love War Stories*, with every new story I would start at the bottom of the mountain again. I would have a kernel of an idea for a story. Then I would just write crap, crap, crap, crap, trying to find the story. Somewhere midprocess I would find what the story was about. I would then outline the story. Next, I would get all the scenes in place—meaning in the right order. The last step was to focus on language and really fine-tune the text. During this process, there was always a point where I hit a wall, and I would think, "I'm never going to finish the story because it's not coming together." But then I would have a breakthrough. By the fourth story, I thought to myself, "Okay, I know what's going to happen. I know that I'm going to write crap for a while and then have a breakthrough." Learning my whole writing process really helped to allay my fears and insecurities.

JAVIER: The first short story in *Love War Stories* takes place in Puerto Rico. The characters throughout the collection are always visiting Puerto Rico, reflecting on its history, its cultures. Can you speak to the role that Puerto Rico has in your work?

Ivelisse: I wanted to start in Puerto Rico and then go to Holyoke, Massachusetts. A lot of the stories do take place in New York, but I didn't really want to write about New York, even though I did. For me, what was important in that collection was the focus on the Puerto Rican enclave in Western Massachusetts, because nobody knows we exist and most Puerto Rican literature from the continental US takes place in New York. However, there are all these other enclaves that never get written about. So writing about Western Massachusetts—Holyoke, specifically—was the locale that was most important to me. I didn't want to talk about what I view as the old tropes in Puerto Rican literature. I didn't want to write the same thing about identity and losing language or being cold in the US. What was important to me, again, was highlighting this Western Massachusetts enclave but also this idea that Jorge Duany discusses in *The Puerto Rican Nation on the Move* where he essentially deterritorializes the nation. He says the nation is where the culture is, where the people are. It's not rooted in the place, it's rooted in the people, and the people go back and forth between Puerto Rico and the continental US.

Maceo: You're part of a new generation of writers who not only have an MFA but also have gone on to get their PhD in creative writing. What made you want to pursue your PhD after getting your MFA, and what do you feel you gained from the experience?

Ivelisse: I wanted to teach, which in a way was my fallback career. Though getting a PhD is a lot of work for a fallback career. I taught for a long time. I do like teaching creative writing, but I spent so many years teaching composition. If you've ever taught composition, you know it's hell on earth. It's so time-consuming, and it's also very demoralizing because you're like, "Is anybody listening to me, because I know I gave you explicit directions on how to complete this assignment?" But that's why I got the PhD, because I had some idea that I wanted to teach. The PhD was helpful for me because for my preliminary exams, one of my lists was on US Latino literature. So, then I was able to study Puerto Rican writers in the diaspora and deduce the similarities in their texts. If you're going to write, you should write something new. You shouldn't be telling the same story, and in order to do that, you need to be well versed in the literature or the body of literature that you're entering. That's how the PhD is helpful—you get to study in depth a body of work.

Another one of my preliminary exam lists was on a comparison of Blackness in the US, the Spanish-speaking Caribbean, and Brazil. It allowed me to see the different ways that Black bodies are incorporated into the state after emancipation and also the different identities that are formed in different countries after emancipation. In the US, African Americans became a separate group. I know there's all this talk about racism in Puerto Rico, but we're one people. I take a little umbrage with the term "Afro-Latino," but that's a different story. We integrated and became one people, and our bodies were constituted as multiracial bodies to begin with. At least that's the way the nation aims to represent itself, which is very different from the way the US represents itself. All this information allowed me to see the different ways that identity is constructed. For example, through my research I realized that the subscription to the idea that African American identity is the only Black identity is faulty, as throughout the African diaspora, there are numerous Black identities that are not tied to the US. People are critical of Brazil and its hundred categories of racial identity, but I find these multiple categories interesting because it shows us that there are multiple and varying ways to racially categorize people. This is a wonderful reminder that the racial classification system from the US is not the only possible way to look at race.

Maceo: What are the literary traditions that you've inherited or that you feel part of?

Ivelisse: I would say a continental US Puerto Rican literary tradition. Again, my aim is to move beyond the normative tropes. For example, the *Memoirs of Bernardo Vega* was published in the '70s, but he's chronicling the time he's in New York in 1916. Then in the early '90s, we had Esmeralda Santiago's *When I Was Puerto Rican*, which is also a story of migration. I think that we can do more than just offer stories of migration, especially over an eighty-year period. I was looking to pin down what those continuing tropes were and see what I could do differently. There's no story in my collection that's about learning English, or how cold it is in Massachusetts, or Puerto Rico as a nostalgic homeland. I wanted to move beyond that. Yes, you can be from a literary tradition, but you have to add something to it and not just repeat the same patterns. Otherwise, the literary tradition doesn't grow.

Javier: In *Love War Stories*, the female characters understand their own situations through already written stories—literature, telenovelas, salsa music, myths. Can you speak a little bit more about the influence of this broader story tradition on the lives of your characters?

Ivelisse: I think a lot about the way that girls are raised, and there's so much emphasis on heterosexual girls growing up and getting married. We see that everywhere. What are you going to do when you grow up? You're going to get married and you're going to have kids. I'm coming from a culture that expects that. When I was younger, every time I would go to Puerto Rico people would ask, "When are you going to get married?" And I would say, "Never." "When are you going to have kids?" "Never." Then the facade would drop. The women would say, "Yes, don't do it." Everybody toes the party line, but then when you push against it, everybody tells the truth. These are the same women who were so invested in asking when I was going to get married. But these are just the expectations within Latinx culture. My mom complains that I don't know how to cook or clean, and I'm like, "Look, I can't be good at everything. I can't be this perfect Latina."

So, there's pressure for girls to grow up and get married, but then at the same time we are told that men are sucios. Men can't be trusted. Even as a little girl, you're told not to be in a room alone with a man because you never know what he'll do. Men are a perpetual threat. When I grew up there was a lot of violence, and I remember at an early age feeling sorry for women who had men in the house because I assumed they were getting beat up. From my own experience, I hated it when men were in the house because they were violent. So, you have these very incongruous ideas: "Grow up and get married," but, "Men are terrible." Beyond Latinx culture, that's just a problem of heterosexuality. I don't know how heterosexuality is expected to work when you're supposed to get with somebody who you've been told your entire life is terrible and can't be trusted. I find that odd in many ways.

The girls in my stories are dealing with all this external pressure, including the stories that they've internalized. We see the way that these stories hurt them. In "El Qué Dirán," Lola tells Noelia it's a terrible thing being a woman, but Noelia is hellbent on becoming a woman, so she ends up having sex with Ricardo and risks being ostracized just like Lola. In the story "The Belindas," we see how Belinda is hurt in small ways, how her boyfriend David attacks her verbally. There are all these small transgressions that happen before the actual abuse begins, but she has this idea that love supersedes everything, supersedes concern for self, supersedes boundaries that she should have for self-preservation. Too many stories are focused on narratives that women must fall in love, but my stories are really anti-love stories because they look at how detrimental love is. If we forge new paths for women, we'd have stronger women, and maybe we'd have stronger men, too.

MACEO: Many of the older women in your stories, like the mothers in "Love War Stories," have been scarred by love and fear that their daughters will be similarly scarred, yet their advice goes unheeded. How did you come to understand this generational divide and its impact on your young female characters?

IVELISSE: It's a generational divide, but then there's also a divide based on people who have had lived experiences and people who are naive. When I was younger, I'd be like, "If you love somebody, you do blah, blah, blah." Young people can have really strong notions about love, or anything, but it's not always based in reality. It's more often based on these external narratives that they've been told about and that they're hoping to regurgitate and participate in.

I remember in the book *Nilda* by Nicholasa Mohr, Nilda's mother is dying, and she's telling Nilda not to have kids because they will hamper her life and that she should do something different. I think of all the previous generations that were hampered by society in terms of what they could do and what they could be. I think about the women who had to get married because of capitalism, who had no other choice but to stay in terrible places and situations. Each generation can do something better, but there are still so many barriers to knock down. Now it's normalized that women can work, that you don't have to be married, that you can be a single mother, but it's still not normalized that you don't have to participate in this heterosexual rite called love. It remains this all-consuming thing and is put on a pedestal. The idea of love also becomes more important than the self. Past generations of women have suffered in more ways than we have. The newer generations are more naive, but they also have more opportunities. Change is slow, but each generation will keep pushing away from these gender norms, and I hope that one day love isn't the most important thing that we teach our girls.

Javier: How do you perceive your role as a writer in relation to your community, to US society, and to literature itself?

Ivelisse: I'm trying to further Puerto Rican literature. I'm making a mark that way. I'm the first Puerto Rican to have ever been a finalist for the PEN/Faulkner Award for Fiction. I'm writing literary fiction. I'm engaging in thoughtful art-making practices. In terms of community, I had a series where I interviewed Puerto Rican writers, and there were so many Puerto Rican writers I did not know. So it was a wonderful experience to learn how much bigger our writing community is. Ultimately, I want to elevate Puerto Rican literature so there is a wider readership. When I was at the PEN/Faulkner Awards ceremony, I said different ethnic groups are in vogue at different times, but that nobody really cares about Puerto Ricans or wants to read about Puerto Ricans, and in an ideal world, that would change.

It's important to be a literary citizen. For me, being a writer and just having a little bit of prestige, I'm always willing to help younger people because I was there just a little while ago, so I know how they feel, and I don't ever want to forget that feeling. We should be here to help each other up. There were a bunch of people that helped me when they didn't need to, and that's what we need to do for each other. I do that for my students when I teach them creative writing. I got one of my students at University of Arizona published in the *Boston Review*. I'm always extending a hand back because I want to bring them forward. I'm also looking for new Latinx narratives. I just guest-edited an issue of *Kweli*, and it was an exploration of the African ancestry of Latinx people. There were stories I didn't want, though. I didn't want "pelo malo" stories, I didn't want slave stories. I wanted to see engagement with African ancestry in ways that we don't normally explore. I'm helping to create a body of work that moves beyond the obvious and allows people to wrangle with ideas that they may not normally engage with.

In terms of literature overall, what interests me as a writer is writing the types of books I love to read: books that have beautiful language, sentences that make you stop, and sentences that are like a balm on your heart that you can carry with you and think about for the rest of your life. Like when Paul D says to Sethe in *Beloved*, "You your best thing." These are lines that I remember. They are encouraging, and you can carry them with you for the rest of your life. I want to read something that's going to teach me something new and that it is going to be done with rapturous language. As a writer, I want to do the same. I want to write things that are very humanistic and that people can use as a way to think about their own lives and how they can change their lives. With *Love War Stories*, the whole idea is that love is detrimental to women. A woman can read it and realize, "I don't have to be a pendeja. I can move away from those norms." That might be too grandiose, but that's what I'm hoping literature can do.

Maceo: Your stories often deal with the intersection of race, class, gender, and sexuality. These are heavy themes, but the voices of the narrators, most of them young, are always very direct and clear. The book is dedicated to Holyoke girls, which made me wonder who you were thinking about in terms of audience when writing these stories?

Ivelisse: Even though a lot of the voices are teenage girls, I'm writing for adults. As far as my approach to audience, I'm always concerned with how much to explain about culture. My first audience is Puerto Rican, and so that's who I'm going to focus on. I'm not going to explain X, Y, and Z in super detail. I hate when I see a Spanish word in a text and then the translation right after. It's inorganic. After Puerto Ricans, I'm writing for people of color. Then women in general, and just people in general after that. I remember at two different readings, people said they felt left out based on the information I provided about quinceañeras and Santería, which I thought was interesting. I'm not trying to keep people out, but that's just part of the reading experience. I think of Junot Díaz's *The Brief Wondrous Life of Oscar Wao*. As an author, Díaz is using multiple languages to write his text. He's using Dominican Spanish, highbrow language, and nerd language, among others, and I'm like, "I don't know what this nerd language is, but I'm just going to roll with it because there are plenty of other languages in the text that I do understand."

You can make your text accessible, but it's still not going to be accessible to everybody. What's most important is the accessibility of the voice, the openness of the voice that welcomes you in, but there are always cultural aspects that you have to think about. There's slang. Is somebody going to understand this? I remember I had to change one of the slang words I used to make my meaning more clear. With a story like "Holyoke, Mass.," I was also worried that I was feeding into stereotypes. The same thing with Santería: "Here's another Latina writer with her Santería story." Those are the concerns I had. Am I being cliché here, or am I being disruptive in the way that I describe the Holyoke girls? I don't know if I got it right. I hope I did. It goes back to this question of, What do you hide from white people? Do you air your dirty laundry or not? Or are we just going to have characters who are in college, which is not realistic? For me the biggest negotiation is how to write about characters without feeding into stereotypes.

JAVIER: Do you perceive yourself and your work as political?

IVELISSE: Yes, it's all political, but political can mean a lot of things. My collection *Love War Stories* is political in a very feminist sense. With the book I'm writing now, it's political in the sense that I'm talking about nation building and how we become a people. I don't know if that's the way we normally think about "political," but I'm thinking of it as making a particular statement, exploring a significant question that not only has to do with the individual but also has to do with the community. What are the collective problems that we have, and how do we collectively change?

MACEO: In your story, "The Simple Truth," you show that truth depends on the teller. In this case, you're the teller of these stories. When did you start to see the common theme of love and relationships in your stories, and how did you come to understand your own unique perspective when it came to these themes?

IVELISSE: I was always writing about love. That was what I was most interested in. I started the collection in fall '96; that's when I started the first story. I still didn't know how to write. I was young. It was my senior year in college, and these were the things that were important to me. I don't think I would write about love now. Let me go back a little. I'm always like, "It took me twenty years to write this book. Boo-hoo." The fact of the matter is, if I hadn't learned certain things, then it would not be the book that it is. It'd be something a lot more simplistic about love. As a woman, a heterosexual woman, spending so much time thinking about men and relationships and love, if I could have that time back, I would. At some point, my analytical mind started to break away from these cultural norms. I think being in bad relationships gives you that vantage point where you start to see how abuse happens. Small transgressions. It's not just something that happens overnight. You realize your boundaries were too porous.

A lot of self-reflection gave me the sensibility to write about love and to think about it in a unique way. It really started to shift for me around the time I was in my PhD program and afterwards. Part of my revision process was asking, "What's new in this story? What new idea am I putting forth?" Or if I had a distinct idea that I wanted to convey to the world, I would put it into the story. For example, with "The Belindas," Belinda sees herself as broken down while David has gone on with his life and flourished. At the end, she realizes that she was the one who was changing all along. That really flips the narrative, and it's an important message. From the outside, a guy can look successful, but internally he's not. Even though the stories in my collection are depressing, there's still a modicum of hope in them. There's a little nugget in each one that tells you, "This is how you get over this. This is how you move forward."

Maceo: What have been the formative moments in your journey as a writer?

Ivelisse: In elementary school, I think I was in fifth grade, we all had to write a story. I don't remember what I wrote, but I remember using the word "grotesque" in it. The principal came, and she said I had the best story in the whole school, and she gave me a bar of chocolate. I love chocolate, so I was like "I want to be a writer." That's what happened, and then I spent a lot of time not writing. This is going to sound terrible, but I felt special early in life, and I thought, "I'm going to be somebody." Then my book didn't get published, and it was hard. I was like, "You lied to me, universe. I'm not special." I was depressed for a couple years, and even my therapist got annoyed with me. She was like, "You've got to get over it." But I kept thinking, "I was supposed to be a writer." The path is not easy. You're doing this thing in this dark room, and you don't know what's going to happen, and you're spending a lot of time with it, and you're not doing X, Y, and Z, which is probably much more fun, because you have this dream, this difficult dream in a capitalist society. There were times where I just wanted to quit.

Life would be so much easier if you didn't have the desire to write. If you just wanted to do this one reachable thing, like going to law school; a career like that has specific steps already laid out for you to follow. As a writer, you can do 101 things, and it doesn't mean it's going to work out. You can be very good at what you do, and it doesn't mean you get the attention that you think your book deserves. There's no guarantee at all, and there's no simple process to follow, and so you're always caught between feeling "I should be doing this," or, "I should be making more money." So I was super depressed, and I said, "I'm not sending this collection out anymore. It's over. It's time to move on." Then I saw that the Feminist Press had their first book contest for women or nonbinary people of color. I said, "Well, this is just sitting there. I'll just send it." Then it was a finalist. It didn't win the contest, but they wanted to publish it anyway. That's what happened, but there was a lot of time spent frustrated and sad. My friend has this joke that being a writer is like being on *Survivor*: the last person standing is the one who gets the book deal. I tried to quit, but then I thought, "What am I going to do with all this time? What am I going to do with my life?" That's what it came down to. "What am I going to do with my life if I don't write?" That's what kept me going.

Now that I have a book, I'm over that hump. That was one hurdle. Another big moment was being a finalist for the PEN/Faulkner. That was a huge deal for me. Because it took me so long to get the book published, I feel grateful for everything, and I don't take things for granted. During the first year of publication, I'd get excited every time I knew someone was reading my book. It still seems like a miracle, just getting invitations to do things like this interview and to speak at schools. It never gets old. The fact that you have an audience and that people are listening to what you're saying, that you can have an impact on somebody who reads your work. I don't like platitudes, and I don't like the idea that everything works out, but at this moment things have worked out.

Maceo: We've interviewed authors who have agents and publicists and are publishing with these giant publishers. Feminist Press, which published your story collection, is a small publisher. Do you have a sense why your book didn't get picked up by a bigger publisher?

Ivelisse: I didn't get an agent until after I was a finalist for the PEN/Faulkner. I had to get a book published, and I had to be a finalist for a major award. The day after the announcement, I got emails from different agents, but I went with one that had been talking to me for a while. It took the PEN/Faulkner for these agents from big literary agencies to see my potential. Before that, they weren't interested. There's a narrow idea of what sells and what books are meaningful. I always assumed it was because people weren't interested in Puerto Rican girls. That's something that I thought about the whole time I was writing the book: Who's going to care about my Puerto Rican girls? But I said, "Well, I care about them."

There was this #PublishingPaidMe hashtag on Twitter, maybe two years ago, that was meant to show the disparity between what white writers received for their advances and what African American writers received. It was demoralizing. Jesmyn Ward had to fight for an advance of $100,000 after she won the National Book Award, twice. Then there were these debut white writers who got like $800,000. I definitely didn't get that kind of money. I was just talking to a writer friend recently, and she told me about her offer, and I was like, "Oh my God, that's so much money," but she was unimpressed. I told her, "Look, I only got a $1,000 advance." I made more money doing events and teaching classes. But the benefit of a small publisher is that my publicist worked really hard, and I ended up getting a lot of press for the book. With a big publisher, the publicists are focused on the books that they've decided are already going to be the main books of the season. With a publisher like Feminist Press, they're going to work hard for all their books.

JAVIER: What are the milestones of Latinx literature so far in the twenty-first century, and which directions do you see Latinx literature taking as we continue into this century?

IVELISSE: The book *Olga Dies Dreaming* was on The New York Times Best-Seller List this last week. Last year, Patricia Engel and Naima Coster were both on The New York Times Best-Seller List. They were both on it the same week, and I thought, "This has to be historical. That's super amazing." There are more opportunities for our stories to be heard. We're also moving beyond literature focused on the four largest groups: Puerto Ricans, Mexican Americans, Cuban Americans, and Dominican Americans. Now, we're hearing from Latinx people from different countries. For example, Patricia is Colombian. We're getting a lot of new Latinx narratives. When I did my interview series, I saw that there were Puerto Ricans writing about different topics than what I had normally read. They were telling new stories. We've seen such inroads in YA and middle grade literature. We have romance writers. I don't know too much about horror writers, but somebody had an Instagram post about it, and I was like, "Oh, cool. I didn't know there were these Latinx horror writers."

We're expanding. Again, I've seen a lot with YA writers. That's where we've made most of our marks. Naima and Patricia were not only on bestseller lists but also picks for national book clubs. I think Patricia had the Reese Witherspoon Book Club, and Naima had the Jenna Bush Book Club. Someone like Lin-Manuel Miranda would be considered a great American artist and he's Puerto Rican. Our stories are getting the possibility for more global stature. We see a lot more opportunities, but at the same time there are still issues, such as the whole *American Dirt* fiasco. There's a little flicker of movement, but there's still a lot of work that needs to be done.

—January 21, 2022

21

YESIKA SALGADO

Salvadoran American poet Yesika Salgado is the author of the best-selling trilogy *Corazón*, *Tesoro*, and *Hermosa*, one released each year since 2019 by the independent publisher Not a Cult. She also has over one hundred thousand social media followers at the time of this interview, an audience far beyond the reach of most poets. She has used social media not so much as a tool to promote her poetry but as an integral part of her poetics. According to a 2019 *LA Times* profile, "Salgado thinks of herself as outside of the literary world, particularly when she receives backhanded compliments using the term 'Instapoet' in contempt." From the beginning of her writing career, Salgado understood the importance of cultivating an audience, whether performing a poem live on the slam scene or posting a poem late at night on Instagram that will connect with followers, most of them young women, experiencing a difficult period in their life. Her work feeds off of the synergy of creator and reader. Based in Los Angeles, Salgado writes about love and relationships, her fat body and the ways that society has disconnected her from it, family trauma, her Salvadoran roots, and her home city—specifically, the Silver Lake neighborhood where she grew up. She sees her poetry, which often mentions streets, highways, and place names, as inscribing herself and her community into the history of the rapidly gentrifying city so that it doesn't forget that they existed. Salgado's work is deeply personal, something she doesn't try to hide or create distance from. In her poem "Credit" from *Tesoro*, she writes, "Every poem I have ever written is about me." And in "Blind Date," from her first collection, she's posed the question, "What are your poems about?" and her response is, "Mostly about me." But Salgado's poems are also about family, community, and migration and how those inform the self, most evident in her collection *Tesoro*, where she tells the stories of Salvadoran migrant women in relation to her own experiences. Salgado is an activist in addition to a poet and travels the country sharing her work and growing her fans and followers, whom she affectionately calls her "mangoes."

Javier: How has the pandemic impacted your writing? And can you speak more generally about your writing process?

Yesika: It has made me rethink the way that I create completely. I live at home with my family. We live in a small two-bedroom house. In the past, whenever people left the house, I knew that I had periods to work. I was also on the road a lot doing speaking engagements. I had downtime in hotel rooms where I would write. Finding time to be alone wasn't much of a challenge pre-COVID. During the pandemic, everybody was home, so finding quiet spots to create was nearly impossible. Now that things have gone a little bit better, I started venturing out to coffee shops. Even that is different. Some of my favorite places have closed, or they've changed their seating out of necessity. It has been difficult to create through the grief and through relearning the world through a whole different lens. For the last two years I've been on pause a little bit. I released a book right before the pandemic hit, so at least I got that one out.

I've always written as a reaction to something. I've been writing since I was in the first grade and I learned and understood that everybody can write. It has always been a tool to help me make sense of whatever is happening in my world at that moment. Then in my adulthood, I was really good about being disciplined to write every day, but it's because there was so much urgency in what I needed to do. There was so much urgency in the stories I was telling because I wasn't eating off my art yet, and that was the goal. The goal was to publish a book; the goal was to have an audience and readers. Now, years later, that urgency has dissipated, and I've had to treat writing like a job, a chore. It's weird. I've had to reintroduce writing into my life in a different way, understanding that what was once my coping mechanism is now my job. I have to find other ways to cope.

JAVIER: You have a very substantial following on Instagram, and the content you create is part of your art practice. Can you speak to what goes into curating your poetry and other kinds of posts for social media? As a writer, how do you view this work?

YESIKA: Early on in my career, I decided that I wanted to be accessible. I'm a high school dropout. I have no "formal education" as many of my peers do. Does that make me better or worse? No, it just makes it a different route than they've taken. In sharing my work through social media, not only am I making it accessible to folks but I'm also making it part of their everyday lives. You could open your Instagram to look at a meme but instead find a poem that might be speaking to you and speaking to something that you didn't even know you needed at that moment. Sometimes in the middle of the night, I'll get an urge. I'll notice that there's a lot of people on my Instagram, and I'm like, "I need to put up a sad girl poem." I'll post something that I feel is in the air and in the energy, and it'll resonate with who it needs to resonate with. It's totally great to have views and likes and follows, but that's never been the goal for me. My goal has always been to speak to the young person or the person that's scrolling and not feeling seen, because at the end of the day, poetry is a constant reminder that we're not alone.

That's how I approach my work, especially on social media. It's not to show off that I can write. It's to say, "Yo, I'm dealing with some heartbreak right now, and maybe you are too," or, "What you're dealing with right now, I already dealt with it, and I went through it," or whatever message that I've chosen. I'll try to share something relevant to a holiday. I have a Father's Day poem that I share every year since my father passed away. There are some folks that that speaks to. I have a Mother's Day poem, because I'm someone who has had three miscarriages, and I know that's a story that speaks to a very specific group of people. I try to use poetry in a different way. I've always said that I have no interest in climbing the mountain, I want to teach the mountain how to kneel. It's not some insult toward folks that have worked within institutions, but I think that we also have the power to teach the institutions to listen to the readers and to listen to the audience and to give folks not only what they need but what they deserve. With my platform—I call them "my mangoes"—together with my mangoes, we've been able to show people that a writer can have a direct relationship with their readers and build something completely beautiful together.

MACEO: What have been the formative moments in your journey as a writer?

YESIKA: The moments that have led me to be the Yesika that folks know now have been hard—really hard moments where I hit a wall and whatever was happening in my life, or whatever I was doing, wasn't working. I've been writing forever, journaling in my journals, posting it anywhere: on Blogspot, on Tumblr, on MySpace, and all these different places as the internet has evolved. Even my own personality has changed. One of the most formative moments for me was realizing that the disconnect between me and a readership was my relationship with myself. Folks couldn't connect with me if I wasn't truly speaking to my own story because that's the story I can tell best. Some folks are really good at writing fiction, writing imagined worlds. I'm really good at telling my own story. That wasn't going to happen until I accepted all of it. The first time that I truly connected with folks was when I wrote this poem called "My Honest Poem." It was about being a fat woman and how I did not love myself, but I wanted to learn how. The poem itself is a simple poem that I've completely outgrown, but this was when the body positivity movement started to pick up and when things going viral started to happen. It was paired with another poem about being a fat woman called "How Not to Make Love to a Fat Woman," and those two poems were responsible for opening so many doors for me.

Moving forward, *Corazón*, my first book, was a book that I wrote my whole life. It took me about two weeks to put it together because I have weird work ethics and I work best under pressure, but all those poems had been written for many years, and it was just about compiling them together, editing them, and writing what was missing within the storyline. Before that book, I don't think I understood the connection I had with readers. When I had my book release, it was so full, people weren't allowed to come in anymore, and it was a huge venue. There are stories of people opening the back door and sneaking in. I had just quit my job at CVS, and an uncle told me, "You're just going to be home all day eating. You're just going to get fatter at home." Some fatphobic thing. My family perceived me as being lazy and that I had quit my job just to do my hobby at home. My uncle got to the event late and they didn't let him in. He had to sit outside. He was seeing folks come, excited, crying, waiting to at least be able to get their book signed. I think that was a moment where I learned to trust myself and to trust my readers. *Corazón* changed my life.

MACEO: Who was it that you looked to when you started to write your stories? What literary traditions do you feel you've inherited or that you're a part of?

YESIKA: The first person that I ever read where I was like, "Oh, people like me write things," was Sandra Cisneros. I was a junior in high school and going through my first heartbreak, and my history teacher, this Chicano man, told me, "I think you would like this," because he knew I wouldn't do my schoolwork because I would be writing poems in the back of the class. Then he said, "You got to give it back to me because it's signed, but you can hold onto it as long as you want." I read that book front to back the entire semester and reluctantly gave it back to him. I wanted to keep it. So hearing Sandra's stories was important, and then becoming part of the spoken word scene and seeing Elizabeth Acevedo win the National Poetry Slam and go on to win the National Book Award. Her trajectory and her career have made so many of us who are just going to open mics and reading poems realize, "I could write a New York Times Best Seller. That's tangible because my homegirl did it. If my homegirl did it, I could do it." She is one of my contemporaries who has made me dream and aspire.

I still look up to people. There are so many people killing the game right now. So many Latinx folks are getting published and getting amazing book deals. I have a cousin that just turned fourteen, and she wanted books for her birthday. I bought her four books, and all of the books were written by women I'm friends with. That's beautiful because when I was in high school, all I had was Judy Blume and *Sweet Valley High* and *The Baby-Sitters Club*. None of those homegirls had my life or looked like me or had anything that related to me. Now, we have Elizabeth Acevedo, Elisabet Velasquez, Gabby Rivera, and Melissa Lozada-Oliva—all these amazing people. It's a really exciting time for literature. I sound like such a nerd about it, but I still continue to be inspired to this day.

Maceo: What have been your experiences in getting your works published?

Yesika: When I was still working retail jobs, cashier jobs, I published a couple of zines, chapbooks. The first was the *Luna Poems*, then *Woes* and *Sentimental Boss Bitch*. I only did *Luna Poems* because my friend was like, "Yesika, shut up and send me your poems. I'll do the layout for you." So he did the layout, and I would go to Staples, print out whatever I needed, and go to shows and sell them. The first time that I ever printed zines, I didn't sell any for three years. That box sat in my room from 2013 until I think I sold the last one in 2017. By the time I did *Woes* and *Sentimental*, I already had more confidence, but I still didn't feel I deserved to have a book. I was seeing my friends go off to get their MFAs, and I was just like, "Well, I don't have access to that. I'm going to keep writing my poems and sharing them on Instagram." That was working for me. I had sold over a thousand zines. I was just like, "I'm making money. I'm selling them. People are still taking my poetry to their home."

Then Daniel Lisi, the cofounder of Not A Cult, an independent publisher here in LA, reached out to me and asked if I would be interested in doing a book. They really liked *Sentimental* and wanted me to extend that into a book. I always knew that my first book was going to be titled *Corazón*. I have it tattooed on me. It's a nod to Sandra Cisneros's *Caramelo*. My father also used to call me corazón. He passed, and I wanted to bring him into my art. We signed the contract, and in a couple of months I turned in the manuscript. My publisher and I expected it to do well because I already had a following, but we did not expect what happened. *Corazón* sold over one thousand copies on the day of its release. It's four years old, and a copy of it has been sold at least once a day in the world since it was published. Because of my connections with the community, I knew people who worked at We Are Mitú. We did a series. I was interviewed by my homegirl who worked at a different publication and another one that worked at another one, and then somebody would bring me in for a podcast interview. It was my community riding with me, my mangoes asking their libraries to carry me. So when we released *Corazón*, I was just like, "I have a bunch of poems that did not go into this book. Let's do *Tesoro*." I wanted *Tesoro* to be this big story of my family and how toxic masculinity has put us through hell. *Tesoro* is my middle child, my problem child. She's heavy. She's my little goth baby. Then I was just like, "You know what? I do things in threes. It's a trilogy. I want to do *Hermosa*."

So we were going to do *Hermosa*, but it wasn't coming. I was a mess. I should've taken a break. I kept crying, andaba chillando all over the place. Then I sat down with my friend Gabby Rivera and she said, "You know who I haven't seen in a book yet? This Yesika, the acrylic nails and the hoops and the lipstick Yesika." That's how *Hermosa* happened. *Corazón* was the book that I wrote to live my dream. *Tesoro* was the book that I felt I owed my family. And *Hermosa* was the book I gave myself. There were a lot of things that I wove in and out of the books because I wanted them to be in conversation with each other, but I also wanted my readers to see how you grow as a person as time goes by. What was once my heartbreak can be my joy, and what once was my joy can be my heartbreak. Maybe I don't want the same things anymore. I just became bolder and more sacrilegious along the way. Some people haven't liked *Hermosa* because I use a lot of Catholic imagery, but you have to push the envelope.

JAVIER: Los Angeles is an important aspect of your trilogy. In "Blood Right," the speaker says, "I know the city the way I know heartache." How did you come to view the geography of Los Angeles as a map of your own history?

YESIKA: I realized that a lot of us who are children of migrants, we romanticize the migration, we romanticize what our parents did. Early on in my writing career, I would always try to write about my parents crossing the border because I felt that's what someone like me had to write about. I had to write about my parents being immigrants and undocumented for most of my childhood. But as an adult, being in conversation and listening to undocumented folks, I realized that wasn't my story to tell. My story is to tell what happened once my parents got here. They came to a new country, but the migration wasn't finished. This city has been taken. It's another migration without us having to leave. I live in Silver Lake, in Los Angeles, and it's one of the most gentrified neighborhoods in the country. When you hear hipsters, it's Silver Lake and Portland. I grieve every time I walk out my door because what I knew to be my childhood has been uprooted and changed and lost. Homegirl across the street moved, la señora up the street is gone. A whole building swept out. Where did that family go? I could tell you what each storefront was before gentrification. I do it almost like a prayer. "This was here, this was here, this was here, this was here." I have to repeat it to myself so that I can remember what the LA that I knew was because this new LA does not feel like home. I had to write it down because if I don't, the story will be that I was never here; the story will be that this neighborhood has always been a wealthy white neighborhood, and that is the furthest thing from the truth. My people, the people that I grew up with, Filipino immigrants, Latinx immigrants, a lot of queer couples who moved here to be around migrant families because they felt part of us—we made this neighborhood feel like home.

Gentrification is such a quiet violence. Not so quiet nowadays. It happens gradually, and many times nobody talks about it, and it comes and goes. On the corner where I live, there's a mural of Silver Lake artists, of artists that came out of my neighborhood, and they're all white men. My goal has been that if I write—and I don't mean this to sound self-important. But I have a readership, numbers don't lie. One hundred thousand people on my Instagram—I know that if I claim this in my writing, it's going to be mine forever. The first time I ever got paid to go perform outside of LA was San Antonio. The woman that brought me knew that I'm a huge Sandra Cisneros fan, so she drove me to see her house and we passed by Taco Haven, which is a restaurant that Sandra would go to every day and sit at the same table. I think she wrote *Woman Hollering Creek* there. The woman pointed at the restaurant and said, "Sandra wrote there." I wouldn't be able to pick the restaurant out of a lineup, but I do know that it belongs to Sandra. In the neighborhood where I live, there's a café called Café Tropical, and it has always been POC-owned. I made a point to write all three of my books there. I would get my stuff, walk over, sit there eight hours a day, every day. I would post about it on my Facebook and on my Instagram. Some of my followers would come and try to bump into me. We did my first big feature in the *LA Times* there. The *New Yorker* interviewed me there. I was filmed for a bunch of other stuff. I'm not trying to flex, it's just I know that this is all being archived, and whenever anybody looks up Yesika Salgado, or whenever anybody looks up Salvadoran poets or Latina poets, Yesika Salgado is going to come up and they're going to see that I was born and raised in Silver Lake. No one can ever take that away from me, or my family, or my people. This is the neighborhood that produced me and that will always be the narrative. That's why I talk about LA so much in my work—because people want to say the story of the city is different than what it is. I refuse to let that be the story that gets told.

MACEO: Your poem "The Almost Death" pushes back against the taboos of a woman's body; specifically, the euphemisms we use to describe it, like "down there" for vagina. How did you come to see the naming or the renaming of the body as transformative and empowering?

YESIKA: I spent years catfishing, which is when you go on the internet and pretend to be someone you're not. I was pretending to be a thin, white-passing Latina, because I thought people didn't want to hear stories from somebody that looked like me; because being a fat person of color in this world is very violent, especially a woman creating on the internet. I separated myself from my body so much. I had body dysmorphia. I would turn the mirrors in rooms. I would avoid my own reflection at all cost. Then I realized I needed help—therapy, poems, all of that happened—and now I'm in a place where I live in my body. I don't escape my body and its complications, the ways that it's divided and chopped up and discussed and criticized.

I understand that in many ways my body speaks for me before I do, so the only way that a writer can have any power is how she speaks about herself in her own work. That is how you educate people about how they're going to speak about you. I use the word "fat." I don't run from it. My bio says, "She writes about her own fat body." Whenever I go to an event and someone has to stand up there and read my bio, they have to address me as a fat woman. That is my way of not running from it. This is who I am and I have the right to love myself, and therefore I will rename every part of me that needs to be renamed. There are so many ways that my body has been taken from me throughout my entire life, and the only way that I can tell people "no, no, no" is by giving my body the names that I choose, and when I say those names, my readers can see themselves and learn to reclaim themselves as well.

I used to think that I was the only one that hated her body the way that I did, and I was ashamed of it. I've been given the gift of amazing readers. A lot of them come to my events and they bring their younger siblings or their parents with them. I've had a father come to my event and FaceTime his daughter in college so that she could be there too. I know that when I'm saying these things—and most of my readers are young women—I'm having the conversations that they feel they can't have at home. If I'm talking about my sexuality, if I'm talking about my body, if I'm talking about how when you refer to me as "down there" you're shaming me out of my body, I'm providing the jumping off point for them to build better, more honest relationships. That's the part that excites me the most—that someone can be like, "Amá, read this," and the conversation can be had.

Maceo: In your poem "Credit" from *Tesoro*, you write, "Every poem I have ever written is about me." How do you go about transforming your experience into poetry?

Yesika: For most of my life, I was trying to escape a lot of things, including my home environment. I was also diagnosed with bipolar disorder in high school. There was a lot of noise in my head. The only time that I could cut through the noise was when I was writing. Sandra Cisneros says she writes about the pain and then it doesn't hurt so much. That's how I've always approached my writing. When I tell my story, it's not about trying to save anybody, or trying to do anything for the world—all I'm trying to do is keep myself alive. It's that simple for me. It's not easy, but the intention is simple. It has allowed me to be able to move forward without clouding my writing and complicating it. That's what makes it resonate with people. I'm just telling what it is and with accessible language. Everybody has different purposes for their writing, and mine isn't fancy. I just have to get the feelings out, and I got a whole lot of them.

Javier: Do you perceive yourself and your work as political?

Yesika: Yes and no. I'm aware that everything is political. I'm a fat woman in LA and everything is political, but I truly believe that every poem anyone ever writes is a love poem. Its presence, its absence, the yearning, our love for our people, our love for our community, our love for the bigger cause, our love for something. So I just treat poetry like it's a love poem. Even the most political poems are love poems because passion is what drives us forward. Is love political? Yes, it can be, but I think a lot of times we forget that. We've created these labels, and we're all trying to create spaces for each other, and we're all trying to get it right, but what I try to do in my work is say, "Let's put all of that down. Let's make space for the ugly icky feelings because if we know that we're not all perfect, we're going to be kinder and more patient with each other." I used to joke that I would perform poems that I thought were unique to my experience and then somebody who looked completely the opposite—a thin blonde woman—would come up crying over my poem about being a fat woman of color. I was sharing this with someone and they said, "We never know what people are going through. That could be somebody who couldn't even fathom speaking about their body in the way that you just did, and you just gave them permission to do so." We get so caught up in trying to have this bigger purpose, this bigger message, but there's space for all of us. There's space for Yesika Salgado and there's space for Matt Sedillo, who is a phenomenal political poet. I can't do what he does. That's not my calling. I'll let homeboy do that, and I'll support him and champion his work, and I'll write my love poems. I'm a sucker for love and romance. As a kid, I would pick up stuff and I'd be like, "Are there any love poems in this?" If there wasn't, I would put it back down. I write the things that I enjoy writing, and I leave my more skilled colleagues to write the other stuff.

JAVIER: Your work speaks about heartbreak, but your poetry isn't just about pain. It also expresses a belief in love or in the search for it. Do you think that's something that your readers connect to?

YESIKA: After a reading and I'm signing books, I get to talk to people about how my work communicated to them. They'll tell me, "I read you when I was going through my first heartbreak," or, "My cousin gave me your book when I was heartbroken, and you got me through it." The message isn't, "We're in pain together." It's more like, "You helped me keep believing." Every religion has the same message: "We're all in this together. Try to be the best person you can. Be nice to each other and there's hope. Something is coming and it's going to be better." The Catholic girl in me has put that into all of her work. The most universal thing we have is love. In every language, in every culture, in every country, love is a driving force. I don't think I intentionally set out to be a writer about love and relationships. I write about many things. I wrote about the trauma of my parents' relationship. My father was an alcoholic and would occasionally be abusive. He was also trying hard to be a good man, but he did hurtful things. The only way that story makes sense to anybody is knowing that I loved my father. Everybody with a complicated parent who they have a difficult relationship with can understand my story once I say that. My dad was not the best dad, but I loved him. I think that at the end of the day if we bring it back to the universal feeling, the instinctive feelings that we all feel, that's what makes poetry transcend into a universal language. For me, it's the language of love—not the sappy stuff but its real complexities.

MACEO: I've heard a lot of poets say that poetry isn't therapy, only therapy is therapy. But I also can't help but see the things you name in your poetry—say, the harmful habits of love that you inherited from your parents—as a way of moving forward, of not repeating the same mistakes. What do you feel poetry does for you?

YESIKA: Nothing replaces therapy but therapy, but some of us can't afford therapy. I can afford therapy now, and I've been fortunate to be able to have a lot of it throughout my life. There were some years there that there wasn't any therapy and it was just me and really big, scary feelings. The only thing that made me get through multiple nights was being able to write, being able to put all of the noise in my head and in my chest somewhere outside of myself. This is why I champion writing workshops so much, and I try to offer as many of them as I can. Therapy is important for those of us who have access to it. Just like those of us who have access to higher education. It is our obligation to bring it back to our people. That's what poetry does. I come back and I talk about the things that other people don't want to talk about. Things that I didn't see people talking about when I was growing up. I'm an open book because I know how dangerous it is to keep your secrets. Secrets eat you up.

In the poem "Judas" I talked about how my father was abusive. I mentioned it in school, and a social worker came to our house. Then my father called me Judas. I said, "The truth doesn't always set you free." Some of us think that just by writing down our pains that they're going to go away. No, they don't. But it allows us to document them so that later on, we can see what we came from, what we grew from, or we can keep the world and ourselves from gaslighting ourselves. I forget the things I survived because more often now my life has been bright and beautiful. Sometimes someone will go through hard stuff and I'm like, "My life has been pretty easy." And I need to say, "Girl, no. Go back and read your poems." If I hadn't been writing it down, I wouldn't have a way to remember the darkness. Also, there wouldn't be proof that I've gotten out of it before.

I once did an event with Gloria Steinem, and we were talking, and she was saying how important poets are in this world. She said, "The difference between the past and history is that the past doesn't get written down and history does." I'm going to write everything down because my life is worth being history. When I write, I'm not only writing for myself, I'm writing for the people that I'm in a community with. Poetry doesn't replace therapy, but it is a powerful tool to help you in between. I always tell people who I give writing workshops to that we must have integrity with our own art and not push ourselves, not traumatize ourselves for the sake of the poem. I try not to write about things if I'm not ready to let it live somewhere else. I've had traumatic things happen and I thought I owed the world that story, but when I tried to share it publicly, I realized, "Oh, no, that's still very much just for me." When I'm ready to share it, then I will, but I have to be able to check in with myself. That's the only disclaimer that I have. I think it's important to keep ourselves safe in telling our stories, but also, if you are being called to it, tell that story porque somebody else might be in that mud and they need to know that there's an exit to it.

JAVIER: Earlier you mentioned the importance of Elizabeth Acevedo winning the National Book Award. What are other milestones of Latinx literature so far in the twenty-first century, and which directions do you see Latinx literature taking as we continue into this century?

YESIKA: We aren't trying to use broad strokes anymore. We're trying to get as specific as possible to tell the most specific stories that we can. We have so many brilliant Afro-Latinx writers. We have so many people of different genders writing and making us aware of those genders and sexualities. The space keeps growing and growing, and we're wiggling around to make more space for each other. If someone says, "My kid wants a book suggestion," I can ask, "What is your kid into?" "Oh, my kid loves cooking." Here's *With the Fire on High*. "My kid is from the Bronx, and we grew up with not many resources," Here's *When We Make It*, by Elisabet Velasquez. There is so much more. It's no longer just like, "All right, *House on Mango Street* for all of you." I have a ten-year-old niece who is going to be a young adult in a couple of years. I have shelves full of books ready for her, for her to be able to pick up and que se encuentre. Then I let her find herself in whatever resonates. I have specific Salvadoran writers. I have specific LA writers. I have writers that are Salvadorans from LA, myself included. I have writers that are Harry Potter geeks. I'm just really excited to see how we keep growing. There are so many ways to get published now, so many avenues. There's a little less gatekeeping, and also larger publishers are paying attention to what we need. For those young writers aspiring to have the accolades and to have the success that so many other people are having, there are people that are fighting for you that don't even know you, myself included. Dope things are happening, and most of the voices are women, or femmes, or queer. I don't know where the men are at, maybe y'all can tell me.

—February 3, 2022

ABOUT THE AUTHORS

Maceo Montoya is an author, artist, and educator who has published books in a variety of genres, including four works of fiction: *The Scoundrel and the Optimist*, *The Deportation of Wopper Barraza*, *You Must Fight Them: A Novella and Stories*, and *Preparatory Notes for Future Masterpieces*. Montoya has also published two works of nonfiction: *Letters to the Poet from His Brother*, a hybrid book combining images, prose poems, and essays, and *Chicano Movement for Beginners*, which he both wrote and illustrated. Montoya is a professor of Chicana/o Studies and English at the University of California, Davis, where he teaches courses on Chicanx culture, literature, and creative writing.

Javier O. Huerta is the author of *American Copia: An Immigrant Epic* and *Some Clarifications y otros poemas*, which was awarded the thirty-first Chicano/Latino Literary Prize from the University of California, Irvine. He earned his MFA from the bilingual creative writing program at the University of Texas at El Paso. His most recent book is a translation of Nicaraguan poet León Salvatierra's collection *Al Norte*. Currently, he teaches at Mission College in Santa Clara and lives in Oakland, California.

INDEX

INDEX